Negotiating the Political
in Northern European Urban Society, c.1400–c.1600

MEDIEVAL AND RENAISSANCE
TEXTS AND STUDIES

VOLUME 434

ARIZONA STUDIES IN THE MIDDLE AGES
AND RENAISSANCE

VOLUME 38

Negotiating the Political
in Northern European Urban Society,
c.1400–c.1600

Edited by

Sheila Sweetinburgh

ARIZONA CENTER FOR MEDIEVAL

ACMRS

AND RENAISSANCE STUDIES

Tempe, Arizona
in collaboration with
BREPOLS
2013

THE ARIZONA CENTER FOR

⚑ MEDIEVAL &
RENAISSANCE

STUDIES

Published by ACMRS (Arizona Center for Medieval and Renaissance Studies)
Tempe, Arizona
and Brepols Publishers, n.v., Turnhout, Belgium.

©2013 Arizona Board of Regents for Arizona State University
and Brepols Publishers, n.v., Turnhout, Belgium.
All Rights Reserved.

ASMAR Volume 38: ISBN 978-2-503-54666-7   D/2012/0095/143

Library of Congress Cataloging-in-Publication Data

  Negotiating the political in Northern European urban society, c.1400-c.1600 /
edited by Sheila Sweetinburgh.
        pages cm. -- (Medieval and Renaissance texts and studies ; Volume 434)
    Includes index.
    ISBN 978-0-86698-482-9 (alk. paper)
    1. Sociology, Urban--Europe, Northern--History--15th century. 2. Sociology,
Urban--Europe, Northern--History--16th century. 3. City and town life--
Europe, Northern--History--15th century. 4. City and town life--Europe,
Northern--History--16th century. 5. Power (Social sciences)--Europe,
Northern--History--15th century. 6. Power (Social sciences)--Europe,
Northern--History--16th century. I. Sweetinburgh, Sheila, author, editor of
compilation. II. Arizona Center for Medieval and Renaissance Studies, issuing
body.
    HT131.N44 2013
    307.76094809'031--dc23

                                                                    2012044338

Front Cover: Dover, plan of proposed harbour works, c. 1531–1532.
Illustration in BL, Cotton Augustus I.i.19.
Photo: reproduced by permission of the British Library.

∞

This book is made to last. It is set in Adobe Caslon Pro,
smyth-sewn and printed on acid-free paper to library specifications.
Printed in the United States of America

TABLE OF CONTENTS

THE VIEW FROM THE INSIDE: URBAN POLITICS, POWER, AND IDENTITY

The View from the Outside:
Relations between Crown and Town

CONTRIBUTORS

Caroline M. Barron is a Professorial Research Fellow at Royal Holloway, University of London. Her historical research has focused on the history of London, on medieval women and children, late medieval religion, and the reign of Richard II. Her latest book, *London in the Later Middle Ages: Government and People,* was published by the Oxford University Press in 2004.

Claire Bartram lectures on Renaissance literature at Canterbury Christ Church University. Her research is interdisciplinary and centres on gentry culture in the sixteenth and seventeenth centuries. In particular, she is interested in the diverse reading and writing practices of the gentry and is currently editing a volume of essays on book culture in provincial society. Recent publications include articles on gentry identity and material culture in *Clothing Culture c. 1300–1600* (2004) and *Pieties in Transition c. 1400–1640* (2007).

Serge ter Braake gained his doctorate in history at the University of Leiden in 2007. He is the author of several books and articles on late medieval and early modern Dutch political history. His main publications are *Met Recht en Rekenschap: De ambtenaren bij het Hof van Holland en de Haagse Rekenkamer in de Habsburgse Tijd (1483–1558)* (Hilversum: Verloren, 2007) and *De Deductie van Johan de Witt: Manifest van de Ware Vrijheid uit 1654* (Arnhem: Sonsbeek Publishers 2009). Since 2007 he has worked as a researcher and editor for the Jewish Historical Museum in Amsterdam.

Mary Dixon has worked extensively on early modern Dover. As well as her doctoral research on the social and economic history of the town in the sixteenth and early seventeenth centuries, she has also undertaken several research projects in association with Dover Museum on crime and punishment and other aspects of urban society.

Christian-Frederik Felskau received his doctorate in 2005 at the University of Berlin. His thesis was entitled "Agnes von Böhmen und 'Zu St Franziskus'—Anežka Česka a 'Na Františku': Leben und Stiftung, Legende und Verehrung." Recent publications include articles on medieval religious history in *Slezsko země korung české: Historie a 1300–1740* (2008) and *Die Landespatrone der Böhmischen Länder: Geschichte—Verehrung—Gegenwart* (2009). He has worked at several academic institutions including the CEU, the Fachhodschule für Archiv-, Bibliotheks-und Dokumentabonswesen Potsdam, the Universität Kassel, and the Universität Köln.

Peter Fleming is Principal Lecturer in Medieval History at the University of the West of England, Bristol. He has published on the history of rural and urban elites in later medieval England, as well as migration and political culture. He is currently historical consultant to the Museum of Bristol project and is working on a monograph on later medieval Bristol.

Karsten Igel gained his doctorate at the University of Münster in 2002. His thesis examined late medieval Greifswald ("Zwischen Bürgerhaus und Frauenhaus: Stadtgestalt, Grundbesitz und Sozialstruktur im spätmittelalterlichen Greifswald," Städteforschung A71 [Cologne, 2010]). He now teaches medieval history, especially urban history, at the University of Münster and the University of Osnabrück. His new project is entitled "Stadt, Raum, Herrschaft. Handlungsfelder des Osnabrücker Rates zwischen Stadt, Land und Reich im Spätmittelalter."

Mark Merry has recently taken up the position of Digital Projects and Training Officer at the University of London's Institute of Historical Research, after eight years as Senior Research Officer in the Institute's Centre for Metropolitan History. He has contributed to a number of research projects at the CMH, notably "People in Place: Families, Households and Housing in Early Modern London" (AHRC) and "Housing Environments and Health in Early Modern London 1550–1750" (Wellcome Trust). He continues to act as a consultant on a number of research projects at London and elsewhere. His research interests are interdisciplinary, and are principally concerned with the workings of urban social groups in London and Bury St Edmunds c.1400–1700. He also has an interest in the techniques of the digitisation of historical sources, and in how these can inform historical methodologies.

Paula Simpson completed her doctorate at the University of Kent in 1997. Her thesis was entitled: "Custom and Conflict: Disputes over Tithe in the Diocese of Canterbury 1500–1600." She worked as a Research Associate on the *Taxatio* Project at the University of Manchester between 1997 and 2000. She is a contributor to *Pieties in Transition c. 1400–1640* (Ashgate, 2007).

Sheila Sweetinburgh teaches history at the University of Kent and is Research Fellow on the University of Huddersfield's research project "The Great Books of Anne Clifford" (Leverhulme). Her research interests are interdisciplinary and focus primarily on late medieval urban society. Using predominantly Kentish examples, she has published on the history of urban piety and civic society in medieval England, and is the editor of *Later Medieval Kent, 1220–1540* (2010).

Illustrations

Front cover: Dover, plan of proposed harbour works, c. 1531–1532. Illustration in BL, Cotton Augustus I.i.19. *Photo: reproduced by permission of the British Library.*

Figure 2.1, p. 51. Osnabrück, Old Town market c. 1350. *Photo: author.*

Figure 2.2, p. 54. Osnabrück, Old Town market and cathedral close (Wenzel Hollar, c. 1630) A: Market, B: Cathedral close, C: The lion. *Photo: reproduced by permission of the Museum of Osnabrück.*

Figure 2.3, p. 55. Osnabrück, Old Town market, early sixteenth century. *Photo: author.*

Figure 2.4, p. 58. Osnabrück, Town Hall and Old Town market (Georg Berger, 1607). *Photo: reproduced by permission of the Museum of Osnabrück.*

Figure 2.5, p. 59. Osnabrück, Town Hall and Old Town market (Christian Ludolph Reinhold, c. 1777). *Photo: reproduced by permission of the Museum of Osnabrück.*

Figure 2.6, p. 63. Osnabrück, council chamber with the crown. *Photo: author.*

Figure 3.1, p. 76. Sandwich, north aisle, St Peter's church. *Photo: Sarah Pearson.*

Figure 3.2, p. 77. Sandwich, chapel at St Bartholomew's Hospital. *Photo: Sarah Pearson.*

Figure 8.1, p. 203. Prague, Vladislav Hall at Hradschin castle. *Photo: Petrus Silesius (GNU Free Documentation Licence: available at www.commons.wikimedia.org/wiki/File:Prag_Vladislav-Saal.jpg)*

INTRODUCTION

SHEILA SWEETINBURGH

Self-awareness is a defining characteristic of human beings, which we share with our close cousins the primates. For us, therefore, our identity is a crucial aspect of our being, and how we see ourselves and are seen by others, and the familial, fraternal, and communal relationships that underpin our sense of self, are fundamental to our position within society. Moreover, such concerns about selfhood require frequent negotiation, involving us in differing and often fluid relationships. Nor is this confined to individuals, for groups, too, seek to define themselves through their relationships to others. As anthropologists and others have highlighted, there are considerable difficulties of interpretation regarding questions of identity in modern society and the choices, motives, fears, and ideas expressed by people through what they say and do. Historians are confronted by even greater difficulties in their desire to gain a better understanding of past lives and communities. Nonetheless, as the essays collected here demonstrate, by examining the interactions among individuals, groups, and institutions — the forging, breaking, and sustaining of relationships and alliances — a clearer picture emerges of the ways people constructed their identity in the past. This goal is of considerable importance for the study of all eras, but is particularly pertinent for those who seek to investigate times of change and dislocation that often produced heightened feelings of anxiety and thus the need felt by contemporaries to affirm or re-affirm ideas regarding individual and communal identity.

Northern European society experienced such a period between c. 1400 and c. 1600 when the continent witnessed far-reaching political, religious, and social changes. Furthermore, towns were at the forefront of this transformation, and the lives of urban dwellers across northern Europe were deeply affected by these upheavals. By focusing on the relations among townsmen and others, both inside and outside the town, at this crucial period, this book offers an opportunity to examine not just how people in the historic past may have viewed themselves, individually and collectively, but also how they responded to these momentous shifts in their worlds, and the implications for the history of urban society.

Such an enterprise takes into account developments within the historiography that have witnessed a burgeoning interest in the ways individuals and groups within late medieval and early modern society apparently sought to 'place' themselves communally through the construction of individual and collective identities. These aspects of individual/collective identities may relate to such issues as power, authority, honour, and wealth, but fundamentally they constitute matters concerning status and reputation, and a sense of belonging.[1] Such fundamental concerns were important in terms of personal and/or communal 'well-being' but were also vital pragmatically, for individuals and groups needed to establish methods of protecting themselves where the stranger was treated with suspicion and where survival might rest on one's 'good name and fame'.

Of special concern in the construction of identity is the matter of process — how do or did people fashion their identities? — which has led some historians to consider ideas from other disciplines, notably anthropology.[2] One result of this opening of history to a range of theoretical influences has been the growth of differing fields of enquiry.[3] The study of conflict is one such development, and, as Warren Brown and Piotr Górecki have noted, negotiation is part of the process through which participants in conflict pursued their goals.[4] This has led to an awareness of the need to investigate practice, since people used a broad range of options in their dealings with others depending upon their particular circumstances, which in turn has highlighted the complexity of the strategies they employed to position themselves within society and so construct their identities. As a consequence of such developments, one area that has come to be

---

[1] In his assessment of popular politics in early modern England, Andy Wood highlights the dynamic nature of politics which he sees as the active attempt by individuals and/or groups "to extend, reassert or challenge the distribution of power": *Riot, Rebellion and Popular Politics in Early Modern England*, Social History in Perspective (Basingstoke: Palgrave, 2002), 13.

[2] Amongst others: Victor W. Turner, *Image and Pilgrimage in Christian Culture: Anthropological Perspectives* (New York: Columbia University Press, 1978); idem, *The Anthropology of Performance* (New York: PAJ Publications, 1986). *Belonging: Identity and Social Organisation in British Rural Cultures*, ed. Anthony P. Cohen (Manchester: Manchester University Press, 1982); idem, *The Symbolic Construction of Community* (London: Routledge, 1985); idem, *Self-consciousness: An Alternative Anthropology of Identity* (London: Routledge, 1994). Clifford Geertz, *The Interpretation of Cultures: Selected Essays* (London: Hutchinson, 1975). Michel Vovelle, *Ideologies and Mentalities*, trans. Eamon O'Flaherty (Cambridge: Polity Press, 1990).

[3] For two useful assessments of the implications of such developments, see Peter Burke, *History and Social Theory* (Ithaca: Cornell University Press, 1992; 2nd ed., Cambridge: Polity Press, 2005). Elizabeth A. Clark, *History, Theory, Text: Historians and the Linguistic Turn* (Cambridge, MA and London: Harvard University Press, 2004).

[4] Warren C. Brown and Piotr Górecki, "What Conflict Means: The Making of Medieval Conflict Studies in the United States, 1979–2000," in *Conflict in Medieval Europe: Changing Perspectives on Society and Culture*, ed. eidem (Aldershot: Ashgate, 2003), 1–35, at 9.

seen as especially important by historians is ritual. For example, there has been a growing number of studies exploring the ways individuals and groups deployed ritual through processions, feasts, gift-giving, courts, and other ceremonial occasions, and thus the use of objects, spaces, memory, written texts, and oral testimony. At the same time, there has also been an increasing awareness that the different aspects of a particular ritual were open to contested meanings, which in turn had implications for their apparently intended use in the construction of shared ideas and ideals. This dimension, as Miri Rubin has demonstrated (see below), is challenging, but has nevertheless provided a further spur to historians, leading to an increasing desire to explore ideas regarding reception as part of the study of urban rituals.

In many ways, in terms of the writing of history, this is a long way from the works of earlier scholars of urban history such as James Tait, F. W. Maitland, and Mary Bateson.[5] Yet their studies on incorporation and the particularities of borough custom in medieval towns did and still do offer evidence with regard to the ways individuals and groups in English urban society negotiated relations both within the town and with outside authorities. The studies of mid-twentieth-century Marxist scholars, though primarily concerned to highlight what they saw as the relationship between the rulers and the ruled in class terms—the feudal lords, whether members of the aristocracy, the Crown or the Church, and the peasantry or their urban counterparts—nonetheless also provided ideas about the ways different groups saw themselves through their relations with others. Still, this dichotomy, employed by historians such as Rodney Hilton and Christopher Hill, does have certain limitations, and recent scholarship has adopted a more nuanced approach.[6] Detailed town studies, such as Christopher Dyer's assessment of factional disputes at Shipton-upon-Stour around the year 1400, and Spencer Dimmock's analysis of the instigation of "a large yeoman and gentry oligarchy" at Lydd by 1550, have indicated the types of strategies individuals and certain

---

[5] *British Borough Charters, 1216–1307*, ed. Adolphus Ballard and James Tait (Cambridge: Cambridge University Press, 1923); F. W. Maitland, *Township and Borough: Being the Ford Lectures 1897* (Cambridge: Cambridge University Press, 1898); *Borough Customs*, ed. Mary Bateson, 2 vols., Selden Society 18 and 21 (London: Quaritch, 1904, 1906).

[6] See, for example, Rodney Hilton, "The Small Town as Part of Peasant Society," in *The English Peasantry in the Later Middle Ages: The Ford Lectures for 1973 and Related Studies* (Oxford: Clarendon Press, 1975), 76–94; idem, "Status and Class in the Medieval Town," in *The Church in the Medieval Town*, ed. Terry R. Slater and Gervase Rosser (Aldershot: Ashgate, 1998), 9–19; Christopher Hill, *The World Turned Upside Down: Radical Ideas during the English Revolution* (Harmondsworth: Penguin Books, 1975).

groups employed to situate themselves politically, economically, and socially in their respective communities.[7]

The value of such an approach has been recognised by those more directly concerned to explore the nature and creation of civic identity in late medieval and early modern urban society. For the Middle Ages, perhaps the earliest exponent of this method was Charles Phythian-Adams, whose analysis of urban ritual led him to believe that ceremonial events were intended primarily to emphasise the correctness of the elite's place as urban governors within the town 'community'.[8] However, he did allow that such matters as precedence in processions, and thus the civic hierarchy, were capable of adjustment to reflect changes in the relative economic status of different groups. Others have followed his lead. Gervase Rosser, in particular, has been especially prolific, producing a number of studies that examine the ways groups such as fraternities, craft and parish, as well as the civic authorities, used rituals and myths to provide ideas about longevity, authority, and community.[9]

As Heather Swanson has indicated, such lines of enquiry have been exceedingly fruitful, not least because they have opened up debates among scholars concerning "who ran the town, and for whose benefit?" where Rosser and Susan Reynolds have sought to emphasise integration among the various groups within

---

[7] Christopher Dyer, "Small-Town Conflict in the Later Middle Ages: Events at Shipton-on-Stour," *Urban History* 19 (1992): 183–210; Spencer Dimmock, "English Small Towns and the Emergence of Capitalist Relations, c. 1450–1550," *Urban History* 28 (2001): 5–24.

[8] First published: Charles Phythian-Adams, "Ceremony and the Citizen: The Communal Year at Coventry, 1450–1550," in *Crisis and Order in English Towns, 1500–1700*, ed. Peter Clark and Paul Slack (London: Routledge, 1972), 57–85; repr. in *The English Medieval Town: A Reader in English Urban History, 1200–1540*, ed. Richard Holt and Gervase Rosser (London and New York: Longman, 1990), 238–64.

[9] Including Gervase Rosser, "Communities of Parish and Guild in the Late Middle Ages," in *Parish, Church and People: Local Studies in Lay Religion 1360–1750* (London: Hutchinson, 1988), 29–35; idem, "Myth, Image and Social Process in the English Medieval Town," *Urban History* 23 (1996): 5–25; idem, "Crafts, Guilds and the Negotiation of Work in the Medieval Town," *Past and Present* 154 (1997): 3–31; idem, "Conflict and Political Community in the Medieval Town: Disputes between Clergy and Laity in Hereford," in *The Church in the Medieval Town*, ed. Slater and idem, 20–42; idem, "Big Brotherhood: Guilds in Urban Politics in Late Medieval England," in *Guilds and Association in Europe, 900–1900*, ed. Ian A. Gadd and Patrick Wallis (London: Centre for Metropolitan History, 2006), 27–42; idem, "Party List: Making Friends in the Medieval English Guilds," in *London and the Kingdom: Essays in Honour of Caroline Barron*, ed. Matthew Davies and Andrew Prescott (Donington: Shaun Tyas, 2008), 118–34.

the urban community.[10] Among those strongly opposed to this view is Stephen Rigby, whose extensive work on later medieval society employs the sociological concept of closure, where exclusion rather than inclusion is the *modus operandi*.[11] Another who has looked critically at what might be called the 'holistic' approach is Rubin, including the equating of ceremonial exclusively with the maintenance of the status quo and problems of language: just what did *communitas* mean, and is the term 'community' overused in modern historiography?[12] With regard to the latter, Rubin certainly believes that it is, and she has robustly attacked the use of the term by many late twentieth-century medievalists because she considers that in their hands it had become "a static notion [that] obscures difference and conflict."[13] Instead Rubin wants us to consider identity in the late Middle Ages as "complex and changeable," where issues of "gender, class, ethnic affiliation, region, learning, and occupational identity" were integral to the process.[14] As a result individual and collective identities and their formation should be seen, according to Rubin, as dynamic developments that took account of these constituent aspects in the construction of multiple selves, and, as outlined above, this view also needs to consider ideas about how such processes of construction were received by others. Rubin's response is part of the realisation that medieval society was exceedingly complex, and that diversity, fragility, fluidity, and factionalism were inherent features of lived experience. For the contributors here this has significant implications because it highlights the need to explore the heterogeneity of urban society in terms of people's differing experiences and thus the importance of particular circumstances in space and time, as well as shared matters and conditions in common.

Turning again to Dyer, he too sees a complex and changeable society where the concept of community was seemingly used by different groups to mean what was relevant to their needs and aspirations.[15] Even though many of his examples are taken from late medieval rural society, the careers of men such as Roger Heritage of Warwickshire and Robert Parman of Suffolk probably had much in common

---

[10] Heather Swanson, *Medieval British Towns*, Social History in Perspective (Basingstoke: Macmillan, 1999), 89–90. See Susan Reynolds, *Kingdoms and Communities in Western Europe, 900–1300* (Oxford: Oxford University Press, 1984).

[11] Stephen H. Rigby, *English Society in the Later Middle Ages: Class, Status and Gender* (Basingstoke: Macmillan, 1995), 9–14.

[12] Swanson, *Towns*, 92. Miri Rubin, "Small Groups: Identity and Solidarity in the Later Middle Ages," in *Enterprise and Individuals in Fifteenth-Century England*, ed. Jennifer Kermode (Stroud: Alan Sutton, 1991), 132–50.

[13] Rubin, "Small Groups," 134.

[14] Rubin, "Small Groups," 134–35.

[15] Christopher Dyer, *An Age of Transition? Economy and Society in England in the Later Middle Ages* (Oxford: Oxford University Press, 2005), 244–45.

with Rubin's townsmen.[16] For Dyer, his concern for these individuals stems primarily from his study of them as early capitalists, and while this is interesting, of greater relevance here is his assessment of the multiplicity of their activities over time on behalf of themselves, their family and their community. In particular, one wonders about the tension that might result from these competing constituencies and thus what implications for the roles, as well as ideas about individuality, Heritage and Parman may have had. This more competitive model of late medieval society remains controversial, especially its implications for the timing of these and associated cultural changes, but Dyer believes "it should not be a cause of surprise or disappointment that such a momentous historical episode [modern capitalist economy] began before 1300 and was complete only after 1800."[17]

Nevertheless, there are those who view the sixteenth century as the watershed owing to the twin transforming influences of religion and the marketplace. In his investigation of the proliferation of court cases in late sixteenth-century England, Craig Muldrew believes he is seeing a very important shift in contemporary perceptions concerning man's normative state from "the medieval notion of community [as] a positive expression of social unity through Christian love and ritual" to one where "men . . . were increasingly seen as fundamentally competitive, and community now had to be *justified* in the negative terms of necessity in order to protect the Christian virtues of love and charity."[18] Muldrew considers that the phenomenal growth in the market in the early modern period is the fundamental cause, but the Protestant emphasis on man's fallen nature may also have a bearing on this change. Even though Muldrew is not interested in individual or small group identity per se, his assessment of the role and place of judicial conflict in urban society offers insights regarding identity construction through the ways relationships were negotiated in the courtroom and elsewhere, ideas that are explored in several essays here. Moreover, the ongoing debate over the value of seeing such cultural shifts through the lens of periodization underlies this collection, and for many this apparently simple binary—medieval/early modern—masks more than it reveals of the history of northern European society.

Another issue that historians have begun to consider with respect to the ways people in the past negotiated relations is the use of space. For some the works of French scholars such as Henri Lefebvre and Michel Foucault have proved to be useful, not least because these theorists have highlighted the political importance

---

[16] Christopher Dyer, "Were There Any Capitalists in Fifteenth-century England?" in *Enterprise and Individuals in Fifteenth-Century England*, ed. Jennifer Kermode (Stroud: Alan Sutton, 1991), 1–24; idem, "A Suffolk Farmer in the Fifteenth Century," *Agricultural History Review* 55 (2007): 7–22.

[17] Dyer, *Age of Transition*, 245–46.

[18] Craig Muldrew, "The Culture of Reconciliation: Community and the Settlement of Economic Disputes in Early Modern England," *Historical Journal* 39 (1996): 915–42, here 920–21.

of spatial dynamics.[19] In particular, there has been a growing interest among historians and archaeologists in the ways ecclesiastical, civic, and other public urban spaces were employed, both in terms of the locating of physical structures and the movement of individuals and groups within them. Many of these studies have indicated a high level of sophistication on the part of those involved, as well as demonstrating their awareness of the complex meanings — neither homogeneous nor static — that they as participants and others might bring to the use of urban space.[20] Among those historians whose findings are especially relevant with respect to this volume is Robert Tittler, who has investigated the construction of corporate identity in early modern urban society through the building of town halls and the deployment of such artefacts as portraits in the creation of corporate identity.[21] The latter highlights the significance of objects as indicators of status, power, and authority, the study of the role of material culture in the development of relations having benefited from cross-cultural comparisons through the works of anthropologists such as Daniel Miller.[22]

Ideas about the production and reception of texts are considered by a number of contributors here. Again, many of the earlier influential studies were contributed by mid- to late twentieth-century French scholars.[23] The continuing debates that have followed from such works covering issues like authorship, textual

---

[19] Henri Lefebvre, *The Production of Space*, trans. D. Nicholson-Smith (Oxford: Blackwell, 1991); Michel Foucault, *Discipline and Punish: The Birth of the Prison*, trans. Alan Sheridan (New York: Vintage, 1977).

[20] See essays in *The Archaeology of Reformation 1480–1580*, ed. David Gaimster and Roberta Gilchrist, The Society for Post-Medieval Archaeology (Leeds: Maney, 2003); *Cities, Texts and Social Networks, 400–1500: Experiences and Perceptions of Medieval Urban Space*, ed. Caroline Goodson, Anne E. Lester and Carol Symes (Farnham: Ashgate, 2010).

[21] Robert Tittler, *Architecture and Power: The Town Hall and the English Urban Community 1500–1640* (Oxford: Clarendon Press, 1991); idem, *Townspeople and Nation: English Urban Experiences, 1540–1640* (Stanford: Stanford University Press, 2001); idem, *The Face of the City: Civic Portraits and Civic Identity in Early Modern England* (Manchester: Manchester University Press, 2007); idem, "Faces and Spaces: Displaying the Civic Portrait in Early Modern England," in *Everyday Objects: Medieval and Early Modern Material Culture and its Meanings*, ed. Tara Hambling and Catherine Richardson (Farnham: Ashgate, 2010), 179–87.

[22] Daniel Miller, *Material Culture and Mass Consumption* (Oxford: Blackwell, 1991); idem, ed., *Material Cultures: Why Some Things Matter* (London: UCL Press, 1998).

[23] Michel de Certeau, *The Writing of History*, trans. Tom Conley (New York: Columbia University Press, 1988). Paul Ricoeur, *Time and Narrative*, trans. Kathleen McLaughlin and David Pellauer (Chicago and London: University of Chicago Press, 1984–1988); idem, *Memory, History, Forgetting*, trans. Kathleen Blamey and David Pellauer (Chicago and London: Chicago University Press, 2004). Roland Barthes, *Image, Music, Text*, trans. Stephen Heath (Glasgow: Collins, 1977).

production, and ways of reading have proved to be especially beneficial. Among those whose studies have been influenced by these ideas are Natalie Zemon Davis, Paul Strohm, Chris Wickham, and Patrick Geary; and the close-reading techniques they have applied to their chosen texts have provided fascinating insights on the importance of narrative and memory in the negotiating of relations as the protagonists constructed their identities.[24]

A further issue investigated by several contributors is the process of gift-giving and reciprocity. Of special concern is how, when, and where gifts were given and received, the apparent balance between pragmatism and strategic planning, and the sometimes far-reaching implications of these exchanges. An understanding of the value of this topic owes much to earlier studies by anthropologists such as Marcel Mauss, as well as recent scholars like John Davis, Annette Weiner, and Arjun Appadurai, who have considerably enhanced our understanding of the complexity of the process itself and the meanings seemingly applied to the various aspects of the gift-exchange by those involved.[25] Historians have followed their lead, and have increasingly demonstrated the complex ways gifts might be deployed to negotiate matters of inferiority, power, and authority, ideas that were relevant to the citizens of a number of fifteenth- and sixteenth-century northern European towns discussed here.

Though many of the resultant studies in the current literature on urban identity consider either the late medieval or the early modern, there is a growing realisation that cross-cultural continuities over time did occur, in addition to significant changes, and it is this complex pattern which makes the period between 1400 and 1600 so interesting. Equally, the topics of cultural difference and similarity among European towns are increasingly becoming the foci of urban studies, and the essays here develop many of the current themes outlined above through the study of richly detailed court records, testamentary materials,

---

[24] Natalie Z. Davis, *Fiction in the Archives: Pardon Tales and Their Tellers in Sixteenth-Century France* (Cambridge: Polity Press, 1987); eadem, *The Gift in Sixteenth-Century France* (Oxford: Oxford University Press, 2000). Paul Strohm, *Hochon's Arrow: The Social Imagination of Fourteenth-Century Texts* (Princeton: Princeton University Press, 1992). James Fentress and Chris Wickham, *Social Memory* (Oxford: Blackwell, 1992). Patrick J. Geary, *Furta Sacra: Thefts of Relics in the Central Middle Ages* (Princeton: Princeton University Press, 1978); idem, *Living with the Dead in the Middle Ages* (Ithaca: Cornell University Press, 1994); idem, *Phantoms of Remembrance: Memory and Oblivion at the End of the First Millennium* (Princeton: Princeton University Press, 1994); idem, *The Myth of Nations: The Medieval Origins of Europe* (Princeton: Princeton University Press, 2002).

[25] Marcel Mauss, *The Gift: The Form and Reason for Exchange in Archaic Societies*, trans. W. Halls, intro. Mary Douglas (orig. 1915; New York and London: Routledge, 1990). John Davis, *Exchange* (Buckingham: Open University Press, 1992); Annette B. Weiner, *Inalienable Possessions: The Paradox of Keeping-While-Giving* (Berkeley and Oxford: University of California Press, 1992); Arjun Appadurai, ed., *The Social Life of Things: Commodities in Cultural Perspective* (Cambridge: Cambridge University Press, 1986).

Crown documents, and literary texts, as well as other resources such as civic or quasi-civic and religious spaces and objects. As a consequence this collection is informed by, builds on, and seeks to extend work done in the Anglo-American academy, as well as studies undertaken in northern European universities (see essays for specific references). The early urbanization of the Low Countries and the sophistication of the civic apparatus that developed to administer and regulate trade, for example, have attracted modern scholars, their individual and collective research on such aspects as the use of ceremonial processions, the multiple employment of ecclesiastical buildings, and the role of gifts providing fruitful comparative materials and theoretical perspectives.[26] Moreover, even though the cities of the Low Countries have been the focus of considerable attention, the desire to place this research in a broader pan-European context has led, for instance, to an interest in the German *Reichsstädte*. One such study that seems to exemplify this approach, both theoretically and topographically, and is now available in English, is Valentin Groebner's monograph on the (political) role of gifts and gift-giving in Swiss and south German cities in the fifteenth and sixteenth centuries.[27] His work and other such studies demonstrate the move to investigate urban power relations through case studies of geographically dispersed communities, a development that has highlighted similarities and differences, as one would expect, but also shows that distance between towns was not always the overriding cause—"what counted as unseemly in one city was permissible a couple of hundred kilometres away."[28] These findings are extremely interesting, not least because they suggest the value of thematic comparisons based on research concerning diverse (size, location) late medieval and early modern urban communities. As a way of exploring this notion, the towns discussed here encompass a wide range from those of moderate size in southern England to large cities in modern-day Germany and Poland. The resulting case studies highlight, through their examination of the ways individuals and groups negotiated matters of status, reputation, and belonging as manifested through honour, commemoration, authority, and power, both the significance of the particular within

---

[26] Among such European projects are 'Stadscultuur in de laatmeddeleeuwse Nederlanden' (Urban culture in the late medieval Low Countries) and 'De interactie van Kerk en wereldlijke overheden bij de godsdienstige hervormingen in de Nederlanden tussen 1370 en 1560' (The interaction between the Church and the secular authorities with regard to the religious reforms in the Low Countries between 1370 and 1560).

[27] Valentin Groebner, *Liquid Assets, Dangerous Gifts: Presents and Politics at the End of the Middle Ages*, trans. Pamela E. Selwyn (Philadelphia: University of Pennsylvania Press, 2002); originally published as *Gefährliche Geschenke: Politische Sprache und das Reden über Korruption am Beginn der Neuzeit* (Konstanz: Universitätsverlag Konstanz, 2000).

[28] Koen Goudriaan, "Conclusion," in *The Use and Abuse of Sacred Places in Late Medieval Towns*, ed. Paul Trio and Marjan de Smet (Leuven: Leuven University Press, 2006), 223.

contemporary cultural developments and points of similarity that apparently, to a greater or lesser extent, transcend geography and period.

Arranged thematically, the first group of essays looks primarily at the ways townsmen, either individually or collectively, sought to establish their place within the urban political arena of their town. For some townsmen, this involved negotiating relations principally with their fellow citizens, but for others it also included negotiations with different institutions such as religious establishments or representatives of the Crown. Although such activities might be ongoing as the various constituencies within the town attempted to negotiate their position continually, there were important points of 'crisis', and it is these that provide the focus for the studies on towns in what is now England and Germany.

Considering two urban societies very different in terms of size and civic organisation, Mark Merry and Karsten Igel assess how the elite of Bury St Edmunds and Osnabrück, respectively, in the fifteenth century sought to position themselves vis-à-vis other townsmen, and the previously dominant religious institutions of the abbey at Bury and the cathedral chapter at Osnabrück, as authoritative and benevolent civic governors. As Merry discusses, John Smyth and his fellow leading townsmen, having no town council, employed the Candlemas guild as a quasi-civic organisation, and as an essential part of this deployment they, through Smyth's will and associated documentation, constructed an ideal citizen, what Merry calls a stylised 'living' biography of a benefactor, who 'freed' the town symbolically and actually from the abbey. Furthermore, since John Smyth was situated at the pinnacle of Bury's elite, his annual commemoration and the ceremonies linked to the Candlemas guild estates provided the townsmen with important civic rituals that proclaimed the special nature of their town and its most prominent citizen.

As Igel demonstrates, even though the elite of Osnabrück did not construct an elite biography in the same way, the leading citizens did similarly value the concept of the civic benefactor, as shown by the highly symbolic and elaborate decorative scheme on their new town hall. Moreover, this was only one element in their reordering of relations with other townsmen and the cathedral. Whereas in Bury exclusivity had been enacted through membership of the Candlemas guild, at Osnabrück it was through participation (including witnessing) in the different sections of the town council election process. This process was changed significantly in the late fifteenth century as a consequence of the spatial reorganisation of the commercial city centre. Igel's analysis of these alterations, which involved considerable demolition and construction of new buildings, highlights the leading citizens' use of civic ritual to underline their power and authority as aspects of their corporate identity. Nonetheless, as he also shows, the elite's aspirations as powerful civic governors were at times tested, and this aspect of negotiating the political was also significant in early sixteenth-century Sandwich.

The disruption of a civic ritual in 1532 is the starting point of Sheila Sweetinburgh's assessment of religious and political tensions in Sandwich. Like the other essays, this investigation considers the circumstances of events in a particular town in the context of wider developments, in this instance the early years of the Reformation in England. Both this and the succeeding analysis by Paula Simpson of tensions in Elizabethan Canterbury consider in detail the implications of a specific event and the repercussions it had for contemporaries. At Sandwich, as Sweetinburgh shows, the disrupted St Bartholomew's day procession and its aftermath was the result of and had serious implications for civic–clerical relations in the town. Nor was this a simple division between the two sides but apparently involved alliances between clerics and townsmen, and between townsmen—vertically and horizontally—as well as with certain outsiders. As a consequence, certain senior town officers saw it as necessary to re-establish their authority, a vital element in their envisaged civic identity.

The negotiating of relations among the clergy, and their lay supporters, to re-establish 'harmony' in late sixteenth-century Canterbury was vital, as Simpson notes, because of the perceived damage to the Anglican Church. Simpson assesses Anthony Kingsmill's vitriolic sermon in which he accused certain ecclesiastical judges of corruption and shows that it is important for a number of reasons, not least the public forum in which it was delivered. Though not a ritual per se, Kingsmill's 'performance' from the pulpit in the cathedral's Sermon House employed ritual, such elements being understood (as Kingsmill expected they would be) by his fellow clerics, the city's officers, and others in the congregation. In addition, as Simpson demonstrates, as recorded in the ecclesiastical court registers the resulting case brought against Kingsmill highlights how narratives could be constructed by those called upon to testify, the spoken and written word being seen as part of the negotiating process in the creation of clerical identity—the godly minister.

The importance of the spoken and written word and its deployment in the construction of personal identity is also analysed in the last essay in this first section: Claire Bartram and Mary Dixon's discussion of John Tooke's discourse on the proposed new harbour in late Elizabethan Dover. Through their close reading of his text, Bartram and Dixon reveal the broad range of rhetorical devices used by Tooke as he sought to situate himself as the authoritative voice of Dover in opposition to certain local mariners, especially William Tiddyman, whom he categorises as having none of the virtues he is able to display. Moreover, as they show, the negotiations in Dover and London surrounding the development of the new harbour bring into sharp relief changes in Dover's oligarchic governmental structure as the differing constituencies within the town sought to strengthen their positions relative to one another. Nor were the formation of alliances among the various groups confined to the town, and, as Bartram and Dixon show, the involvement of particular royal officers and members of the county gentry highlights the important place of negotiation in relations between the Crown and provincial urban society.

The vital role negotiation played in Crown–town relations is explored in the second section of three essays that consider *longue durée* studies of Bristol, the cities of Holland and Zeeland, and Prague. Having provided an assessment of Bristol's earlier political history, Peter Fleming focuses his attention on the town's fortunes under successive Lancastrian and Yorkist kings by examining the interactions among Bristol's leading citizens, local magnates, and the Crown. As he shows, the townsmen understood, for example, the necessity of forming alliances with certain parties in their bid for survival, but equally the town might at specific times be able to negotiate such relations from a position of strength rather than weakness. Furthermore, the balance between local and national political concerns for Bristol's civic authorities is a recurrent feature of Fleming's analysis, and, as he notes, their desire to safeguard the town's rights and privileges, and thus Bristol's identity, was of prime importance.

Local and national political relations are also discussed by Serge ter Braake in his assessment of relationships between six major cities in Holland and Zeeland and the Emperor Charles V. In particular, ter Braake concentrates on the men who acted as mediators between the civic governors and royal authority, and on the methods used by the different and often competing constituencies to try to ensure the well-being of 'their' town. For example, familial links are shown to be important in the establishing of good relations between individual cities and the emperor, and in terms of the negotiation process gift-giving was a highly valued component. Nevertheless, as ter Braake explains, in the sixteenth century religious and later political changes in Holland had profound effects on town–Crown relations. At times this deterioration in relations led to violent conflict, and, as at Amsterdam, might also have implications for how the city was envisaged by those inside and outside.

The significance of violence as part of the negotiating process is similarly explored by Christian-Frederik Felskau in his study of power relations in Prague during the fifteenth and early sixteenth centuries. The city's history is extremely complex during this period, not least because some of its citizens embraced new religious ideas, the city comprised several towns all of which had particular interests, a number of local noble families had concerns there, and royal authority was generally weak. In his survey of the resulting oscillations in Prague's power structure as the different political, religious, and social factions jostled for control, Felskau draws attention to the importance of alliance-making as a means of seeking power and authority, as well as of creating a degree of stability that benefited the commercial life of the city. Even though such periods were somewhat intermittent, Prague's role as the Bohemian capital meant that it continued to be an important national centre. Nonetheless, as he notes at the conclusion of his review of Prague's medieval history, the citizens had failed to achieve autonomy during more than a century of absent and/or weak royal power, leaving them politically vulnerable once a strong Habsburg presence was established in the mid-sixteenth century. Thus this final urban study underlines the importance for the leading citizens of negotiating relations with others both inside and outside the town, but also of *how* they engage in these negotiations, which in turn has implications for their individual and collective identities.

Having a wide-ranging and detailed knowledge of late medieval London, demographically the only English city comparable to the major cities of northern Europe, Caroline Barron in the Afterword brings important insights from her own work to her assessment of the broad range of town studies explored here. Thus she provides a valuable concluding essay that highlights the particularity of urban politics as seen through the detailed town studies, as well as the comparable nature of certain practices found within the negotiating process, such as the use of processions, gift-giving, and the construction of civic buildings and texts that were employed by townsmen to negotiate relations with others inside and outside the town.

This essay collection has its origins in a conversation with Simon Forde of Brepols in Copenhagen several years ago. His support over the intervening period has been invaluable. John Arnold, too, has been a keen supporter of the project and I am delighted to be able to acknowledge both men's help towards the completion of this collection: thank you both for all your assistance. I am also extremely grateful to Helen Parry, a freelance editor, who has generously given of her time and expertise. I should also like to thank Roy Rukkila, Managing Editor at Arizona Center for Medieval and Renaissance Studies, for his expertise in the completion of this volume; and also Leslie MacCoull and David Budgen for their aid in the final stages. Finally, I owe a considerable debt of gratitude to the contributors who have shown great patience and fortitude on the long journey from first idea to completed book.

The View from the Inside:
Urban Politics, Power, and Identity

'Specyall Lover and Preferrer of the Polytike and Common Weale': John Smyth and Ideal Citizenship in Fifteenth-Century Bury St Edmunds

Mark Merry

Introduction:
Biography, the Individual, and Community

This paper will consider the ways in which a form of biography in a late medieval urban context can be used to understand the relationship between people and places, and in particular the way that individuals, communities, and localities interacted in the construction of identity. 'Biography' here is taken to be a form of representation of individual lives within communities, one which provides evidence of the mechanics of the interaction between individual and community. This is a kind of biography which attends to individuality as something experienced in relation to society, and which therefore needs to take local social and cultural forms into account, and where particularities of place should affect how we read evidence about people.

A whole body of work wrestles with the concept of the interrelationship between the individual and the community, and more specifically with how the one influences the perceptions and behaviour of the other.[1] The brand of enquiry

---

[1] Historians who have engaged with these concepts include Craig J. Calhoun, "History, Anthropology and the Study of Communities: Some Problems in Macfarlane's Proposal," *Social History* 3 (1978): 363–73 and idem, "Community: Toward a Variable Conceptualization for Comparative Research," *Social History* 5 (1980): 105–29; and Aron Gurevich, *Categories of Medieval Culture* (London: Routledge, 1985); idem, *Medieval Popular Culture: Problems of Belief and Perception* (Cambridge: Cambridge University Press, 1988); and idem, *Historical Anthropology of the Middle Ages* (Chicago: University

Negotiating the Political in Northern European Urban Society, c.1400–c.1600, ed. Sheila Sweetinburgh, MRTS 434 (Tempe: ACMRS, 2013). [ISBN 978-0-86698-482-9]

which saw individuals as the *result* of community, with its imposition of culture and ideology, as opposed to the raw stuff from which communities were shaped, has, one is glad to observe, been re-appraised. As one anthropologist has remarked, to treat individuals "as merely socially or culturally driven, ignoring the authorial or '*self*-driven' aspects of behaviour, is to render them . . . fictitious ciphers of the anthropologist's theoretical invention."[2] Historical biographers have struggled alongside Cohen with the structural determinism of anthropologists, preferring instead to acknowledge the role of agency in lives and the impact of the individual upon his/her community.[3]

I want to suggest that lives, and subsequent biographical treatment of them, can change local structures, and further, that biographies in an urban context can be created in order to achieve idealised civic goals. These biographies can then develop and take on a 'life' of their own, self-perpetuating and adaptive to social change. A case from fifteenth-century Bury St Edmunds is discussed here involving the formalisation of an emerging communal identity through the public actions of a leading townsman, an identity which became concretised through the production of a series of records that amount to municipally sponsored biographical commemoration.

The value of biography, especially medieval biography, as an historical endeavour is something that is perennially revisited.[4] But while this paper does not wish to visit it, it is interested in examining an example of contemporary life-writing within its cultural and social context. The tradition of biographical writing that was available to medieval Bury's townsmen was one of

---

of Chicago Press, 1992). Amongst social anthropologists, Anthony P. Cohen, Nigel Rapaport, and Amélie O. Rorty are representative of this work. Good introductions to this material can be found in: A. P. Cohen, *The Symbolic Construction of Community* (London: Routledge, 1985) and idem, *Self Consciousness: An Alternative Anthropology of Identity* (London: Routledge, 1994); idem and Rapaport, eds., *Questions of Consciousness* (London: Routledge, 1995); and A. O. Rorty, ed., *The Identities of Persons* (Berkeley: University of California Press, 1976).

[2] Cohen, *Self Consciousness*, 7.

[3] See for example Pauline Stafford's appraisal of the structuralist approach to individual lives in *Queen Emma and Queen Edith: Queenship and Women's Power in Eleventh-Century England* (Oxford: Blackwell, 1997).

[4] See for example the introduction in David Bates, Julia Crick, and Sarah Hamilton, eds., *Writing Medieval Biography 750–1250* (Woodbridge: Boydell Press, 2006). Whilst K. B. MacFarlane concluded that medieval biography was a hopeless endeavour, more recent medievalists allow that biographical focus on an individual's *persona* facilitates the analysis of medieval perceptions: *Writing Medieval Biography*, 10; K. B. MacFarlane, *The Nobility of Later Medieval England* (Oxford: Clarendon Press, 1973), ix.

commemoration, exemplification, and polemic.[5] From the classical pedagogic function of exemplifying morality and celebrating the dead, espousing civic virtue and public duty, to the stylised and conventional hagiographical form which layered these models in Christian philosophy, the biographers of Bury had a store of rhetorical forms with which to create the individual (and by extension collective) life that they attempted in the latter half of the fifteenth century. Moreover, they had an awareness of the reasons for commemorating a life, especially in terms of the political applications of the medium, and it is these 'reasons' which allow us to investigate the relationship between individual, community, and identity in the particular social, cultural, and political environment of Bury in the period.

Bury St Edmunds in the Fifteenth Century

Appreciating the social and political structures at work in Bury St Edmunds in the latter half of the fifteenth century is crucial to understanding the way in which identity operated within it.[6] Bury was a monastic borough, governed by the great abbey of St Edmunds. The town's secular population had no civic administrative structures within its own control, and all administrative power was held in the hands of the abbey's sacrist. The sacrist, the direct landlord of every holding within the borough, had been the focus of the townsmen's disaffections for over two centuries, enflamed during the unrest of the fourteenth century, which had been the inevitable result of a number of economic and both regional and national political developments.[7] As the town developed in its role as a centre for the supply, production, and marketing of wool and cloth, bringing increased prosperity to the ever-growing numbers of Bury individuals involved in the industry, the demand for the machinery for political and civic expression

---

[5] K. Sharpe and S. N. Zwicker, "Introducing Lives," in eidem, *Writing Lives: Biography and Textuality, Identity and Representation in Early Modern England* (Oxford: Oxford University Press, 2008), 2–4; Bates et al., *Writing Medieval Biography*, 1–6.

[6] The history of late medieval Bury St Edmunds is something that needs readdressing. Mary Lobel's account of the town's struggle for political independence, and Robert Dinn's thorough study of popular religious practice in the town, have provided us with much information about the structural organisation of the town: M. D. Lobel, *The Borough of Bury St Edmunds* (Oxford: Clarendon Press, 1935); R. Dinn, "Popular Religion in Late Medieval Bury St Edmunds" (Ph.D. diss., University of Manchester, 1990). Robert Gottfried's study of the social and economic aspects of secular life in the town raises many important issues regarding the development of burghal identity, but remains problematic: R. Gottfried, *Bury St Edmunds and the Urban Crisis 1290–1539* (Princeton: Princeton University Press, 1982).

[7] For the role played by the sacrist in the running of the town's affairs, and the secular community's resistance to this, see Lobel, *The Borough*, 17–19, 31–59.

naturally developed as well. The townsmen had never been granted any form of incorporation, and the minimal privileges that they had accrued since the eleventh century were held at the sufferance of the abbot and sacrist of St Edmund's. The lack of political self-determination, and the jealous guarding of prerogatives and customs on the part of the abbey, generated friction as it did elsewhere in other monastic boroughs.[8]

In keeping with the economic decline suffered by the great landowners of the late fourteenth century, the officials of St Edmund's adopted the short-sighted policy of alienating and dispersing its vast holdings in an attempt to recoup its losses. With the continual reduction of its landed power base, the ultimate source of its authority within the Liberty of St Edmund's and the town of Bury, the increasingly prosperous secular community of the fifteenth century had no need to try to wrest increasing privileges from the abbot and sacrist: the officers of the abbey found themselves granting concessions as a matter of financial policy at a time when the town was consolidating its economic strength.[9] This led to a loosening of St Edmund's grip on the running of civic affairs in the town, and the stabilisation of relations between town and abbey: the fifteenth century saw no return to the outright violence that flared during the fourteenth century, violence that was replaced with litigation as the medium of opposition to monastic rule.[10]

By the middle of the century, the increasing freedom enjoyed by Bury's townsmen led to the establishment of an 'unofficial' secular town government centred on the resurrection of the town's moribund fourteenth-century Candlemas Guild, originally created in the wake of the punitive closure of the town's Gild Merchant after the 1327 rising.[11] The Candlemas Guild was ostensibly an exclusive social and religious guild with no administrative function, but increasingly it was recognised as the locus of civic interests, directed by Bury's burghal elite, taking on a series of duties on behalf of the whole secular community.[12] The guild was endowed with a number of often substantial grants of land and

---

[8] N. M. Trenholme, *The English Monastic Boroughs: A Study in Medieval History* (Columbia: University of Missouri Press, 1927).

[9] Gottfried, *Bury St Edmunds*, 86–127.

[10] Lobel, *The Borough*, 18, 159; Gottfried, *Bury St Edmunds*, 238; Trenholme, *English Monastic Boroughs*, 68. The origins of this stability may be partly found in the personalities of several of the early fifteenth-century monastic officials of St Edmund's, most noticeably the conciliatory abbot William Curteys. The role played by Curteys in ameliorating relations with the townsmen might be indicated by the renewal of the secular community's attempts to acquire political independence after his death in 1457: J. W. Elston, "William Curteys, Abbot of Bury St Edmunds 1429–1446" (Ph.D. diss., University of California at Berkeley, 1979).

[11] Trenholme, *Monastic Boroughs*, 19–23, 71; Lobel, *The Borough*, 82.

[12] A comparison of the 1389 returns for the Candlemas Guild (London, The National Archives, C 47/46/406) and the ordinances it drew up in 1471 (London, British

property with which to defray the tax burden of the town, a programme which was begun by John Smyth in the 1470s, and which was subsequently built upon for at least two centuries.

Late medieval communities were self-conscious and able to construct identity, and were motivated to do so when self-determination and administrative autonomy was an aspiration rather than the reality enjoyed in other, constitutionally independent, towns. It is clear that in terms of burghal pride the management of communal aspirations: the desire to provide and maintain favourable economic conditions for trade and industry in Bury, and the ambition to attain a degree of independence, was adopted by the town's elite. For example, the fact that they were powerless to enact ordinances which might have shaped the communal identity of the town did not prevent them from producing documents designed to do precisely this, such as the 'ordinances' drawn up by Bury's alderman Robert Gardiner in 1470, and the bill of fourteen complaints made against the abbot of St Edmund's in 1478.[13] Both documents asserted that the role of the alderman included the responsibility to "fight diligently" to maintain the rights of the town and to correct transgressions against the townsmen. These transgressions included costs associated with the alienation and inheritance of *hadgovel* tenements, various types of non-monetary service owed to the sacrist, the passing of various taxes owed by the abbey to the townsmen, the interference of the abbey in the election and privileges of the town's (largely figurehead) alderman, manipulation of the town's view of frankpledge, and so on. Perhaps the most hated imposition was that of the 'Abbot's Cope', the hundred-mark payment owed to a newly installed abbot: extensive litigation throughout the fourteenth century signifies the efforts the townsmen went to to avoid paying this, and it was still a focus for discontent in the 1470s. While the 1470 ordinances and the 1478 articles may well have been conservative (the demands they made were those that had been traditionally made against St Edmunds since the twelfth century),[14] the fact that they were drawn up at all is evidence of the resurgent desire by the town's elite for civic independence at a time when in essence this was some way from being established. The motivation behind these documents must therefore have been the desire for *recognition* as an independent political entity, when the

---

Library, MS. Harley 4626) indicates quite eloquently the wider social and administrative remit it had adopted in the intervening years.

[13] Reproduced in Trenholme, *Monastic Boroughs*, 98–104. The articles of complaint are found in London, British Library, MS. Add. 17391, fols. 156ᵛ–157. See Lobel, *The Borough*, 182–85 for the abbot's response to the complaints, found in London, The National Archives, Star Chamber Proceedings, Henry VIII bundle xxii no.6.

[14] Lobel, *The Borough*, 160; Dinn, "Popular Religion," 126. Gottfried suggests that throughout the period the burghal elite of Bury was "staid and conservative": *Bury St Edmunds*, 91, 136.

reality was that by the 1470s Bury's townsmen enjoyed more self-determination than ever before.

The documents of the 1470s (including John Smyth's enfeoffments—see below) portrayed an overtly political collective identity, and were only one component of what appears to have been a concerted effort. Other components may be seen in the townsmen's attempts to assume control of certain institutions from the obedientiaries of St Edmund's: the hospitals, the guildhall, and the gaol, for example.[15] The nature of relations between town and abbey throughout the thirteenth to the fifteenth centuries was itself a substantial factor in the communal identity of the secular community, and it has been suggested that the prolonged struggle acted as a cohesive social force within the community, serving to bind the townsmen together despite the social and economic distinctions between various groups in the town.[16] The 1470s constituted the high-water mark of the townsmen's efforts to construct a communal identity for themselves, efforts which appear to have met with some success.

In order to better analyse the relationship between individual and community, a model of the social behaviour of the secular population of Bury St Edmunds has been developed.[17] The model is not the focus of this paper, but it has been employed to draw out facets of Bury-specific identity at the level of the individual. The model uses the town's rich probate materials to elucidate a wide variety of aspects of urban living, such as occupation, property ownership, guild membership, literacy, life-cycle status, religious affiliation, charitable giving, local and regional connections, patronage of the arts, and so on. It treats the behaviour of the individual as an abstract, using all the evidence available for the whole community at the same time, in order to provide a context for examining the behaviour of specific individuals. The model provides a community- and

---

[15] See Mark L. Merry, "The Construction and Representation of Urban Identities: Public and Private Lives in Late Medieval Bury St Edmunds" (Ph.D. diss., University of Kent, 2000), 122–40.

[16] Gottfried, *Bury St Edmunds*, 131. Gottfried probably over-emphasises the homogeneity of Bury's secular community, however: the wealthier members of the secular community had close ties with the abbey, as suggested by their will-making strategies, as well as their membership of the abbey's confraternity, and requests to be buried in the abbey grounds. A unified identity of the community may have been more of an ideal than a reality in Bury's secular community: for example, the disputes between the elite and rest of the townsmen over the levying of the fine in the wake of the 1381 violence; the disassociation of the elite from the rebels throughout the fourteenth century; and so on. See also Lobel, *The Borough*, 88 for examples of prominent townsmen disputing between themselves over financial and political matters.

[17] The model and the discussion of the methodology used are presented in Merry, "Construction and Representation," 129–75. The model was constructed using data on 9,054 named individuals mentioned in wills proved in the sacrist's court of St Edmunds, and a variety of sources with a non-monastic provenance between 1354 and 1493.

period-sensitive amalgam against which specific individuals can be judged in the quantified context of those around them in their time and place. The degree of divergence of the individual from the model is useful in elucidating which individuals stood out from their peers.

One of the things which the model facilitates is the identification of the individuals that might be described as Bury's elite. Indicators of elite status in Bury include those one would expect: fulfilling the role of town alderman;[18] demonstrable wealth; entrepreneurial involvement in mercantile or textile enterprises;[19] active public life, as manifested in repeated appearance in the records;[20] guild

---

[18] Office-holding can be seen as an outward sign of good reputation and of social and economic success: David H. Sacks, *The Widening Gate: Bristol and the Atlantic Economy, 1450–1700* (Berkeley and London: University of California Press, 1991), 162. Civic office might be seen as a sign of "real status," where wealth and status are "fused together in a social institution": Charles Phythian-Adams, *Desolation of a City: Coventry and the Urban Crisis of the Late Middle Ages* (Cambridge: Cambridge University Press, 1978), 116, 123. In Bury, whilst office-holding was largely limited to that of alderman, the inhabitants of Bury served on their own commissions of the peace and gaol delivery; see Diarmaid MacCulloch, *Suffolk and the Tudors: Politics and Religion in an English County 1500–1600* (Oxford: Oxford University Press, 1986).

[19] Occupations categorised as entrepreneur/textile marketing, textile manufacture, and clothing/furnishing manufacture account for 34 per cent of all fifteenth-century secular Bury occupations. The town's textile workers were principally involved in trades connected with finishing cloth and marketing it: Merry, "Construction and Representation," 136–43; Gottfried, *Bury St Edmunds,* 101–2, 107–21. The other substantially prominent category is that of specialist professional and retail occupations, reflecting Bury's urban context, within which 24 per cent of individuals with specified occupations fall in the century. Without the standard of office-holding in Bury against which to assess status and 'success' it is of course difficult to match occupational life-cycle with social status and official authority: however, of the forty-one known Bury aldermen for the period 1347–1472, fourteen (and probably nine others) can be identified as a mercer, merchant, draper, or grocer: see Bury St Edmunds, Suffolk Record Office [hereafter SROB], Osbern, fols. 1, 1ᵛ, 11ᵛ, 16ᵛ, 31, 34ᵛ, 36, 38, 46ᵛ, 54, 61ᵛ, 68ᵛ, 79ᵛ, 127ᵛ, 180ᵛ, 182ᵛ, 225ᵛ, 244ᵛ, 253ᵛ, 255ᵛ; SROB, Hawlee, fols. 29ᵛ, 30, 39ᵛ, 62, 64, 80, 83ᵛ, 95, 125ᵛ, 145, 192ᵛ, 232, 253ᵛ; *Calendar Close Rolls, 1360–64,* 248, *Calendar Close Rolls, 1435–41,* 180; *Calendar Close Rolls, 1476–85,* 329; SROB, H 1/5/21, 3; SROB, H 1/5/18; London, The National Archives, PCC PROB, 11/6/32; Merry, "Construction and Representation," 186–221.

[20] When someone is recorded in any form of document it marks an interaction between his social activities and the legal and institutional structures that bound that person into the community. Frequent appearance in the records might indicate an active public life. What is more, frequent appearance, as executor or overseer for example, in the material used for this model (that is, primarily testamentary) suggests a high social profile and perceived authority.

membership;[21] significant land or property holding;[22] conspicuous consumption of material goods; the employment of servants;[23] book ownership;[24] and so on. Other patterns emerge. Membership of the Candlemas Guild and therefore en-feoffment in John Smyth's lands were the clearest flags of elite status.[25] Other

---

[21] Testamentary bequests made to occupational or social/religious guilds or their brethren have been taken to indicate membership on the part of the testator. Membership of guilds must have comprised one of the most concrete delineators of identity in urban communities, as it brought the individual into contact with others on various overlapping occupational, economic, social, civic, symbolic, and spiritual levels. The formal nature of relationships within guilds (particularly at times of ceremonial observance), prescribed by ordinances and overseen by officials, provided a structure within which individuals could rise and progress as a result of enduring membership or occupational and financial success. Roles within the guilds were apportioned according to status, and in a town lacking an official governmental hierarchy this must have had an effect upon the explication of identity and status. Furthermore, guild membership was not only an indicator of status, but was also a vehicle to developing status, through the multiplex nature of social connections that guild membership engendered. Evidence suggests that only a small proportion of Bury inhabitants belonged to guilds, and that certainly only a few belonged to more than one guild. The 1389 Chancery guild certificates show that there were at least eighteen craft and socio-religious guilds active: London, The National Archives, C 47/45/400, C 47/46/401–17. Guild membership was generally the province of Bury's wealthier testators: Dinn, "Popular Religion," 329–32.

[22] Typically Bury's testators in the period held a single property, which was within the town. Properties held by Bury testators in other towns and villages have been taken to indicate commercial interests, and therefore wealth and status. Only 4 per cent of fifteenth-century Bury testators referred to properties outside Bury.

[23] Not every householder employed servants, and doing so signified the availability of a certain level of resources. In the fifteenth century 10 per cent of Bury testators refer to servants in their employ. Of these the vast majority refer to a single servant only.

[24] Late medieval book ownership in urban communities was the province of the most prominent burgesses: Susan Reynolds, *An Introduction to the History of English Medieval Towns* (Oxford: Clarendon Press, 1977), 85. Perhaps surprisingly, less than 3 per cent (forty-seven) of wills in the period 1346–1493 indicate testators' possession of books. In comparison, 12 per cent of testators in Norwich during the period 1370–1490 owned books at the time of their death: Norman P. Tanner, *The Church in Late Medieval Norwich 1370–1532* (Toronto: Pontifical Institute of Medieval Studies, 1984), 193–97. The experience of textual material among the secular community was more than likely facilitated by the presence of the abbey, as not only did St Edmund's possess one of the greatest libraries in the country, but there is also a suggestion that its contents were lent out to the elite: the last entry in Abbot Curteys' register before the index is a letter of admonition to the lay confraternity from the abbot demanding the return of all books to the abbey (London, British Library, MS. Add. 7096, fols. 216ᵛ –217).

[25] Admission to the enfeoffment of John Smyth was reserved to the twenty-four most substantial burgesses of the town, and promotion to this status was regulated by quasi-civic ordinances: Merry, "Construction and Representation," 209–18.

components included patronage of particular religious houses in Suffolk and fur-ther afield;[26] the provision of chantries, and support for the town's Jesus cult;[27] personal links with the abbey of St Edmunds;[28] extramural economic connec-tions with people and institutions, particularly in London; longevity of family residence in the town; and certain forms of marriage strategy.

The group of townsmen comprising Bury's elite appears *as* a group with striking clarity, their definition made all the clearer by the fact that these indica-tors apply as a set: only a very few of Bury's townsmen can claim any of them, but those that can usually claim most if not all. In other words, there are very similar displays of attitudes and behaviour among Bury's secular elite, and the similar-ity suggests an acute awareness of what these were.[29] Exclusive, dominated by a small number of long-standing Bury families, and very difficult to break into, the secular elite of the town bore all the hallmarks of a town council; a group was born out of what commentators have identified as generations of solidar-ity amongst a community united in its opposition to St Edmund's.[30] The par-ticular political circumstances in Bury, and the unique way in which the secular

---

[26] In the fifteenth century, 39 per cent of Bury testators across the period made bequests to religious houses, individuals, or parish churches elsewhere in Suffolk. Dinn suggests that giving to the large regional religious houses was unsurprisingly the preroga-tive of Bury's richest testators: "Popular Religion," 475.

[27] For the prevalence of these in Bury, see Robert Dinn, "Death and Rebirth in Late Medieval Bury St Edmunds," in *Death in Towns: Urban Responses to the Dying and Dead, 100–1600,* ed. Steven Bassett (Leicester: Leicester University Press, 1992), 151–69.

[28] The popularity of St Edmund's among the secular community declined during the fifteenth century from the already quite low levels of the fourteenth century: Mac-Culloch, *Suffolk and the Tudors,* 136. The social composition of those making bequests to St Edmund's comprised the wealthier burgesses: see Dinn, "Popular Religion," 430–33. Many of the town's elite had familial connections with the personnel of the monastery, and many may have been members of the monastery's lay confraternity. The wealthiest testators were more likely to choose a burial place in one of Bury's churches rather than in the town's cemetery, with those requesting St Edmund's among the richest of the group: Dinn, "Popular Religion," 595–606. Fifteenth-century examples of testators being bur-ied in St Edmund's can be found at SROB, Osbern, fols. 215, 240ᵛ; SROB, Hawlee, fols. 64ᵛ, 144.

[29] Historians such as Nancy Partner have argued that such self-conscious, intro-spective awareness was a feature of medieval sources every bit as much as for later periods: "The Hidden Self: Psychoanalysis and the Textual Unconscious," in *Writing Medieval History (Writing History),* ed. eadem (London: Hodder Arnold, 2005), 42–64, at 42–45. Others, talking of the early modern period, have characterised communities and indi-viduals as both existing in a framework of "'self-fashioning'. . . the artful construction of identities, selfhoods, public lives" where "not only [. . .] public authority but [. . .] personal identity were produced through a series of constructions and performances": Sharpe and Zwicker, "Introducing Lives," 9–10.

[30] Gottfried, *Bury St Edmunds,* 130–31; Lobel, *The Borough,* 93.

community chose to exploit them, produced specific forms in which identity could be expressed: many of the official mechanisms on which elite urban standing was habitually built elsewhere did not exist in Bury. With no possibility of admission to a freeman body or the various ranks of civic office-holding, other strategies for social organisation took on heightened significance. This is where the impact of individuality could be made: the lack of structures within which to construct identity placed an increased emphasis on the role of social relationships, which left more freedom for social 'strategy' and agency.[31]

Elite status became something more malleable and less rigidly composed, the parameters determined by the community through convention rather than statute. Gottfried decided that Bury's burgesses "submerged their individuality in the amorphous personality of the larger corporate group,"[32] but I would argue that the evidence presented in the following sections suggests that individuality *did* have a significant effect upon the management of identity in Bury, and furthermore could have an impact upon the wider social and political structures in the town.

John Smyth

The renewed expression of political identity in the late fifteenth century, and the demand for its recognition, took its practical form through the actions of Bury's elite, led by John Smyth, mercer of the parish of St Mary's and esquire, who died in 1481. Smyth was alderman of Bury at least five times, and possibly as many as nine times.[33] He fits very squarely within the model-dictated definition of the 'oligarchic' elite of the town, perhaps even epitomises it. His connections to the personnel of St Edmund's were evident. The sacrist John Swaffham received a bequest of 20s, while every brother of the convent received 6s 8d if they were also

---

[31] Elisabeth Salter has seen social relationships as the area in which individuals were "presented with particular possibilities for creativity in their lives": *Six Renaissance Men and Women: Innovation, Biography and Cultural Creativity in Tudor England, c. 1450–1560* (Aldershot: Ashgate, 2007), 1. For a sociological discussion of the role of multiple, overlapping social relations in the construction and performance of identity, see Pierre Bourdieu, "Fieldwork in Philosophy," in idem, *In Other Words: Essays Towards a Reflexive Sociology*, trans. M. A. Adamson (Cambridge: Polity Press, 1990), 3–33.

[32] Gottfried, *Bury St Edmunds*, 136, 150.

[33] Lobel claims that he occupied the office of alderman at least five times, while Gottfried suggests that he held the position nine times between 1423 and 1462 (with the office holder for the years 1444 to 1451 unidentified); however, to have held the office in 1423 and then lived until 1481 would have made Smyth a very young representative of the town's established elite. It is possible that Smyth's father (also John) held the office in the 1420s and 1440s: Lobel, *The Borough*, 161; Gottfried, *Bury St Edmunds*, 141, 271.

a priest, or 3*s* 4*d* otherwise.[34] The prior was given Smyth's "beste stondyng cuppe of sylver and gylte," a somewhat ambiguous bequest.[35] On the one hand the nature of the gift might suggest a personal acquaintance; on the other hand the fact that Smyth requires the cup to revert to the prior's successors transforms the bequest into something altogether more symbolic. The standing cup becomes an object that associates the *memory* of John Smyth with the *office* of prior at times of heightened symbolic awareness. Given the role that the prior is to play in the administration of Smyth's will and the foundation of his two chantries, it might be possible to identify an attempt by Smyth to establish a kind of symbiotic relationship with the abbey, particularly with the prior, a relationship which enhances the prestige of both.

Smyth also made considerable bequests to the town's parochial clergy, its Mary and Jesus priests, and created two substantially endowed perpetual chantries. His religious giving extended further afield in Suffolk as well: friars at Babwell, Sudbury, Clare, and Thetford are remembered, as are nunneries in Redlingfield, Thetford, Bruisyard, Soham, 'Icklyngton',[36] Ixworth, and Campsey.[37] These houses comprise a checklist of those most commonly named in Bury wills throughout the fifteenth century: Smyth neither remembers an unusual religious house nor fails to recall a house that his fellow townsmen favoured. It might be said that Smyth's religious interests within and beyond Bury were typical of his community, and perhaps even indicate an awareness of *exactly* the kind of religious interests that community had, manifesting an acute consciousness of the religious knowledge and interests of the Bury elite.

In similar fashion, his testamentary charity to his parish is both typical and at the same time exemplary of Bury elite status. Smyth's 1480 will suggests a close association with the parish church, with valuable bequests made to the high altar and to named priests of the church, as well as the establishment of the two chantries at the altars of Our Lady and St John the Baptist. He may have been responsible for building the chancel aisles and the sacrarium of St Mary's.[38] He was

---

[34] Samuel Tymms, *Bury Wills and Inventories*, Camden Society 49 (London: Camden Society, 1850), 55.

[35] In 1480 the prior was probably William Mildenhale. He is named in SROB, H 1/6/1 *Feoffment Documents*, fol. 56 as a witness to John Frense's instructions regarding the leper house at the Risbygate (see below); and in the 1479 will of Thomas Cranewys, chaplain and parish priest of St Mary's: SROB, Hawlee, fol. 285ᵛ.

[36] Possibly Icklingham in Suffolk.

[37] All these houses are in Suffolk, except the two friaries and nunnery at Thetford in Norfolk, and Soham in Cambridgeshire.

[38] Margaret Statham, *Jankyn Smyth and the Guildhall Feoffees* (Bury St Edmunds: Guildhall Feoffment Trust, 1981), 2. In the indentures attached to his will Smyth refers to the residue of revenues coming from "a pece of medewe inclosed at the Turret in Bury Seynt Edmunds aboveseid, whiche is assigned to the reparacion of the newe eles in thaforseyd chirche made by me thaforseyd John Smyth": *Bury Wills*, 62.

also responsible for the north chapel or 'Jesus Aisle', which had been constructed by 1463, as well as for the south or Lady Chapel which was completed a decade later, where his chantry priests were to celebrate. The sanctuary and the crypt beneath it had probably been added by Smyth sometime before 1479.[39] The scope of the works undertaken by Smyth would have required official and communal involvement at many different levels, including the highest obedientiaries in St Edmund's (who held the advowson of St Mary's), the clergy of St Mary's, the master mason involved in the construction work,[40] the local suppliers of materials, and the labourers drawn from the area. This would have increased the publicity of Smyth's activities, possibly even beyond the confines of Bury St Edmunds, especially as the undertaking extended over a period of more than a decade.

What makes Smyth stand out from his burghal peers, however, were a number of grants he had made to the townsmen of Bury, forming the core of the communal effort to create a de facto civic government. The probate register Hawlee contains a copy of his will made in December 1480 and proved in September 1481.[41] Annexed to it are copies of several indentures detailing his grants to the town. *Jankyn Smyth's Book* contains an abbreviated copy of an earlier version of the will, made in 1477, reproducing clauses primarily concerned with the enfeoffment of the Candlemas Guild brethren in Smyth's lands and properties.[42] Importantly, the ordinances of the Candlemas Guild drawn up in 1471 but surviving in a later document also contain clauses from earlier indentures as part of their schedule, as well as a summary of what happened to Smyth's feoffment in subsequent years.[43] Similarly the manuscript known as *Feoffment Documents* contains not only several copies of Smyth's will, but also copies of what are called his 'second', 'third', and 'fourth' wills, which are in fact copies of different indentures enfeoffing Candlemas Guild members in various additional grants, as well as a brief account of the subsequent fate of the lands and properties.[44] The

[39] Clive Paine, *St Mary's, Bury St Edmunds* (Bury St Edmunds: Honey Hill, 1986).

[40] Possibly William Leyer, or more probably his pupil Simon Clerk who took over from Leyer as master mason of the abbey: John Harvey, *English Mediaeval Architects: A Biographical Dictionary down to 1550* (Gloucester: Sutton, 1984), 55–60, 172.

[41] SROB, Hawlee, fol. 304. A copy of this version is printed in *Bury Wills*, 55–73.

[42] SROB H 1/2/1 *Jankyn Smyth's Book*, fols. 1–5. This document, drawn up at the end of the fifteenth century, is essentially a detailed and presumably definitive list of the properties and parcels of land left to the Candlemas Guild on behalf of the town by John Smyth and Margaret Odeham. The numerous parcels of land detailed in this manuscript are an exact reproduction of those that appear in London, British Library, MS. Harley 4626, fols. 33–37ᵛ. The 1477 will also appears at fol. 23ᵛ in the same manuscript, while the 1480 will (the version in Tymms) appears at fol. 26ᵛ.

[43] London, British Library, MS. Harley 4626, fols. 23ᵛ–29ᵛ, 33–41. Fols. 23ᵛ–26 comprise a copy of the 1477 will, while fols. 26ᵛ–29 is an indenture of 1480.

[44] SROB, H 1/6/1 *Feoffment Documents*, fols. 12–36, 42, 46, 56, 59–61, 73, 77–83, 88, 95, 98, 103–105, 110, 115, and 128.

proliferation of these interconnecting documents comprises the initial stages of the biography of John Smyth, created by him in collaboration with his leading peers.

Central to the public identity and biography of John Smyth, and ultimately why he was commemorated so carefully by generations of Bury inhabitants to the present day, were the grants he made to the town's Candlemas Guild on behalf of the whole town. Smyth made enfeoffments of several groupings of lands and properties, two being the most significant: a 1470 enfeoffment of everything he held in the south, east, and Vine fields of Bury, as well as in the towns and fields of Berton, Fornham St Martin, Rougham, and Nowton; and a 1473 enfeoffment of a messuage, eighteen pieces of arable land, a piece of meadow, and a piece of wood with liberty of a fold course in Rougham.[45] The 1480 will of Smyth refers to the first enfeoffment which was subsequently reiterated in the second indenture of 1473.[46] Two copies of the 1473 indenture are found in the *Feoffment Documents*, although they do not list the feoffees as the 1480 will does.[47] The feoffees in both versions of this grouping of lands and properties were members of the Candlemas Guild, and all were prominent in the records. Details of the second (Rougham) enfeoffment appear in at least five sets of documents.[48] The feoffees of this grant were largely the same that were to serve in the other. Many of these feoffees were past, present, or future aldermen of Bury, and the surviving testamentary materials indicate that all were men of considerable standing.

The various records of these two grants were codified in two very significant, civically generated documents: the Candlemas Guild statutes, drawn up in 1471, and *Jankyn Smyth's Book*. Both reproduce the same list of eighty parcels of land in the fields of Berton, Rougham, and southern Bury St Edmunds comprising 222

---

[45] Less frequently recorded enfeoffments include a grant made in 1463 to John Walsshe which provided a parcel of land to the north of Eastgate Street in order to provide a payment of 2*d* at Easter and Michaelmas to the alderman. The *Feoffment Documents* also record a grant of a messuage and fifteen pieces of land comprising eighty-two acres in the fields of Berton and Fornham St Martin: SROB, H 1/6/1 *Feoffment Documents*, fols. 1–13. Fold courses were very valuable resources in the region: see Mark Bailey, *A Marginal Economy? East Anglian Breckland in the Later Middle Ages* (Cambridge: Cambridge University Press, 1989).

[46] *Bury Wills*, 68. Copies of this indenture appear in several places, notably SROB, H 1/2/1 *Jankyn Smyth's Book*, fols. 1–1v; SROB, H 1/6/1 *Feoffment Documents*, fol. 16; London, British Library, MS. Harley 4626, fols. 23ᵛ–24.

[47] SROB, H 1/6/1 *Feoffment Documents*, fols. 20, 27.

[48] There are at least five copies of this indenture: *Bury Wills*, 68; SROB, H 1/2/1 *Jankyn Smyth's Book*, fol. 1v; London, British Library, MS. Harley 4626, fol. 24; SROB, H 1/6/1 *Feoffment Documents*, fols. 17, 34.

acres and 24 roods, a number of messuages and tenements, a garden, and a piece
of meadow given by Smyth to the inhabitants of Bury.[49]

The 1470 enfeoffment was made so

> that alle the issuez and pro*fites* comyng and grovyng of the seid meeses,
> lond*es*, and tenement*es* schulde be houly co*n*vertyd and applyid to thuse and
> pro*fitys* of thynhabytauntys of the seid town of Bury and of their succes-
> sourez for ever to discharge certayn y*m*posicionez and charg*es* wonte to be
> boryn be the seid inhabitauntez[50]

while the 1473 enfeoffment was made

> unto the releve & helpe of the alderman burgeyses and of alle the com*myn*-
> alte and poore inh*a*bitaunt*es* of the seyd Toun of Bury and unto the sup-
> portac*i*on of the Chargis dayly lying on them[51]

Smyth's concern seems to have been quite specific: his gifts to the town were to
alleviate the "chargis dayly lying" on the whole population of the town, including
the poorest. The earlier will of 1477, produced in *Jankyn Smyth's Book*, provides
more details of Smyth's wishes with regard to his enfeoffments. This book is a
significant milestone in the biography of John Smyth. Internal evidence suggests that it dates from the end of the fifteenth century, and it codifies Smyth's
grants, as well as detailing the re-enfeoffments that took place in the generation
after his death, framing these in calls for suitable civic comemoration from the
whole town. The *Book*'s very title seems significant, as if by naming Smyth by his
diminutive the authors were encouraging in the townsmen a sense of familiarity
with the man.

After his death the alderman and burgesses of the town, as well as Smyth's
feoffees, were to "solemnly and devoutly" keep his yearday at St Mary's for his
soul and the souls of his wife Anne, their parents, their benefactors, and all
Christian souls.[52] On the vigil of the anniversary the priests and clerks were to
sing *Placebo* and dirige, and on the yearday itself a requiem mass was to be conducted with other prayers. After these civic celebrations of Smyth's life, the

> residue and overpluse of the issues and pro*fitez* of the said [grants] be re-
> servyd and kepyd savely and suerly by the said ald*er*man burgez & feoffes

---

[49] SROB, H 1/2/1 *Jankyn Smyth's Book*, fols. 12–24; London, British Library, MS.
Harley 4626, fols. 33–37ᵛ.

[50] *Bury Wills*, 57.

[51] SROB, H 1/2/1 *Jankyn Smyth's Book*, fol. 2; London, British Library, MS. Harley
4626, fol. 24.

[52] SROB, H 1/2/1 *Jankyn Smyth's Book*, fol. 2ᵛ; London, British Library, MS. Harley
4626, fols. 24–24ᵛ.

for the tyme beyng to that entent that whansoever and howoft soever in tymes to come the abbey of Bury seynt Edmund schalbe vacant of an abbot be the deth of the abbot and a new abbot therre after his deth schall lawfully be chosyn I wyll thanne that of the sayd issues and profitez be payd to the sayd newe abbot for the tyme beyng as moche as may be reservyd and kepyd therof in to a satisfactyon and a recompensacion of a certeyn summe of mony wont of custom to be payd to the newe abbot by the inhabitantes of the sayd toun of Bury seynt Edmund [. . .] Also yf any thyng therof remayne over the said charges I wyll that it be applyed and disposid to the paymentes of tenthis and fyftens taxis tallagys and of alle odir maner charges the which xalbe exact & put to the burgesses and comynalte of the sayd toun in to the releve and discharge of the burgesses & comynalte of the sayd toun of alle and syngler forsayd chargys[53]

The grants, whilst providing practical financial support to the town, are here explicitly cast in a political context by being ostensibly set up to target the imposition of the Abbot's Cope first and foremost, other burdens being a secondary consideration. This is both symbolic and political, and clearly sets Smyth's actions within the traditional context of secular opposition to St Edmund's.[54]

In order for these grants to serve their stated purpose, their perpetuation was clearly vital, and detailed provision was made for it. This was to comprise a continual process of re-enfeoffment: when the twenty-four feoffees were reduced to fourteen, twelve were to release their right in the enfeoffment to the two eldest, who would re-enfeoff them and others of the most substantial of Bury to return to the number of twenty-four, chosen by the alderman and burgesses. Smyth entrusted the enfeoffments always to the most substantial townsmen of Bury to administer on behalf of the town, to be overseen by the most senior burgesses under the supervision of the alderman. The list of feoffees in John Smyth's grants to the town thus constitutes a starting point for an investigation into Bury's civic elite. The current and future feoffees were obliged to take an oath before the town's alderman and burgesses to fulfil the intentions laid out in Smyth's wills and indentures. Each year the alderman and burgesses were to choose four "provyd men & abyll" from the feoffees to supervise the enfeoffments, receive the revenues,

---

[53] SROB, H 1/2/1 *Jankyn Smyth's Book*, fols 2ᵛ–3; London, British Library, MS. Harley 4626, fol. 24ᵛ; *Bury Wills*, 70.

[54] It has been argued that, given the fragmentary and laconic nature of medieval sources, historians should give a privileged place to what *is* mentioned over what is not, and that we should be rhetorically sensitive to the emphases of our texts: Pauline Stafford, "Writing the Biography of Eleventh-century Queens," in Bates et al., *Medieval Biography*, 99–109, at 102.

fulfil Smyth's will regarding the yearday observances, and make account to the alderman.[55]

Crucially, despite the fact that he ostensibly stipulated that the feoffees were to be drawn from the burgesses of the town, what in fact happened was that they were drawn from the brethren of the Candlemas Guild. In terms of the potential pool of individuals this provided there would have been little difference—the senior burgesses would have belonged to the guild—but the fact that responsibility for the enfeoffments was adopted by a formally composed body with a distinctly corporate nature allowed greater control over what happened to the grants in the future. This development was presumably enacted with the assent of Smyth, given that the re-enfeoffment process was embedded in the rules of the guild during Smyth's lifetime. The result was that the Candlemas Guild became the body which perpetually held Smyth's lands, and becomes responsible for administering the funds to pay the tax burden on behalf of the town. In effect, the guild became a self-sustaining body with the resources to operate as a representative council on behalf of the town in its relations with the abbey: a de facto town government run by the secular community.

However, the hierarchy of St Edmund's was drafted into the perpetuation of the grants as well. The abbot, sacrist, and prior all served as witnesses to Smyth's will and indentures, while the sacrist John Swaffham was to perform a more direct service:

> And for perfitte wittenes and knowlege that this is my very will and intent by me the seyd John Smyth made uppon the seyd feffement and that it shuld be undouted to all men I have to this present writyng putto my seel and subscribed it with my owne hand And for as moche as my seell to many folkys is unknowen therfor at my request the Secristen of the Monasterie of Bury Seynt Edmund [. . .] to this present writyng also hath putto his seell[56]

This participation perhaps served to legitimise Smyth's grants and the activities of the Candlemas Guild, and it was probably important that the implicit support of St Edmund's was recorded in the documents that came to take on the form of Smyth's biography.

The relationship between Smyth's gifts and the population of Bury St Edmunds, and the mediation between the two by the Candlemas Guild, are crucial to an understanding both of why Smyth made his grants, and of how the secular community of the town managed its affairs. The Candlemas Guild not only copied the indentures into their statute book, they also chose to incorporate their observance into their day-to-day operation. The enfeoffments, as they are

---

[55] London, British Library, MS. Harley 4626, fol. 25ᵛ; SROB, H 1/2/1 *Jankyn Smyth's Book*, fols. 4–4ᵛ; *Bury Wills*, 70–72.

[56] *Bury Wills*, 67–68.

represented in both the 1477 will produced in *Jankyn Smyth's Book* and the 1480 registered will, make no mention at all of the Candlemas Guild by name. Subsequent references to Smyth's grants suggest that the role of the Candlemas Guild in the administration of the enfeoffments was central, and probably originally implicit, and later management of the enfeoffments makes the developing connection with the guild clearer. For example, the *Feoffment Documents* record the transfer of eighteen acres of land in Berton, and Smyth's property in Bury called 'Recyes' in 1491, 1517, and 1534; the record of the 1491 transfer states that the holdings are

> ad usum & proficium Inhabitantium villate de Bury predicte per Avisamentum & concensum fratrum Guilde purificacionis beate Marie virginis vocatur Candlemas guilde

while the 1517 record indicates that the enfeoffment of the same holdings is to be

> ad opus & usum ac ad proficium ffratrum Guilde beate Marie infra villam de Bury sancti Edmundi[57]

The change in emphasis between these two statements is enlightening, and the role of the Candlemas Guild is evidently central by the end of the century. The ordinances, essentially framed around the enfeoffments, were recorded just over four months after John Smyth made his 1470 grant, and it is evident that they were a direct collaboration. The ordinances' first statute describes the guild's rules regarding the obedience of its members to the alderman, dye, auditors, and "holders" of the guild, and the swearing in of new brethren; and it is significant that new entrants into Bury's most exclusive guild are referred to as "feoffees", indicating that from 1471 John Smyth's feoffees and the members of the Candlemas Guild were to be synonymous.[58]

If the guild had previously existed as a largely social and figurative body, after September 1470 the situation was very different as a result of the substantial landed wealth it suddenly acquired. The grants made by Smyth to the town gave the Candlemas Guild a structure on which to base any authority it may have aspired to, and the machinery designed by Smyth to perpetuate the feoffment would also have served a similar purpose for the guild. The guild statutes qualify the procedures of membership in the same manner as Smyth specifies the process of enfeoffment, by stipulating that promotion to the guild is reserved for men of good name, fame, and conversation, and then only with the assent of the whole guild; and that the number of brethren is to be maintained at thirty-two.[59] The

---

[57] SROB, H 1/6/1 *Feoffment Documents*, fols. 35–36.
[58] London, British Library, MS. Harley 4626, fol. 21.
[59] London, British Library, MS. Harley 4626, fol. 22

number of feoffees required by Smyth's indentures was to be twenty-four *at least*, and the establishment of a definite limit to the membership of the guild resembles the creation of an assembly or council such as formed civic governments in other towns in the period.[60]

Part of the process of being sworn into the guild involved an oath to fulfil the will of John Smyth.[61] The will was to be read to the whole guild every year at their principal meeting and dinner on the feast of the Purification of Our Lady, when the guild chose the four feoffees who were to supervise and account for the enfeoffments as stipulated in the indentures.[62] The book of statutes then goes on to record a copy of Smyth's will and a detailed description of what has been given to the town. The statutes indicate very clearly an existing awareness of the specific details of Smyth's intentions among the civic elite of Bury in 1471.

That Smyth's intentions (and the original documents displaying them) were incorporated into the constitution of the Candlemas Guild is significant for several reasons, as it alludes to the mechanisms involved in a number of social processes. It suggests that the successful accumulation and exercise of political authority in a community that had no official structures for such activity could depend upon the behaviour and personality of individuals. In this kind of community, biography can tell us a lot about how a society worked. It tells us that in Bury St Edmunds in the late fifteenth century it was possible for the political world of the town's secular community to be transformed through the actions of a single individual, and, interestingly, one who had held no formal public office for at least eight years by 1471. Neither Smyth nor his colleagues had any official authority, and yet it is likely that what was achieved had a considerable impact upon the communal life of the town.[63]

Before Smyth's enfeoffments, the secular community had largely been characterised by and derived its identity from its opposition to St Edmund's. During the fifteenth century this cohesive feature of public life in Bury was dissipating as the relative balance of power switched from the abbey hierarchy to the mercantile

---

[60] Some kind of semi-official body of twenty-four may have existed in Bury before this time: in 1385 the fine imposed upon the town after the rising of 1381 was to be assessed and levied by Roger Rose, the alderman, and twenty-three burgesses: *Calendar Patent Rolls, 1381–85*, 586.

[61] London, British Library, MS. Harley 4626, fol. 25ᵛ; SROB, H 1/2/1 *Jankyn Smyth's Book*, fol. 4; *Bury Wills*, 70–72.

[62] These four are also to ensure that the yearday observances (including dirige and requiem) take place at their appointed times: London, British Library, MS. Harley 4626, fols. 21, 23.

[63] It is worth noting, however, that some historians believe that medieval sources inherently overemphasise the impact of the individual upon society by presenting biographical details in isolation from the individual's social context. This reduces the life to stereotype: Stafford, "Writing the Biography of Eleventh-century Queens," 104.

and industrial leaders of the town. Smyth's grants may have provided new foundations for a communal identity which was more positive and forward-looking than that which it replaced. In a town other than Bury, the impact of Smyth's lifetime actions might not have been so pronounced. Smyth's life took on a significance in local affairs to the extent that its commemoration was to become central to the secular community's collective identity.

John Smyth's Legacy and Biography

After his death, the various documents generated by the Candlemas Guild effectively incorporated within them a life of John Smyth, one that was to serve as a reminder of what he had achieved on behalf of the town. The production of documents was one aspect of this, where simple records of grants transmuted into other types of literary forms. Civic ceremony was another aspect. The biography may also have been intended to serve as a symbol of what it meant to be a Bury townsman. The ordinances of the guild, if followed, would have put Smyth and his grants at the centre of the guild's ceremonial activities, placing him at the heart of the town's elite long after his death. But it is clear that Bury's elite were at pains to have Smyth explicitly remembered as the benefactor of the town by the population as a whole. The 1471 ordinances state:

> It is to be called and reduced to the Perpetuall memorye and remembraunce of thinhabytaunt*es* of this Toune of Burie S*an*cte Edmund this great bounteus and p*ro*fytable gifte of that honorable p*er*son John Smythe late of Burie S*an*cte Edmund Esquyre specyall lover and preferrer of the polytike and comon weale of the same Inhabytant whom god assoyle w*hich* deceased in the vygill of s*an*ct Peter the xxvij^te daye of June the yeare of *our* Lorde god a thowsand foure hundered foure scoure & one Of his landes ten*emen*tes rentes services and other com*m*odyties lyeng in the Tounes of Barton Rougham And the feldes of Burie w*ith* other made and geven to the burges and comynaltie of the same Toun of Burye and to ther successoris to the relefe supportac*i*on and ayde of all charges Imposicions taxes & tallages to the said burges and Comonaltie in tyme to come to be put to and speciallye for the dyscharge of a sum*me* of monye wonte of custome to be payde to the abbot at his creac*i*on speciallie in tyme to come w*ith* the revenewes of the sayde landes & ten*emen*tes to be borne and payde[64]

The fact that such an instruction exists among the ordinances of the unofficial secular government is significant, and the statutes come to take on the role of a shrine for Smyth's memory. The rhetoric of the biographical tradition is evident here, with its language of implied virtue and exemplarity. The phrase "specyall

---

[64] London, British Library, MS. Harley 4626, fols. 39^v–40.

lover and preferrer of the polytike and comon weale" stands out, and acknowledges that Smyth's actions were seen to have an explicitly political agenda.

This call for remembrance permeates the quasi-official records of the secular community. Perhaps the most striking (and certainly least pleasing to the ear) is the anonymous verse entitled "John Smythe":

> The whiche John this lyvelode hath geven passed to god he is
> On the peters even at mydsum*m*er as goddis wyll is
> In the yeare of *our* lorde a thowsand fowre hundred fowre score & one
> Lette us all of charytie praye for the soule of John
> We putte you in remembraunce that ye shall not mysse
> The keping of his dirige and also of his messe
> On the peters evin his evin the dirige shall be seyde
> And on the peters evin the messe *with* manie a good beyde
> We put you in Remembraunce all that the othe have made
> To come to the dirige & the messe the soules for to glade

Even though Smyth's will called for only the alderman, the Candlemas Guild, and the most prominent of burgesses to take part in these services, the author of the poem claims:

> All the Inhabit*auntes* of this Toune ar bownde to do the same
> To praye for the sowle of John & Anne ellis they be to blame
> The w*hi*ch John afore rehersed to this Towne hath bene full kinde
> Thre hundered markes for this Toun hathe payde no penie unpayde behinde
> Nowe we have informed yow of John Smythes will in wryting as it is
> And for the gret gyftes that he hath geven god bring his soule to blysse.[65]

Again, the source dispays an obvious literary form, and one which is overtly polemical.

The existence of *Jankyn Smyth's Book* is significant, as it constitutes a record of several important developments within the secular community in the later fifteenth century: the rise of an unofficial civic government; the impact of the public role, reputation, and memory of rich individuals upon the community as a whole; and the ability of a particular interest group (the burghal elite) to organise themselves into a quasi-constitutional body in the face of the declining author-

---

[65] London, British Library, MS. Harley 4626, fol. 26; SROB, H 1/2/1 *Jankyn Smyth's Book*, fols. 5–5ᵛ. The reference to the three hundred marks given by Smyth to the town corresponds to the three 'Abbot's Cope' payments that would have been charged to Bury's population during Smyth's later life, at the installation of the abbots Robert Ixworth, Richard Hengham, and Thomas Rattlesden: Statham, *Jankyn Smyth and the Guildhall Feoffees*, 4–5. The fact that these payments have special attention drawn to them, even though they constitute only a part of Smyth's charities, again underlines their resonance for the secular population.

ity and resources of St Edmund's. It originates from within the secular elite, and serves to celebrate the activities of these individuals, with Smyth as their figure-head, although the projection is designed to represent those activities of the elite as being on behalf of the whole town, rather than simply in their own interests.

The identity of John Smyth that one can extrapolate from the goals he pursued in the last decade of his life is very much a public one: very little of Smyth's private life is reflected in the material. Even in his final will of 1480, there are almost no clues about his life away from his civic activities: of his family we learn that he was survived by a son (John) who was to inherit all his father's lands and properties in Thorpe Morieux, Felsham, Gedding, and Rattlesden; and that his parents John and Hawise, and a daughter Rose, were all dead. The prestigious gentry family, the Yaxles, Smyth's relations through marriage, are remembered in his will, and are to inherit lands in the event of Smyth's heirs dying without issue. We learn also that Smyth had a servant by the name of Elizabeth Theloth or Tyllote.[66] This is the extent of what can be gleaned about John Smyth's private life, as there are no bequests suggesting close personal relations with either family or friends, indeed no bequest that is anything other than entirely prosaic.

What survives of John Smyth's life suggests little of the personal life one might expect from an individual wealthy and prominent enough to have complex social interactions with those around him, and who appears markedly in the records. All we can perceive is the public individual whose identity is constructed by the appropriation and re-alignment of existing social and civic structures. It is a one-dimensinal identity, almost a stereotypical one. The use of his will and indentures as instruments of civic policy might explain the contextual typicality it indicates in terms of his religious, charitable, and civic interests.

The life of John Smyth as represented in the record was clearly a product of a lifetime of activity in the public sphere of political, social, and civic life of Bury St Edmunds and can probably be attributed to a high degree of conscious self-imagining during his lifetime. The impact that Smyth had upon the civic and political ambitions of Bury must have been significant: as long-serving alderman and certainly one of the town's wealthiest individuals he must have been involved in all political and public affairs, and it is possible that during his lifetime his personality may have imbued communal activity with a sense of *how* such affairs were to be conducted. Moreover, the public identity that this particular individual constructed during his life may have had a dramatic effect upon not only the mode of political activity in the town, but also the actual political aims of Bury. The machinery he put in place to fund public affairs via the Candlemas Guild in effect enabled structures to be set up so that the community, always

---

[66] *Bury Wills*, 56–57, 61, 73.

under the supervision of the town's 'best', could express itself *as* a community, something it had not been able peaceably to do before.[67]

Ideal Citizenship in Bury St Edmunds

The calls for Smyth to be remembered by the people of Bury must be seen alongside other forms of commemoration, which are useful in judging the extent to which his constructed identity had been promulgated during and after his life. Most significantly, it can be seen that the memory of Smyth's civic beneficence created a convention for contribution to civic 'causes'.[68] This is not to say that before John Smyth there was no civic charity in Bury; but Smyth's enfeoffments provided a structure to which subsequent benefactors could attach their own grants to the population, thus investing in a secure venture to the profit of the town.

Many examples of this occur in the years following Smyth's death. In 1503 John Salter of Bury left a property in Northgate Street and two acres of land in the Risbygatefield to the brethren of the Candlemas Guild in reversion, to be administered according to the regulations left by John Smyth for the perpetuation of his feoffments.[69] In 1519 Thomas Edon made a grant to the people of Bury utilising the administrative involvement of the Candlemas Guild.[70] Twenty-eight

---

[67] The late fifteenth- and early sixteenth-century references to new enfeoffments being made in Smyth's lands and properties indicate that the machinery for the perpetuation of the grants was successful, at least initially: SROB, H 1/6/1 *Feoffment Documents*, fols. 35–36. However, by 1584 the picture had changed: a commission was initiated after Bury's inhabitants complained about the activities of the feoffees. The commissioners found that the feoffees were not abiding by the conditions of the original enfeoffments, that they "had been in the habit of electing new colleagues on their own responsibility, and had been accounting to themselves instead of making a yearly account to the burgesses [. . .] They had maladministered the property and had been guilty of peculation": Lobel, *The Borough*, 168.

[68] In effect providing the basic framework for what is now the Guildhall Feoffment Trust in Bury: Statham, *Jankyn Smyth and the Guildhall Feoffees*.

[69] SROB, Pye, fol. 141. He was a feoffee of Smyth. A copy of the will appears in SROB, H 1/6/1 *Feoffment Documents*, fol. 52.

[70] Thomas Edon is referred to as 'gentleman' in numerous instances in the documents between the 1470s and 1520, is involved in the will of many significant townsmen and women in that period, and takes some role in every major civic bequest or grant of land and property to the inhabitants of Bury. SROB, H 1/6/1 *Feoffment Documents*, fols. 30, 42, 45–46, 52, 55, 61, 64, 123; London, British Library, MS. Harley 4626; SROB, H 1/2/1 *Jankyn Smyth's Book*; SROB, H 1/5/18 *Fishe Gift*; Thomas Edon's grant to the Purification guild, SROB, H 1/5/19; and Adam and Margaret Newehawe's obit, SROB, H 1/5/21. He was a feoffee of John Smyth.

feoffees, all drawn from the membership of the Candlemas Guild, were entrusted with two pightels of land that Edon had been granted by John Frense, master of St Peter's leper hospital in 1494, to the use and profit of the town's lepers. The grant was closely tied to the administrative machinery and civic perspectives of the Candlemas Guild by Thomas Edon:

> asoftyn as ther shalbe made ony transmutac*i*on of the land*es* & ten*ementes* sumtyme John Smyth Esquyer so often to be made a new feoffament of the seid ij pightell*es* or closes *over* unto the same feoffes of the landys & ten*ementes* late of the seid John Smyth by a pleyn dede of feoffament[71]

A further example is provided by the 1514 will of Richard Kyng, a very prosperous mercer of Bury, the grandson of Richard Kyng alderman, and nephew of Edmund Kyng who served as feoffee in the original grants of John Smyth.[72] Kyng's wealth is immediately apparent from his will: among the legacies he leaves are lands and properties in Bury and throughout Suffolk and Norfolk. The house of Franciscans at Babwell was given the income generated from a parcel of land, with the arrangement that after sixty years the parcel was to pass to the brethren of the Candlemas Guild. He also made a reversionary bequest of all his lands and properties throughout East Anglia: if any recipient of Kyng's lands and properties should die without heir, their inheritance was to pass to the Candlemas Guild, which was to provide 100*s* for the poor and imprisoned of Bury and 33*s* 4*d* per year for the upkeep of the guildhall. The residue of the income from the lands and properties was to be kept in the guildhall by the alderman and Candlemas Guild, and used by them as a contribution to tenths, fifteenths, and other tallages and taxes. The lands and properties were to be kept in feoffees' hands, and the 'covenant' in place for the renewal of John Smyth's enfeoffment was to be invoked for the re-enfeoffment of Kyng's bequest. Kyng also required that copies of his will and indentures were to be kept in the guildhall, and that his was to be read in the guildhall by the clerk of the Candlemas Guild when the wills of John Smyth and Margaret Odeham were proclaimed.[73]

The grant to the townsmen of Bury that has come to be known as the 'Fiske gift', made by William Fishe (or Fiske) and his wife Elen, was similarly attached

---

[71] SROB, H 1/5/19 *Thomas Edon's Land Grant*. The leper house was to receive the profits of the two closes according to the terms of the will of John Frense, who had specified that the closes remain always in the hands of the Candlemas Guild.

[72] London, The National Archives, PCC PROB 11/17, fol. 256.

[73] London, British Library, MS. Harley 4626, fol. 21; London, The National Archives, PCC PROB 11/17, fols. 256ff.; *Bury Wills*, 78. Kyng requests that the alderman and brethren of the Candlemas Guild elect annually an individual to supervise the enfeoffment.

to provisions laid out in John Smyth's wills and indentures.[74] William Fishe in his will of 1499 bequeathed all his lands in Bury to his wife Elen for the term of her life; a year following her death they were to pass to William Darotte, Thomas Clerke, John Aleyn, and "others of the brethren of the Candlemas Guild" in order to contribute towards the customary payment levied on the townsmen at the installation of a new abbot to St Edmund's (the 'Abbot's Cope'), as well as the 'Taske' of the town in general.[75] The revenues accrued from Fishe's lands were to be used in accordance with the instructions of John Smyth. The *Feoffment Documents* provide a summary of a 1503 indenture between Elen Fishe and eight named members of the Candlemas Guild, by which Elen in accordance with the will of her husband assigns all the lands in the south and east fields of Bury to the Candlemas Guild.[76] It is stipulated that the feoffees in Smyth's legacy are to perform the wills of William and Elen Fishe in return for the gift of lands.[77] The residue of the profits coming from the Fishe gift are to be used to benefit the inhabitants of Bury according to the will of William Fishe.

Elen Fishe was by no means the only woman contributing to the civic wellbeing of her community by adapting the feoffments of John Smyth, as the civic beneficence of a final example, Margaret Odeham, indicates. Margaret was the wife of John Odeham, a wealthy draper and burgess of Bury; after his death in 1469, she received a considerable endowment of land and property in Bury, Berton, Nowton, Great and Little Horningsheath, and Westley.[78] Her will of 1492 depicts a woman of very considerable means.

In the context of her connection with the civic activities of John Smyth, the most important elements of her will are the two enfeoffments (one dating from 1478, during Smyth's lifetime) that form the bulk of its text.[79] These saw

---

[74] SROB, H 1/5/18 *Fiske Gift* is a bundle of deeds and indentures detailing the transfer of lands and properties to and from William and Elen Fiske and others.

[75] SROB, Pye, fol. 85. There are several inconsistencies between this will and the summary of it that appears in SROB, H 1/6/1 *Feoffment Documents*, fol. 59.

[76] SROB, H 1/6/1 *Feoffment Documents*, fol. 59.

[77] SROB, H 1/6/1 *Feoffment Documents*, fols. 59–60. The named Candlemas Guild members made a separate indenture dated on the same day agreeing to fulfil the wills of the Fiskes; they also agree to pay Elen a pension of £3 17s 10d every year, and to her assigns for a year after her death, to be paid on the day after Candlemas (that is, the day after the guild's main ceremonial meeting and feast). The duties to be performed are to include an annual 'sangrede' for the souls of William and Elen in both parish churches of Bury, as well as an annual obit for them in St Mary's at which the feoffees are to spend 4s in the same manner as they observe at Smyth's obit. The role of Smyth as exemplar was manifest.

[78] SROB, Hawlee, fol. 129ᵛ.

[79] As with the documents produced by John Smyth, those created by Margaret Odeham appear in several (sometimes slightly different) versions in several documents. *Bury Wills*, 73–81 reproduces SROB, Pye, fol. 8, the will of 1492 incorporating the 1478

a substantial property in Bury's Skinners Row, two tenements in Churchgate Street and "diverse" properties in the "Market sted," and all Margaret's lands in the east, south, and west fields of Bury, as well as in Berton, Nowton, Great and Little Horningsheath, and Westley enfeoffed to twenty-six of the most prominent burgesses and Candlemas Guild brethren. During her life Margaret was to receive the revenues of these holdings, and once she was dead they were to be exploited in a number of ways for the benefit of various souls, notably in specific and perpetual acts of charity for prisoners in Bury's gaol.[80] In 1526 these properties were in the possession of the Candlemas Guild, as the sacrist's rental for that year indicates that money was owed by the holders of the guild for properties identified as three shops late of Margaret Odeham.[81]

Margaret explicitly associated her enfeoffment with that of John Smyth:

> Also I wyll that the same ffeoffees the whyche arn and her aft*er* shall be in the hows lond*es* and tenemen*tes* yoven to the town of Bury by John Smyth esquier shall also in lyke wyse be enfeoffed in all my lond*es* and hows above rehersyd wyth ther app*er*ten*au*nc*es* and the alenacion of that oon always to folowe that othyr[82]

The alderman and officers of the Candlemas Guild were to supervise the revenues of the enfeoffment; and those brethren enfeoffed in her holdings were to take an oath to fulfil Margaret's will before those already sworn to fulfil the will of John Smyth.[83] This is a striking enactment of a civic hierarchy: Smyth's grants, the means of perpetuating them, and the men enacting his will all serve as models of authority and identity operating in Bury St Edmunds. The guild's statutes likewise reflect the connection between the guild and the enfeoffments of both Margaret and John Smyth:

---

indenture; SROB, H 1/2/1 *Jankyn Smyth's Book*, fols. 6–9ᵛ reproduces the 1478 indenture, and provides a detailed list of the properties and parcels of land given to the Candlemas Guild, fols. 25–30ᵛ. London, British Library, MS. Harley 4626 reproduces the 1478 indenture (fol. 29ᵛ) and a part of a will dated 21 July 1483, which includes grants to the Candlemas Guild that do not appear in the 1478 document; it also reproduces the list of lands and properties as it appears in *Jankyn Smyth's Book* (fol. 37ᵛ) as well as lists of rents payable on Margaret's holdings (fol. 39ᵛ). SROB, H 1/6/1 *Feoffment Documents*, has copies of the 1478 indenture (p. 37), the 1483 will (p. 42), and two copies of an indenture of 1480 that is substantially the same as that of 1478 (pp. 45–47).

[80] *Bury Wills*, 75–79

[81] SROB, A 6/2/1, p. 33.

[82] *Bury Wills*, 77. Indeed, twenty-five of her twenty-six feoffees act as feoffees in the grants of Smyth.

[83] *Bury Wills*, 77–78. The officers of the guild were forbidden from selling off any of the enfeoffment. The clerk of the guild was to receive 4d for reading Margaret's will at the annual feast when he was to read the will and indentures of John Smyth.

And also the wyll of Margaret Od*h*am gentlewoman to be fulfilled as it appereth by a payre Indentures wrytten in Englysshe concerning the same will And that these twayne willes ben red everye yeare in the feaste of the puryficac*i*on of blessed marye vyrgin before the Bretherne of the same guylde at dynner[84]

Through the organisation and personnel of the Candlemas Guild Margaret Odeham directly adopted, adapted, and enlarged the enfeoffment made to the population of Bury by John Smyth. This may be seen as a kind of complementary grant to Smyth's: whereas Smyth's intentions were ostensibly civic (to ease the financial burden of the whole town), Odeham's grant was bedded in pious charity, and the 'target' of her benevolence different from that of Smyth. The income generated from Smyth's endowment was to meet the costs of civic existence, both general (taxes and tallages) and specific to Bury (the 'Abbot's Cope') and thus benefiting the majority of the community. Margaret was more concerned with the poor and marginalised of the town, and particularly those incarcerated in the town's gaol. However, by choosing to attach her own significant endowment to that of Smyth she was not only providing security for her enfeoffment (which, it must be remembered, directly benefited the health of her soul) but also embodying some of the civic aspirations indicated by Smyth. Margaret Odeham's enfeoffment served to reinforce and to some extent concretise the memory of John Smyth, and as her will may not have been enacted until late 1492, the timing of her endowment may have proved decisive in establishing the 'civic patron' image of John Smyth within the community soon after his death. That others were involved in the same process in the late fifteenth and early sixteenth centuries, where grants were made to the Candlemas Guild on behalf of the town, the administration of which were to follow the system specified by Smyth, or where the holdings themselves are to be subsumed into Smyth's, suggests that Smyth's peers and successors saw the enshrining of his life as central to public and civic affairs of the late fifteenth century.

The choice made by many individuals to adopt, adapt, or refer to Smyth's enfeoffments as a model for their own acts of charity points to a situation where the memory of Smyth's activities had developed into a model civic identity, a kind of ideal 'citizenship'. This ideal was ratified in the documents generated by Bury's elite: that the disparate grants all refer to one another indicates a wide awareness of the modes of such civic giving. These documents, taken together with their visible ceremonial accompaniments, comprise the biography of John Smyth.

---

[84] London, British Library, MS. Harley 4626, fol. 21.

Conclusions

What we see here is an extraordinary example of a person directly influencing his community on the widest scale, with the community in return creating a stylised 'living' biography of a benefactor, continually acted out through the town's ceremonial life and the processes of re-enfeoffment of the Candlemas Guild estates. Smyth enabled a change of the secular community's political and social condition in the fifteenth century, theoretically freeing the townsmen from both the symbolic and the effective control of the abbey of St Edmund's. He did this with the help of his peers in the Candlemas Guild, but in the 'biographies' of him that survive in the guild documents he is portrayed as a figurehead of the movement. A commemoration of Smyth's life was built into the public life of the community, both amongst the elite and the whole population, which may have taken on the role of something akin to a local cult, which still persists today.

One aspect of the design and enactment of a communal identity constructed for the purposes of attaining political independence is that, in order to advance within that elite group, the individual has to adapt to the structures and espouse the principles of the group. For this to happen the identity of the aspiring individual has to correspond with the collective identity that has been displayed by the dominant group within which he hopes to prosper: he has to toe the 'party line'. The need to impress the urban elite of Bury in order to gain social advancement within the town may have acted to restrict the freedom of any display of identity, as outward modes of behaviour, the public expression of opinion, and the processes of social interaction would all have been prescribed to some extent. In other towns these restrictions upon the forms of public life were imposed through custom and civic ordinances;[85] but in Bury, where these structures were not under the control of the townsmen themselves, the only means by which the identity of *individuals* could be expressed was via the local structures of collective identity.

But for an individual to prosper within a community like that of Bury to the extent achieved by John Smyth, it would have been necessary not only to impress one's peers within the town's elite by embodying the group's self-professed identity and interests, but also to be noticed by those other groups within the town. Essentially, as indicated by the career of Smyth as industrialist, entrepreneur, public officer, and civic benefactor, the method for achieving this would have been to *epitomise* the principles of the group the individual hoped to advance within, while at the same time making oneself conspicuous to the community as a whole. Smyth was evidently instrumental in the initial design of the identity adopted by the elite of Bury, and it is certainly therefore the case that he embodied the

---

[85] See Phythian-Adams, *Desolation of a City*; also Sacks, *The Widening Gate*, for examples of such structures restricting the expression of individual identity.

values of that group. As part of the invention of the tradition of John Smyth, he had to embody the model of values constructed by the elite at that time, but to be as successful as he was, he needed to *more* than embody it. Smyth not only had to begin the process of establishing the model and therefore what should be 'typical' behaviour for the people of Bury: he had to appear to be 'archetypical', an extreme example of the identity that was being promulgated. Paradoxically, this may have been an example of someone expressing their individuality through extreme compliance with a consciously constructed collective identity.

It is clear that, regardless of the degree of self-consciousness involved in the construction of identity, the longevity of such an enterprise depends almost entirely upon the support of the individual's community. In the case of John Smyth this would appear to have been especially so, as the identity constructed through his grants needed and received the direct *practical* administration of the most influential individuals in the community. The relationship between the identity of Smyth and the identity of what was the de facto civic government of Bury was in many ways reciprocal: the Candlemas Guild perpetuated the status and reputation of Smyth through the administration of his grants, the fulfilment of his wishes, and the ceremonial acknowledgement of his achievements and charity; while Smyth's enfeoffments and the machinery to maintain them provided the Candlemas Guild with a structure upon which it could base its own hitherto largely symbolic organisational identity. The choice taken by many individuals to adopt, adapt, or refer to Smyth's enfeoffments as a model for their own acts of charity points to a situation where the construction of his identity had developed in the years following Smyth's death into a model civic identity, a kind of ideal 'citizenship' as described above. The mechanism for doing so was the invention of a tradition; and the success of this tradition may have marked a turning point in the townsmen's struggle for civic and political independence.

Smyth's actions were possible thanks to the peculiarities of Bury's political and social context, and the results were magnified by them. The success he achieved in generating a level of independence for the townsmen in the face of (albeit diminishing) obstinacy from the abbey was owing to the twin facts of the lack of political structures in the town and the long history of resistance to the abbey's rule. If Smyth had lived in a different community, the need for such actions and the opportunity to put them into force would probably have been lacking. What remains to us is a startling example of the individual shaping a community, establishing a collective identity which is solidified and disseminated through a form of official biography.

Rebuilding the City Centre

Karsten Igel

The central act of council rule in the city of Osnabrück was the annual re-election of the council, which was also the moment when this body was able to present and legitimise itself to the city's citizenry and residents.[1] In consequence, some of the rituals associated with the election were intended for the urban public, while others were removed from it, thus casting light on the ways public accessibility and exclusivity—or, more accurately, secrecy—were graduated within the polity of the city.[2] The rituals of the council election took place in urban spaces, inside both sacred and non-sacred buildings as well as on the city's streets and public places. The procedures and forms of the rituals interacted with the shape of the spaces that were incorporated into the procedure: those where rituals

---

[1] On the act of the election see Dietrich W. Poeck, *Rituale der Ratswahl: Zeichen und Zeremoniell der Ratssetzung in Europa (12.–18. Jahrhundert)* (Cologne: Böhlau, 2003).

[2] On the term 'public' (Öffentlichkeit) see Jürgen Habermas, *Strukturwandel der Öffentlichkeit* (Frankfurt am Main: Suhrkamp, 1962); Alfred Haverkamp, "'[. . .] an die große Glocke hängen': Über Öffentlichkeit im Mittelalter," *Jahrbuch des Historischen Kollegs* (1995): 71–112, esp. 82–93; Peter von Moos, "Das öffentliche und das Private im Mittelalter: Für einen kontrollierten Anachronismus," in *Das Öffentliche und Private in der Vormoderne*, ed. Gert Melville and Peter von Moos (Cologne, 1998), 3–83; Gudrun Gleba, "Repräsentation, Kommunikation und öffentlicher Raum: Innerstädtische Herrschaftsbildung und Selbstdarstellung im Hoch- und Spätmittelalter," *Bremisches Jahrbuch* 77 (1998): 125–52; Susanne Rau, "Das Wirtshaus: Zur Konstituierung eines öffentlichen Raumes in der Frühen Neuzeit," in *Offen und Verborgen: Vorstellungen und Praktiken des Öffentlichen und Privaten in Mittelalter und Früher Neuzeit*, ed. Caroline Emmelius et al. (Göttingen: Wallstein, 2004), 211–27; Susanne Rau and Gerd Schwerhoff, "Öffentliche Räume in der Frühen Neuzeit: Überlegungen zu Leitbegriffen und Themen eines Forschungsfeldes," in *Zwischen Gotteshaus und Taverne: Öffentliche Räume in Spätmittelalter und Früher Neuzeit*, ed. eidem (Cologne: Böhlau, 2004), 11–52. On 'secrecy' see Antje Diener-Staeckling, *Der Himmel über dem Rat: Zur Symbolik der Ratswahl in mitteldeutschen Städten* (Halle a.S.: Mitteldeutscher Verlag, 2008).

Negotiating the Political in Northern European Urban Society, c.1400–c.1600, ed. Sheila Sweetinburgh, MRTS 434 (Tempe: ACMRS, 2013). [ISBN 978-0-86698-482-9]

remained hidden and those where contact with the public was sought and the urban environment used as a stage for ceremonial display.[3] This implies that far-reaching changes to parts of the urban environment used in this way must have had an impact on the form and procedures of the rituals, but may also have been prompted by the requirements of those rituals or changes in them that resulted from alterations to the city's political structures. We have a particularly detailed knowledge of the complete reorganisation and restructuring of the city centre around the market of the Osnabrück Altstadt ('Old Town') associated with the building of the new Altstadt Town Hall in the decades before and after 1500. This area was also the political centre of the united city, which had been founded in 1307 by the union of the Altstadt and the Neustadt ('New Town').[4] The present article examines the significance of this spatial reconfiguration within the

---

[3] On the concept of space and its social context as discussed by Pierre Bourdieu see Monika Löw, *Raumsoziologie* (Frankfurt am Main: Suhrkamp, 2001); Karsten Igel, "Der Raum als soziale Kategorie: Methoden sozialräumlicher Forschung am Beispiel des spätmittelalterlichen Greifswalds," in *Städtesystem und Urbanisierung im Ostseeraum in der Frühen Neuzeit: Urbane Lebensräume und Historische Informationssysteme. Beiträge des wissenschaftlichen Kolloquiums in Rostock vom 15. und 16. November 2004*, ed. Stefan Kroll and Kersten Krüger (Berlin: Lit, 2006), 265–300. See also Gerd Schwerhoff, "Öffentliche Räume und politische Kultur in der frühneuzeitlichen Stadt: Eine Skizze am Beispiel der Reichsstadt Köln," in *Interaktion und Herrschaft: Die Politik der frühneuzeitlichen Stadt*, ed. Rudolf Schlögl (Konstanz: UVK, 2004), 113–36.

[4] Karsten Igel, "Vom Gewerberaum zum Repräsentationsraum: Der Altstädter Markt in Osnabrück zwischen dem 13. und dem 16. Jahrhundert," *Zeitschrift für Archäologie des Mittelalters* 34 (2006): 203–14, at 211–13; idem, "Rat und Raum: Ratsherrschaft im Spiegel des Osnabrücker Stadtbildes zwischen Hochmittelalter und Früher Neuzeit," in *Außen und Innen: Räume und ihre Symbolik im Mittelalter*, ed. Nikolaus Staubach and Vera Johanterwage (Frankfurt am Main: Peter Lang, 2007), 193–215; idem, "Ratsherrschaft und Öffentlichkeit im spätmittelalterlich-frühneuzeitlichen Osnabrück," in *Stadt und Öffentlichkeit: Die Entstehung politischer Räume in der Stadt der Vormoderne*, ed. Stephan Albrecht (Cologne: Böhlau, 2009), 161–76. Ilse Eberhardt, *Van des stades wegene utgegeven unde betalt: Städtischer Alltag im Spiegel der Stadtrechnungen von Osnabrück (1459–1519)* (Osnabrück: Verein für Geschichte und Landeskunde von Osnabrück, 1996), 81–86. See also Stephan Albrecht, *Das Bremer Rathaus im Zeichen städtischer Selbstdarstellung vor dem 30-jährigen Krieg* (Marburg: Jonas, 1993), 22–32; Gleba, "Repräsentation," 142–50; Daniel Gutscher, "'solich hus zu slissen sy dem kilchhof zů gut': Bern entdeckt seine Freiräume," in *Berns große Zeit: Das 15. Jahrhundert neu entdeckt*, ed. Ellen J. Beer et al. (Bern: Berner Lernmittel- und Medienverlag, 1999), 82–87; Armand Baeriswyl, *Stadt, Vorstadt und Stadterweiterung im Mittelalter: Archäologische und historische Studien zum Wachstum der drei Zähringerstädte Burgdorf, Bern und Freiburg im Breisgau* (Basel: Schweizerischer Burgenverein, 2003), 156–57, 272–73; Donatella Calabi, *The Market and the City: Square, Street and Architecture in Early Modern Europe* (Aldershot: Ashgate, 2004), reviewed by Karsten Igel in *sehepunkte* 5 (2005), No. 6 [15.06.2005], URL: <http://www.sehepunkte.de/2005/06/6020.html>.

context created by the ritual elements of the council election, its importance to the ceremonial displays staged by the council, and the conclusions that can be drawn from this with respect to the development of specific political structures in the Westphalian cathedral city of Osnabrück. With nearly ten thousand inhabitants in the fifteenth century, Osnabrück was regarded in the late Middle Ages as one of the four major cities in Westphalia, alongside Dortmund, Münster, and Soest. These urban centres had cooperated since the thirteenth century in various alliances and, as the 'Four Cities', had played a significant role in the region's political development.[5] Like nearby Münster, Osnabrück had been able to free itself from church rule as early as the thirteenth century and, in consequence, had gained increasing influence over the episcopal regime in the principality of Osnabrück.[6] In the fifteenth century, the town was described by outside observers as a 'free city', as well as being invited to the Reichstag (Imperial Diet) at Nuremberg in 1430.[7] However, the Osnabrück council did not take up this invitation. Nor did the people of Osnabrück think of themselves as living in a 'free city', since this would have meant the loosening of their ties with the surrounding territory of the episcopal principality of Osnabrück, which constituted the basis for the city's flourishing economy. On the contrary, the council and citizenry were prepared to intervene massively in the politics of the region. For example, at the election of a new bishop in October 1424 they took up arms and brought cannon into position to surround the cathedral. For three days they besieged the clergy assembled within the cathedral, including the newly-elected bishop, so ensuring they would have a say in the election and influence the bishop's rule over the episcopal principality. The city's real position of power was evident from the fact that the treaties adopted under the duress of the siege were confirmed retrospectively by the cathedral chapter and the bishop, who also urged the papal curia to lift the city's excommunication.[8]

---

[5] Klaus Scholz, "Das Spätmittelalter," in *Westfälische Geschichte 1: Von den Anfängen bis zum Ende des Alten Reiches*, ed. Wilhelm Kohl (Düsseldorf: Schwann, 1983), 403–68, esp. 451–57; Jürgen Karl W. Berns, *Propter communem utilitatem: Studien zur Bündnispolitik der westfälischen Städte im Spätmittelalter* (Düsseldorf: Droste, 1991), 57–67.

[6] Hermann Rothert, "Geschichte der Stadt Osnabrück im Mittelalter: Erster Teil," *Osnabrücker Mitteilungen* 57 (1937): 1–325, esp. 185–232.

[7] Hermann Rothert, "Die Geschichte der Stadt Osnabrück im Mittelalter: Zweiter Teil," *Osnabrücker Mitteilungen* 58 (1938): 1–435, esp. 63–65.

[8] Bernd-Ulrich Hergemöller, *"Pfaffenkriege" im spätmittelalterlichen Hanseraum: Quellen und Studien zu Braunschweig, Osnabrück, Lüneburg und Rostock* (Cologne: Böhlau, 1988), 83–103; Karsten Igel, "Von Belagerung bis Mord: Mittelalterliche Sakralräume als Schauplatz von Gewalttaten," in *Topographien des Sakralen: Religion und Raumordnung in der Vormoderne*, ed. Susanne Rau and Gerd Schwerhoff (Hamburg and Munich: Dölling und Galitz, 2008), 200–20, esp. 206–11.

Council Elections in Osnabrück

At the latest from the beginning of the fourteenth century and on into the nineteenth century, Osnabrück's annual council elections were held on 2 January every year, which is called *Handgiftentag* ('Handshaking Day') because the two groups of electors involved shook hands to mark the handing over of their office during the election ceremony.[9] The first reference to the procedure for, and venue of, the election is contained in the treaty on the unification of the Osnabrück Altstadt and Neustadt of 1307.[10] This not only set the date for the election, the day following the Feast of the Circumcision, but also stipulated that it should be conducted in the Altstadt Town Hall. All citizens were required to gather there in order to elect the new council in accordance with the traditions of the Altstadt. A more detailed account of the procedure is given by the Osnabrück election code known as the *Sate* (Low German for 'contract'), which was first issued in 1348 and was to remain in force until the city finally lost its autonomy at the beginning of the nineteenth century.[11] The ringing of the bell of St Mary's,[12] at which all citizens who owned a house were required to assemble in the building where the council would be elected, marked the beginning of the election day. In the *Sate* of 1348, the Town Hall was no longer described as the venue for the election, but simply as the building in which the election took place. From the second half of the fourteenth century, the Town Hall was supplanted as the venue for the election by the great chamber of the Merchants' Hall, which served as a cloth hall.[13] This reveals the spatial division that had become established by this time between the place where the councillors exercised their rule and the venue of the election that legitimised it. There, before the assembled community of citizens, the sixteen councillors of the Altstadt and the Neustadt selected two of their number by throwing dice. The two who threw the highest and lowest numbers subsequently nominated sixteen electors from the Neustadt and the four *Laischaften* (quarters) of the Altstadt. However, this group of sixteen did not directly elect the new council, but first elected a further sixteen citizens, and it was this last group who finally went on to elect the councillors. Each of these three rounds of the election involved an oath in which the two councillors and the two

---

[9] Poeck, *Rituale der Ratswahl*, 67–68.

[10] *Urkundenbuch der Stadt Osnabrück 1301–1400*, ed. Horst-Rüdiger Jarck (Osnabrück: Verein für Geschichte und Landeskunde von Osnabrück, 1989), 60–61.

[11] *Das älteste Stadtbuch von Osnabrück*, ed. Erich Fink (Osnabrück: Verein für Geschichte und Landeskunde von Osnabrück, 1927), 35–36 ; Poeck, *Rituale der Ratswahl*, 67–74.

[12] Sabine Wehking, *Die Inschriften von Osnabrück* (Wiesbaden: Reichert, 1988), 30–31.

[13] Igel, "Vom Gewerberaum zum Repräsentationsraum," 204–5, 209–11.

groups of sixteen electors swore to perform their duties for the good of the city without being influenced by, or making agreements with, outside parties.

Further information about the procedure used in the election is given by various late medieval and early modern sources, including the biography of Heinrich David Stüve, who served as mayor around 1800 and had seen the election in its barely reformed late medieval/early modern form.[14] From at least the mid-sixteenth century, the annual council election began early in the morning of 2 January, when the council that still held office assembled under the great wheel-shaped chandelier in the council chamber of the Town Hall known as the *Krone* (Crown).[15] The *Schützen*, a city guard that had been founded in the mid-fifteenth century and usually consisted of a hundred men,[16] assembled in front of the Town Hall under arms, then formed a guard of honour through which the councillors proceeded to jointly make their way to St Mary's Church. One of its bells was rung as they crossed the marketplace, calling the citizenry and residents to Mass and the ensuing election. In its procession from the Town Hall through the marketplace to St Mary's Church, the old council showed itself once more to its citizens and, with the *Schützen*, displayed its military might and sovereign power. The Mass was followed by the ballot in the cloth hall discussed above, which was opened with a reading of the election code of 1348. After the old council had walked across to the Town Hall to enjoy a banquet together, the ceremonial of the election went on until the evening. Meanwhile, the citizens and residents celebrated the day around the Town Hall and market as a riotous popular festival, which symbolised the absence of government from the city during the election. The gates remained closed and all outsiders were therefore excluded from the urban community. At the conclusion of the election procedure, towards the end of the day, the announcement of the new councillors was marked by the ringing of the bell of St Mary's. The following morning, the old and new councils met once again—as on the previous day secluded from all contact with the public—under the wheel-shaped chandelier in the council chamber, where the secrets of office and the business of the council were handed over behind closed doors.[17]

---

[14] Johann Carl Bertram Stüve, *Heinrich David Stüve Doctor der Rechte und Bürgermeister der Stadt Osnabrück: Zur Erinnerung für dessen Kinder und Enkel* (Jena: Frommann, 1827), 22–25. Poeck, *Rituale der Ratswahl*, 67–74.

[15] *Die Kunstdenkmale der Stadt Osnabrück*, ed. Heinrich Siebern and Erich Fink (Hannover: Selbstverlag der Provinzialverwaltung, 1907; repr. Osnabrück: Wenner, 1978), 230–31.

[16] Heinrich Blömker, "Die Wehrverfassung der Stadt Osnabrück bis zum Westfälischen Frieden," *Osnabrücker Mitteilungen* 53 (1932): 84–90; Eberhardt, *Van des stades wegene utgegeven unde betalt*, 104–5.

[17] Poeck, *Rituale der Ratswahl*, 74.

The Town Hall and the Market

We now turn to the layout of the space that provided the stage for the rituals of the annual council election: the Altstadt market and the Town Hall there formed the economic and political centre of the city and its citizenry. A town hall is mentioned for the first time as early as 1244. This presumably stood somewhere near the market,[18] but only the building that succeeded it, erected after a fire in the city in the early 1250s, can be located with certainty at the corner of the market and Bierstraße, which means it stood on the site of the present Town Hall. Archaeological evidence has been found of market booths to the east, on the other side of an alleyway, at least one of which was used by goldsmiths for a time in the second half of the fourteenth century.[19] There were also booths on the southern side of Marktstraße, including the shops of twenty-seven mercers mentioned in 1347 and the stalls of the bakers and butchers on the ground floor of the Merchants' Hall opposite the Town Hall (Fig. 2.1). To the north of the Town Hall, branching off from Bierstraße, ran the alley with the booths of the *Höker*, grocers who sold a range of foodstuffs. There were also more market booths to the east of St Mary's Church, such as those on the alley of the shoemakers and presumably also the alley of the *Krämer*, small shopkeepers who sold foodstuffs and other goods, such as leather. Furthermore, the mint can be located at the market end of the shoemakers' alley. Not only was the Town Hall largely surrounded by shops, but its ground floor was also used for commercial purposes. At the same time, Bierstraße and Krahnstraße, where the butchers' stalls stood, were integrated into the market area, and there is firm evidence of another merchants' hall on Hegerstraße in the fourteenth and fifteenth centuries, which was owned by the city but leased out at times by the council. The spatial structures that can be identified suggest that the Town Hall faced the junction of Marktstraße, Krahnstraße, Hegerstraße, and Bierstraße, which was also the intersection between the north–south and east–west trading routes that led through the city and so its real centre. At this point in time, St Mary's Church was cut off from the actual market by its churchyard and the adjoining row of booths and was not related spatially to the Town Hall. Until the second half of the fifteenth century, the same was true of the relationship between the Town Hall and cathedral, including its close, which essentially formed a large public square. The Altstadt Town Hall was turned away from this centre of episcopal power, from which the city was still ruled in the mid-thirteenth century, as well as being spatially separated from

---

[18] *Osnabrücker Urkundenbuch*, Band 2: *1201–1250*, ed. Friedrich Philippi (Osnabrück: Verein für Geschichte und Landeskunde von Osnabrück, 1896), 361–62.

[19] Karsten Igel, "Von der Straße zum Platz: Der Osnabrücker Markt—ein Stadt-Raum im Wandel," in *Mercatum et Monetam: 1000 Jahre Markt-, Münz- und Zollrecht in Osnabrück*, ed. Wolfgang Schlüter (Bramsche: Rasch, 2002), 171–96; Igel, "Vom Gewerberaum zum Repräsentationsraum."

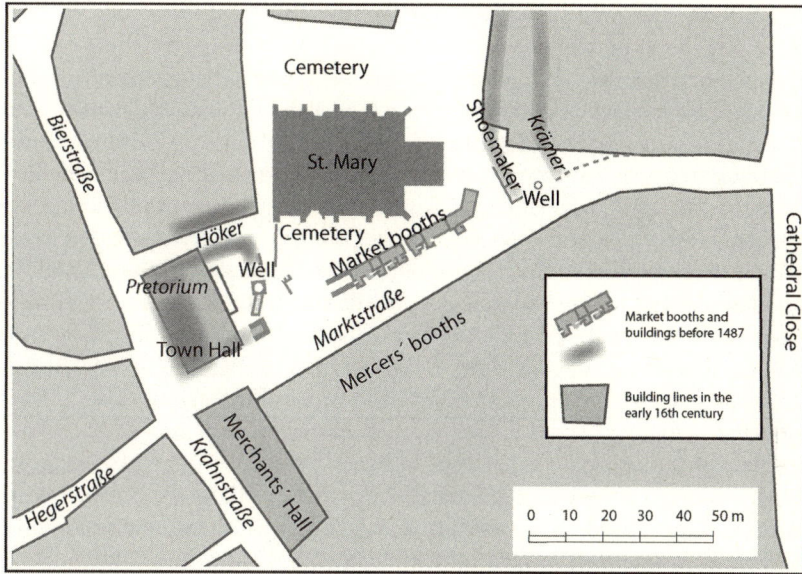

Fig. 2.1: Osnabrück, Old Town market, c. 1350. *Produced by Karsten Igel.*

it by the buildings erected along Marktstraße. Despite its situation at the city's central crossroads, the way it was bound into comparably narrow streets meant that the Town Hall could hardly form a counterweight to the impressive space of the cathedral close, with the cathedral at its centre and the *curiae*, the canons' residences, surrounding it. Rather, the Town Hall remained subordinated to the cathedral within Osnabrück's built urban environment.

The first far-reaching change to the built environment around the market took place in the second half of the fourteenth century: after the middle of the century, the cloth trade moved from the mercers' booths located south of Marktstraße to the cloth hall, which was mentioned for the first time in 1383.[20] Furthermore, the booths that had now become redundant on the southern side of the market probably gave way to purely residential buildings at around this time. The chamber of the cloth hall, which dated from the second half of the thirteenth century, measured about twelve metres by forty (40 ft by 130 ft). Apart from its economic functions, it served, as discussed above, as the venue for the annual council election, probably being used for this purpose from the mid-fourteenth century at the latest. The use of a merchants' hall as an election venue distinct from the town hall can also be proven in other places, such as Minden, Soest, Deventer, and Zwolle. However, it has not to date been possible to determine when this spatial separation between the Town Hall and the venue for the

---

[20] *Urkundenbuch der Stadt Osnabrück*, 889–90.

election took effect and the extent to which the same process occurred in other cities.[21] This functional division during the election very much reflects the spatial opposition between the community and the council that resulted from their respective roles in the city's constitution. The cloth hall may also have been the venue for meetings of the Great Council established around 1400, which consisted of the sixteen councillors from the Altstadt and Neustadt, former councillors, the twenty-two guild masters of the eleven leading craftsmen-guilds, and sixteen representatives of the city's quarters. It is not possible to ascertain with complete clarity how the powers of the Great Council and the smaller ruling council were delimited during the late Middle Ages. While the ruling council dealt with day-to-day business, it is likely that the Great Council assembled primarily in order to make fundamental decisions that concerned the whole citizenry. In 1432, however, a citizen complained that the court proceedings against him had been conducted before the Great Council, a departure from the procedural conventions usually followed in Osnabrück.[22] Given that this body numbered sixty to seventy people, it would seem obvious for it to have initially met in the spacious chamber of the cloth hall as well, for the existing Town Hall had been built at the beginning of the second half of the thirteenth century to accommodate the twelve-man council of the Altstadt and can hardly have had enough space for such a large assembly.

The size of the Great Council, combined with the expanding and intensifying administrative functions required by the running of the city, which had a population of between 8,000 and 10,000,[23] must in itself have been sufficient grounds for the construction of a new Town Hall. However, the council in office at the end of the fifteenth century was not content to merely extend the Town Hall, but combined this with an almost complete reorganisation of the urban environment around the Altstadt market. It is only possible to identify parallels between the building of this totally new Town Hall and a few projects undertaken elsewhere in the German-speaking countries during the same period. Comparisons may be drawn with the construction of the new Bremen town hall between 1405 and 1410, which was also accompanied by a remodelling of the city's market,[24] and the building of the town hall at Meißen from 1471 to 1481.[25] The construction of the Marburg town hall from 1511 onwards was also associated with an initiative to lay out public places, but this first real town hall in Marburg

---

[21] Poeck, *Rituale der Ratswahl*, 80, 91–92, 132, 139–40.

[22] Niedersächsisches Landesarchiv, Staatsarchiv Osnabrück, Dep. 3a1 VIII No. 54/16.

[23] Karsten Igel, "Quellen zur Einwohnerzahl und Sozialstruktur des spätmittelalterlichen Osnabrück," *Osnabrücker Mitteilungen* 106 (2001): 281–87.

[24] Albrecht, *Das Bremer Rathaus*, 22–27.

[25] Stephan Albrecht, *Mittelalterliche Rathäuser in Deutschland: Architektur und Funktion* (Darmstadt: Wissenschaftliche Buchgesellschaft, 2004), 168–69.

was built under the influence of the Landgrave of Hesse and was therefore not an expression of urban independence.[26] Furthermore, the close connections between the construction of the new Town Hall and the far-reaching reorganisation of the market into a communal square make the Osnabrück example one that is exceedingly interesting and unusual in the German-speaking countries. The accounts of the Altstadt, nearly all of which have survived from the middle of the fifteenth century, allow the construction of the Town Hall to be traced in considerable detail.[27] A great deal can be ascertained about the building work that was undertaken, as well as individuals and groups who made donations to support the erection of the new Town Hall. First preparations for the construction work can be noted from as early as 1477 onwards, during which the council began to purchase wood and stones as building materials for the new Town Hall, at least some of which were stored in the churchyard of St Mary's. However, it remains unclear whether there were already firm plans at this point in time that included the reorganisation of the market in addition to the construction of the new Town Hall. The actual construction work then began in 1486 with the demolition of the old Town Hall. The following year, the council purchased two houses that presumably had to make way for the new building, and work began on its foundations. The booths of the *Höker* to the north of the Town Hall disappeared in 1486 or 1487. The same fate also befell the row of booths to the north of Marktstraße and other private houses that had been acquired for this purpose.[28] These may have been located in the area to the east of St Mary's Church, where the frontage of Marktstraße was moved back by as much as fifteen metres (50 ft) to the north. The demolition of houses this involved opened up the view from the cathedral close to the ambulatory choir of St Mary's erected in the second quarter of the fifteenth century.[29] The area between Marktstraße and St Mary's Church had been 'cleared' of all buildings, and the part of the cemetery located here was flattened at the same time to create a large, triangular public space. The base of this triangle along Bierstraße was now taken up by the slowly rising edifice of the Town Hall. It is not difficult to recognise that this was accompanied by a spatial reorientation: thanks to the way the frontage on the eastern side of the market had been pushed back, the choir of St Mary's now stood clearly opposite the cathedral while, with its imposing main façade and the new square placed in front of it, the Town Hall that had essentially been completed by 1505 was also obviously positioned as a counterweight to the cathedral and the cathedral close

---

[26] Ulrich Klein, "Der Marburger Markt in der frühen Neuzeit (1511–1648)," in *Der Marburger Markt: 800 Jahre Geschichte über und unter dem Pflaster*, ed. Elmar Altwasser et al. (Marburg: Magistrat der Stadt, 1997), 71–79.

[27] Eberhardt, *Van des stades wegene utgegeven unde betalt*, 81–103; Igel, "Rat und Raum," 200–5.

[28] Eberhardt, *Van des stades wegene utgegeven unde betalt*, 99–100.

[29] Igel, "Von der Straße zum Platz," 182–83; idem, "Rat und Raum," 213–14.

FIG. 2.2: Osnabrück, Old Town market and cathedral close (Wenzel Hollar, c. 1630). A: Market, B: Cathedral close, C: The lion. *Reproduced with permission from the Museum of Osnabrück.*

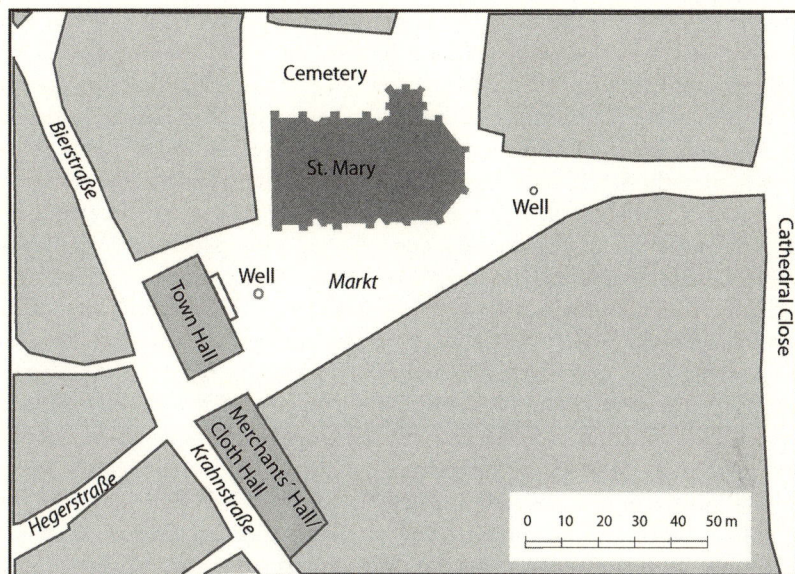

FIG. 2.3: Osnabrück, Old Town market, early 16th century. *Produced by Karsten Igel.*

(Fig. 2.2). In contrast to the earlier arrangement, the Town Hall and St Mary's Church now formed a coherent ensemble that would be supplemented in the following three decades with the council scribe's office and the city scales in the corner between the two buildings that dominated the square (Fig. 2.3).[30]

In parallel to the construction of the Town Hall, the work on its sculptural decoration also commenced. Stones were purchased in Münster as early as 1488. The Osnabrück sculptor Albert Steynsnider used these materials to fabricate sixteen consoles, nine of which were set into the Town Hall façade that same year.[31] The following year, Steynsnider delivered another console and sixteen baldachins, while the remaining consoles, eight in total, were put in place in 1489 as well.[32] This suggests that the construction work had already advanced beyond the bottom of the windows on the raised ground floor, because the consoles that can be traced or are still in place were positioned above this level. However, the walls had not yet risen above the tops of the windows as, according to the accounts, the baldachins found at this level had still not been incorporated into the masonry. This is of significance since there was now a pause in the building work that lasted several years until 1496, even though the Town Hall had not reached the level of the ceilings of the *piano nobile*. At the same time, it is evident that by this point

---

[30] *Die Kunstdenkmale der Stadt Osnabrück*, 235–37.

[31] Eberhardt, *Van des stades wegene utgegeven unde betalt*, 355.

[32] Eberhardt, *Van des stades wegene utgegeven unde betalt*, 362.

consoles for seventeen figures had been prepared in its window zone. A year after
the construction work resumed, Albert Steynsnider made another console and
set the twelve baldachins that had previously been manufactured into the masonry. In view of the height the walls had reached by the time building stopped,
and the eighteen consoles for statues of which there is still evidence today on the
Town Hall,[33] the single console must presumably have been the one above the
door of the Town Hall, on which stands the only figure to have survived there,
Charlemagne (although this is only a copy). Also in 1497, Albert Steynsnider was
commissioned to purchase Baumberger sandstone for eight figures and five capitals.[34] Unfortunately, the biggest gaps in the surviving Altstadt accounts for the
period during which the Town Hall was being constructed are encountered in
the following years, during which most of the work on the façade must have been
done, so that this important phase in the construction work can be traced only
sketchily. Not until 1505 do the accounts once again offer a small, but important, insight into the work on the building's sculptural decoration when they record the settlement of an outstanding debt for the sword of Charlemagne.[35] This
statue had therefore been completed and probably also installed by this time.
In the same year, the construction work was so well advanced that the building
could be used by the council, as an inscription above the entrance to the council
chamber states,[36] even if the remaining work on the Town Hall was still to go
on until 1512.[37]

The construction work on the Town Hall of the Osnabrück Altstadt can be
followed in comparatively close detail, but the question of the original sculptural
programme cannot be answered in any but vague terms. Indeed, it is not even
possible to determine with certainty whether it was ever completed or remained
partly unfinished. Only three figures have been preserved: the Charlemagne, a
copy of which stands prominently today on the Town Hall, as well as a Ceres and
a Flora which are now to be found in the grounds of a castle near Osnabrück.[38]
Finally, a reference to a fourth figure is found in the city accounts: in 1495, the
merchant Hermann Lancksmed and his wife donated *fl.* 20 for a statue of Mary

---

[33] Madelaine Pfeffer, "Zur Fassadengestaltung des Osnabrücker Rathauses"
(Diplomarbeit der Fachhochschule Hildesheim/Holzminden/Göttingen, 2002); see
also Hermann Queckenstedt, "Die Geschichte der Restaurierungen von Rathaus und
Friedenssaal in Osnabrück," in *[. . .] zu einem stets währenden Gedächtnis: Die Friedenssäle
in Münster und Osnabrück und ihre Gesandtenporträts*, ed. Karl Georg Kaster and Gerd
Steinwascher (Bramsche: Rasch, 1998), 65–100.

[34] Eberhardt, *Van des stades wegene utgegeven unde betalt*, 425.

[35] Eberhardt, *Van des stades wegene utgegeven unde betalt*, 460.

[36] Wehking, *Die Inschriften*, 91.

[37] Eberhardt, *Van des stades wegene utgegeven unde betalt*, 85.

[38] Pfeffer, "Fassadengestaltung des Osnabrücker Rathauses," 12–14.

on the Town Hall, although no remains of it have survived.[39] Some of this money went to Albert Steynsnider in 1497, when he was commissioned to purchase Baumberger sandstone for eight figures.[40] It is difficult to reconstruct a particular sculptural programme from the four figures of which we know. Further questions are prompted by the early-modern depictions of the Town Hall. The oldest extant picture of the market and Town Hall is a very precise depiction in the *Bergersches Bischofsbuch*, an illustrated history of the bishops of Osnabrück dating from 1607—which means it was produced a good hundred years after the building was completed (Fig. 2.4). It shows Charlemagne on the main façade above the portal with four figures to his right, but the other four consoles are empty. By contrast, however, another three statues can be made out on the narrow southern side of the Town Hall. Its accuracy is confirmed by the view of the Osnabrück marketplace engraved before 1780 by the Osnabrück copper engraver Christian Ludolph Reinhold, which also depicts the Town Hall with great precision (Fig. 2.5). In this image too, empty consoles are shown to the left of Charlemagne, as well as baldachins for the missing figures.

The sole reference to the sculptural programme of the main façade states that there were nine figures already in place or at least planned, with Charlemagne located at the centre. This means that the Nine Good Heroes, a very frequently depicted theme, should probably be regarded as the most likely programme,[41] without complete certainty being possible in this respect. This sculptural programme, which has its roots in the world of chivalry, is also to be found decorating the town halls at Cologne, Lüneburg, Hamburg, and Mechelen, as well as the well in front of the town hall at the Brunswick Altstadt. In all likelihood, the town halls at Lübeck and Tangermünde also featured representations of the Nine Good Heroes, whose feats of arms served as models for those charged with the defence of these cities, in addition to making reference to the lifestyle cultivated by the urban ruling elites that involved a number of chivalric elements.[42]

---

[39] Eberhardt, *Van des stades wegene utgegeven unde betalt,* 87.

[40] Eberhardt, *Van des stades wegene utgegeven unde betalt,* 87.

[41] Ulrich Meier, "Vom Mythos der Republik: Formen und Funktionen spätmittelalterlicher Rathausikonographie in Deutschland und Italien," in *Mundus in imagine: Festgabe für Klaus Schreiner,* ed. Andrea Löther et al. (Munich: Fink, 1996), 345–87; idem, "Freiheit und Recht, Rat und Tat: Zur Selbstdarstellung des Stadtbürgertums in den Bildprogrammen niederdeutscher Rathäuser des späten Mittelalters und der frühen Neuzeit," in *Mittelalterliche Rathäuser in Niedersachsen und Bremen: Geschichte — Kunst — Erhaltung,* ed. Ursula Schädler-Saub and Angela Weyer (Petersberg: Michael Imhof, 2003), 35–48; Stephan Selzer, *Artushöfe im Ostseeraum: Ritterlich-höfische Kultur in den Städten des Preußenlandes im 14. und 15. Jahrhundert* (Frankfurt am Main: Peter Lang, 1996), 83–85; Werner Paravicini, "Rittertum im Norden des Reichs," in *Nord und Süd in der deutschen Geschichte des Mittelalters,* ed. idem (Sigmaringen: Thorbecke, 1990), 147–91, esp. 166–73.

[42] Meier, "Freiheit und Recht," 40–42.

FIG. 2.4: Osnabrück, Town Hall and Old Town market (Georg Berger, 1607). *Reproduced with permission from the Museum of Osnabrück.*

Ceres, Flora, and Mary would then have to have been on the narrow side or rear wall of the Town Hall facing Bierstraße. If the sculptural decoration did indeed remain incomplete, as is suggested by the fact that four figures on the eastern façade and probably one on the southern façade can be identified as missing in 1607, the eight sculptures commissioned in 1497 may actually have remained the only ones that were ever finished. Even if the reconstruction of this sculptural programme must therefore remain largely hypothetical, yet another entry is to be found in the city's accounts that is of significance in this context: in 1489 the

FIG. 2.5: Osnabrück, Town Hall and Old Town market (Christian Ludolph Rein-hold, c. 1777). *Reproduced with permission from the Museum of Osnabrück.*

two Altstadt mayors, Ertwin Ertmann and Hinrich von Leden, the long-serving Neustadt mayor Hinrich Vrese, and the councillors Gottschalk von Ankum and Gerd Dumpstorp paid a total of twelve and a half marks amongst them to have their coats of arms carved into the capitals of the Town Hall. It seems obvious to connect this payment of money with the consoles installed that same year, which were probably intended for the front façade, given that the city accounts specify there were eight of them.[43] This would, of course, have been the ideal place for local figures of this kind to immortalise themselves as the 'builders' of the Town Hall, at the same time securing their place in the historical memory of the city. The likely programme, the Nine Good Heroes, would have been highly appro-priate in reflecting the lifestyle of the city's leading families, who identified with a chivalric model of conduct.[44] Since the three mayors who are mentioned were also parish councillors at St Catherine's, they would have been responsible for the construction of the church tower from 1493 onwards. This monumental structure rose to a height of more than 100 metres (330 feet) once it had been completed in 1511, dominating views of the city for miles around.[45] Earlier, when the church

---

[43] Igel, "Rat und Raum," 204.

[44] Igel, "Rat und Raum," 206.

[45] Igel, "Rat und Raum," 207–8.

vaulting was being built in the 1420s, the families who contributed financially to the construction work, such as the von Ledens and the various branches of the Dumpstorp family, had their involvement recorded by arranging for the coats of arms to be set around the keystones of the vault.[46]

The completion of the Town Hall was also accompanied by the laying out of the newly created square in front of it, which had taken the place of the original market characterised by its cramped roadways and alleys. A stone path in front of the Town Hall was paved in 1505. Whether the rest of the square was also paved cannot be determined from the city accounts during this period, of which only an incomplete record has survived, and archaeological investigations have also found no evidence of this.[47] However, it is quite probable that the square was paved, particularly as work on stone paving in other streets around the city can be proven during this period.[48] When this work was finally completed, new walls were built around the two wells on the market in 1512 and the pillory erected over the well to the east.[49] The western well, known as the *Ratsbrunnen* (Council Well), remained incomplete for the time being, but was given a protective wooden roof in 1517.[50] It was probably only towards the end of the sixteenth century that its decorative pillars and roof, which featured sculptural figures, were eventually finished. This well has remained largely disregarded until now, but it is shown in great detail in the depiction from the *Bergersches Bischofsbuch* and, in an identical form, the engraving made by Reinhold before 1780 (Figs. 2.4 and 2.5). Above the well, there are presumably four figures on the columns, with four more figures higher up surrounding the base of the dome, which is crowned by a single monumental figure with a staff in its hand. According to a description dating from the early nineteenth century, this figure had two heads,[51] which indicates it was probably Prudence depicted as one of the Virtues. Furthermore, the fact that there were four figures on its lower tiers suggests a representation of the Four Cardinal Virtues. All that has survived of these wells is a carving of Christ and the Samaritan Woman from the *Jakobsbrunnen* (Jacob's Well), which

---

[46] Igel, "Rat und Raum," 208.

[47] Wolfgang Schlüter, "Die Ausgrabungen in der Marienkirche und auf dem Marktplatz," in *Die Marienkirche in Osnabrück: Ergebnisse archäologischer, bau- und kunsthistorischer Untersuchungen*, ed. Karl-Georg Kaster and idem (Bramsche: Rasch, 2001), 19–125, here 98.

[48] Eberhardt, *Van des stades wegene utgegeven unde betalt*, 213–56.

[49] Eberhardt, *Van des stades wegene utgegeven unde betalt*, 489–90.

[50] Eberhardt, *Van des stades wegene utgegeven unde betalt*, 499.

[51] *Osnabrück vor hundert Jahren: Aufzeichnungen des Senators Gerhard Friedrich Wagner*, ed. H. Forst (Osnabrück: Kisling, 1891).

is preserved today at Osnabrück's Kulturgeschichtliches Museum and has been dated circa 1580.[52]

With its far-reaching intervention into the urban environment, the reconfiguration of the Altstadt market in the years around 1500 created an urban space in which the newly created marketplace formed the foreground to the imposing Town Hall, which looked somewhat reminiscent of a castle building.[53] Furthermore, in its flanking position, the now more exposed St Mary's Church was subordinated to the Town Hall in the arrangement of the square. In consequence, an urban space that had previously been overwhelmingly used for commercial purposes became reshaped into an arena for ceremonial display that expressed the power and confidence of a city at the peak of its prosperity. At the same time, the council now had a stage at its disposal on which it could create performative representations of its power, especially on the occasion of the annual election. The marketplace, where the non-participant majority of citizens and residents assembled, linked the spaces involved in the rituals of the election: St Mary's Church, in which the Mass was held before the election, the cloth hall, in which the electors met behind closed doors, and the Town Hall, in which the council partook of a large meal and plentiful quantities of wine for the rest of the day.[54] The sculptures that probably decorated the Town Hall and later the Council Well promoted the just rule of the council. However, the Nine Good Heroes who may have been represented on the Town Hall façade would have referred to a lifestyle more strongly oriented towards chivalric ideas. This gave the group of families that dominated the council an opportunity to proclaim their claims to leadership of the city at the same time as asserting the influence over the surrounding region to which they aspired within the episcopal principality of Osnabrück. At this level, they were in competition with the cathedral chapter, most of whose members came from the lower nobility and were now trying to stop members of commoner families from being accepted into the chapter.[55]

---

[52] Bärbel Hedinger, *Plastik des Osnabrücker Landes vom 14. bis zum 18. Jahrhundert im Kulturgeschichtlichen Museum Osnabrück* (Osnabrück: Museums- und Kunstverein, 1977), 48–49.

[53] Igel, "Von der Straße zum Platz," 181–83; Albrecht, *Mittelalterliche Rathäuser*, 106–9.

[54] Stüve, *Heinrich David Stüve*, 22–24; Poeck, *Rituale der Ratswahl*, 72–74.

[55] Lambert Huys, *Das Verhältnis von Stadt und Kirche in Osnabrück im Mittelalter* (Leipzig: Noske, 1936), 5–6.

The Loci of the Council

The procedure for the election shows clearly how the accessibility of places and spaces was graduated: all the city's citizens and residents assembled in St Mary's, at least as many of them as could fit into the church, and later on the market and in the streets around the Town Hall. In the chamber of the cloth hall, participation was limited to those citizens who owned houses and were therefore entitled to take part in the election. The two sixteen-strong groups of electors isolated themselves from the assembly of house-owning citizens, as did the departing council, which consumed a ceremonial banquet in the Town Hall, where they were spatially separated from the crowds on the streets and the electors during the day. Finally, two constituent acts took place solely in the presence of the members of the council: the departing council assembled on the morning of the election in the Town Hall and then once again the following morning together with the newly elected councillors. At the latest from the sixteenth century, this happened each year under the *Krone* in the council chamber (Fig. 2.6). An almost identical wheel-shaped chandelier is to be found in Münster, and there are similar or slightly different chandeliers in many German town halls. It symbolised the order of the world into which the council had integrated itself and from which it drew its legitimacy.[56] Its topmost point showed Paradise with the Tree of Knowledge, Adam and Eve. Below them was the Firmament, with the Sun, Moon and Stars, then Mary with the Christ Child and three other figures representing the members of the *Weisheit* (Wisdom—the old council), the *Gilde* (the twenty-two masters of the eleven leading craftsmen-guilds), and the *Wehr* (sixteen members of the Great Council elected to represent the city's quarters). The ruling council itself is absent, although Mary, the patron saint of the market church where the service was celebrated before the election, can probably be regarded as a symbol of the council.[57] Finally, the lowest tier of the chandelier may be understood iconographically as a depiction of the Heavenly Jerusalem and therefore the ideal city.[58] Attached to this level is a shield bearing a depiction of the six-spoked wheel, which links the chandelier to Osnabrück as the city's coat of arms and seal. In assembling under the wheel-shaped chandelier, the council emphasised its legitimacy, which was ultimately based on the divine order of the world, remaining behind closed doors as it did so. The council took its place in the council pews of St Mary's Church in public, but its members had already been inaugurated into office in the shared secrecy of the meeting between the old and new councils under the *Krone*. So not only was the city itself recognised as a community in the course of the council election, but the council also affirmed its own position as a ruling body desired by God—as such it was publicly

---

[56] Diener-Staeckling, *Der Himmel über dem Rat*.

[57] Poeck, *Rituale der Ratswahl*, 69–70.

[58] Hans Sedlmayr, *Die Entstehung der Kathedrale* (Freiburg: Herder, 1993), 125–30.

FIG. 2.6: Osnabrück, council chamber with the crown. *Photograph by Karsten Igel.*

represented in St Mary's Church—something that was done out of the public gaze under the *Krone* in the Town Hall. However, its withdrawal during the day of the election, combined with the position of the Town Hall, raised above the gathering on the market, and the secret elements of the ritual, also illustrates the supreme position of the smaller ruling council, which ruled in practice as a patrician oligarchy.

The Altstadt Market in the Structure of Public Spaces

The strong position of the council and, despite the establishment of the Great Council, the rather modest opportunities for broader circles of the citizenry to have any direct input into decision-making from about 1400 onwards naturally raise questions about the reactions this state of affairs provoked, in particular the forms of any 'counter-public sphere' and the spaces and places where this may have been constituted. The reading of the 1348 election code at the beginning of the ballot discussed above was apparently only a remnant of what had once been a complete reading of the city ordinances, which were recorded in the municipal register. Hence the demands made by the Rampendahl Society on 1 January 1430—the day before the election—in which this group of rebels against the

existing form of council rule called, among other things, for the municipal register to be read out in full once again on the day of the election or in the course
of the following days.[59] Initially, the council seems to have responded positively
to the rebels and had these and other demands made by the Rampendahl Society
recorded in the municipal register. Subsequently, however, once the uprising had
been put down and its two ringleaders executed, the council added a note of their
invalidity.[60] In 1488 too, during the Lenethun Uprising, which had been partly
sparked off by the high costs incurred for the construction of the Town Hall and
was probably the reason why the building work on it halted for several years, demands were once again made for the municipal register to be read out before the
assembled citizenry.[61] While the Rampendahl Society could at least point to the
inclusion of the statutes it had drawn up in the municipal register in 1430 as an
achievement, even if it was short-lived (which may also suggest that the municipal register was actually read out when this was done), the tailor Lenethun and
his fellow rebels were denied even such fleeting success.

The apparent significance of the municipal register in these two conflicts
shows that the restriction of public access—here in terms of the accessibility of the
city ordinances—was integral to the exercise of rule by the council, and any opposition had to break through these restrictions if it was to test the legality of acts
of government against the city's statutes.[62] At the same time, such rebellions and
uprisings contained the idea of a 'counter-public sphere', within which a more or
less strong dissatisfaction with council rule could spill over from grumbling within
small circles and go as far as the mobilisation of larger groups in which the reality
and ideals of urban self-rule were also discussed. It has to be asked, of course, although the medieval sources hardly allow a clear answer to be given, whether this
counter-public sphere was to a certain extent constantly present or occasioned more
by the particular factors of any given situation.[63] According to tradition, the Rampendahl Society took its name from an inn that served as a meeting place,[64] and

---

[59] Hans-Bernd Meier, "Unruhen und Aufstand in Osnabrück im 15. und 16. Jahrhundert," *Osnabrücker Mitteilungen* 89 (1983): 60–121, here 84–93.

[60] *Das älteste Stadtbuch von Osnabrück*, 63–66.

[61] Meier, "Unruhen und Aufstand," 87.

[62] Jeannette Rauschert, "Gelöchert und befleckt: Inszenierung und Gebrauch städtischer Rechtstexte und spätmittelalterliche Öffentlichkeit," in *Text als Realie*, ed. Karl
Brunner and Gerhard Jaritz (Vienna: Verlag der österreichischen Akademie der Wissenschaften, 2003), 163–81.

[63] On the term 'counter-public sphere' see Schwerhoff, "Öffentliche Räume," 126–
33. On inns in this context see B. Ann Tustly, "'Privat' oder 'öffentlich'? Das Wirtshaus
in der deutschen Stadt des 16. und 17. Jahrhunderts," in *Zwischen Gotteshaus und Taverne*,
ed. Rau and Schwerhoff, 53–73; and Beat Kümin, "Wirtshaus und Gemeinde: Politisches
Profil einer kommunalen Grundinstitution im alten Europa," in *Zwischen Gotteshaus und
Taverne*, 75–97.

[64] Meier, "Unruhen und Aufstauds," 84.

the Lenethun Uprising of 1488 also seems to have started in one or several inns. A contemporary satirical poem describes the course of the uprising in a critical tone. Although, given the author's standpoint, exaggerations are to be suspected, above all in his characterisations of the protagonists, the account of the places where events took place certainly appears to be reliable.[65] The actual uprising began on 26 August with the ringing of the *Burgglocke* (Citizens' Bell), one of the bells of St Mary's that was rung on especially notable occasions. Now it was used by the rebels as a means of sending signals, something it was possible for them to do because they had also been joined by the city guards. The reference to the ringing of the bell is indicative of the seriousness of the situation: for it was the same bell that announced the election of the new councillors every year on 2 January.[66] At this moment, it was the acoustic signal for the rebels to launch their (attempted) seizure of power. Over the following days, the members of the citizenry called together in this way launched continual attacks from the gates of the city, plundering and laying waste to the estates held by the Benedictine nunnery situated outside the city as well as other areas that had been taken out of communal ownership. (Attacks on this nunnery occurred repeatedly despite its close links to the urban ruling class. It had previously been burned down by the whole citizenry in 1280/81 because it was located in a strategically important position on a hill just outside Osnabrück and represented a threat to the city in its conflict with Bishop Konrad von Rietberg around 1280.[67] During the Lenethun uprising and other episodes of urban unrest, however, it was more likely to have been economic competition that prompted attacks on the nunnery.) At first, the council appears not to have intervened, but to have looked on powerlessly or to have hoped that the dissatisfaction ventilated in this way would cool down if it were allowed free rein. On the fourth day, the rebels finally met under the lime tree in St Mary's churchyard and turned directly to, or against, the council with their demand that the municipal register be read out. Under the leadership of the mayor, Ertwin Ertmann, the council initially agreed to this request, but Ertmann read out only selected statutes, above all those that applied to rebellion against the council and the relevant punishments (one of the first bylaws in the municipal register dating from the beginning of the fourteenth century threatened conspirators against the council with the death penalty).[68] At the moment of the uprising, the public reading of the city's legislation remained

---

[65] *Die niederdeutsche Bischofschronik bis 1553: Beschrivinge sampt den handelingen der hoichwerdigen bisschopen van Ossenbrugge. Übersetzung und Fortsetzung der lateinischen Chronik Ertwin Ertmanns durch Dietrich Lilie*, ed. Friedrich Runge (Osnabrück: Verein für Geschichte und Landeskunde von Osnabrück, 1894), 199–211.

[66] Wehking, *Die Inschriften*, 20: "Wann ick sla an einen bord, is dar upror, brand oder mord. Wann ick sla an beide banden, sind dar nye heren vorhanden."

[67] Karsten Igel, "Von der Vorkommunalen zur kommunalen Stadt," *Osnabrücker Mitteilungen* 109 (2004): 27–67, esp. 49–51.

[68] *Das älteste Stadtbuch von Osnabrück*, No. 5.

under the control of the council—and the statutes read out certainly excluded the ones added to the municipal register nearly six decades earlier in the course of the Rampendahl Rebellion. The immediate response from the rebels was to move over to the cathedral close, where they discussed the situation and their demands.[69] In the close, they were removed from the immediate legal authority of the council for the time being. Simultaneously, however, they had also stepped onto the territory of the group against whom a large part of their pent-up anger was directed: the clergy. Apart from the release of areas of common land that had been enclosed by clergymen and leading city families, the rebels' demands included a call for any women who had a relationship with a priest to don a short coat with a stripe of the kind worn by prostitutes, so making these relationships public—which provoked Ertmann to the laconic response that people would be amazed how many respectable women would be seen with such stripes in the city![70] In view of the size of the crowd that had assembled, the legal authority of the cathedral chapter over the close was hardly enforceable any longer. The council's lack of authority there was probably not decisive to the rebels' choice of this meeting place, for it appears to have possessed a significance for the entire society of the city across the clerical–secular legal boundary. For instance, in 1511 the council authorised expenditure on the repair of woodwork and masonry under the lime tree on the cathedral close, so undertaking work on its own authority there at this particular place of assembly.[71] The lime tree is mentioned as early as 1311 in the terms of a foundation established to pay for various activities at the cathedral church, from which the bell-ringers were paid to carry water to the lime tree and perform other tasks there.[72] In the fourteenth and fifteenth centuries, it was used again and again as a venue for negotiations about a very diverse range of legal transactions, and it also served as a communal place of assembly for the cathedral chapter and council well into the sixteenth and seventeenth centuries—in particular for the discussion and mediation of questions at dispute between the two parties. The significance of this place extended beyond the walls of the city when, as in 1525, the *Landtag*, the diet of the episcopal principality, met there.[73] As criticism of the city's clergy was also particularly central to the Lenethun Uprising, this public space may well have appeared a suitable place to hold negotiations, even if the clergy are most likely to have stayed away from the rebels' assembly. As previously in 1430, the uprising of 1488 petered out without having any impact on the powers and composition of the council.

---

[69] *Die niederdeutsche Bischofschronik bis 1553*, 203, lines 151–152.

[70] *Bischofschronik*, 204, lines 174–191.

[71] Eberhardt, *Van des stades wegene utgegeven unde betalt*, 480–81.

[72] Bistumsarchiv Osnabrück, Dompfarrarchiv No. 5 — 1311 November 23.

[73] *Urkundenbuch der Stadt Osnabrück*, No. 1256 — 1399 Oktober 19; Friedrich Philippi, *Die ältesten Osnabrückischen Gildeurkunden (bis 1500): Mit einem Anhange über das Rathssilber zu Osnabrück* (Osnabrück: Kisling, 1890), 47; Rothert, "Die Geschichte, 2. Teil," 328–29.

To date, it has not been possible to clarify from the sources quite how the lime tree in the cathedral close related to the *Gogericht* (district court), the high court of the city and the areas immediately surrounding it, because it too was located in the close. There was a lion sculpture outside the court, a copy of which still stands on this site, and at the beginning of the fifteenth century it was known as the *Gericht zum Löwen* (Lion Court) after this sculpture (Fig. 2.2).[74] The *Gorichter*, the district judge who presided over this high court, was an episcopal official, but swore an oath of loyalty to the city council, while his duties were limited to summoning the accused and proclaiming judgements that had already been reached by the council. It was a reflection of the council's power over the court that its seat was moved in the fifteenth or sixteenth century from the lion located on the border between the legal space of the city and that of the cathedral—about halfway between the cathedral and the market—when the Town Hall became the courthouse.[75] The relocation of the high court fits in with the spatial concentration of government functions on the Altstadt Town Hall and its immediate environs,[76] which was strikingly expressed in the reconfiguration of the market area as the political heart of the city, a project that was begun towards the end of the fifteenth century. This transformation of spatial structures and relationships, which shifted the new Town Hall to the centre of attention and activity, made plain the oligarchic structure the council had already taken on, which was also evident during the Lenethun Uprising and in the restrictions on public readings of the municipal register. Moving the court to the Town Hall, the steps of which were then used for the proclamation of judgements, also meant a reduction of public access in comparison to the previous Lion Court: the new marketplace did offer enough space for large crowds to attend court cases, but the actual proceedings took place within the walls of the Town Hall: public access could now remain guaranteed only if the windows and doors were kept open.[77] The building of the new Town Hall meant a similar transformation for the court of petty jurisdiction, the *Burgericht* (citizens' court), which was responsible for civil-law affairs, above all the recording of non-contentious matters such as land sales and similar transactions.[78] Half of this court had been purchased by the citizenry from the bishop in 1225, and by the fifteenth century it had become identical to the

---

[74] Philippi, *Gildeurkunden*, 53, no. 102.

[75] Philippi, *Gildeurkunden*, 51–53; Rothert, "Die Geschichte, 2. Teil," 86–90.

[76] See also Schwerhoff, "Öffentliche Räume," 118–26.

[77] Jürgen Weitzel, "Gerichtsöffentlichkeit im hoch- und spätmittelalterlichen Deutschland," in *Information, Kommunikation und Selbstdarstellung in mittelalterlichen Gemeinden*, ed. Alfred Haverkamp (Munich: Oldenbourg, 1998), 71–84.

[78] Rothert, "Die Geschichte, 2. Teil," 47–60.

council as a body of lay magistrates.[79] At least since the second half of the thirteenth century, the *Burgericht* had possessed its own courthouse, the *pretorium*, which was first mentioned around 1250 and apparently stood immediately next to the older Town Hall (Fig. 2.1), but was probably arranged as an open arcade on the ground floor along Bierstraße.[80] If it was still being used for this purpose in the 1490s, the *pretorium* must, like the old Town Hall, have had to give way to the new Altstadt Town Hall that was being built, for the *Burgericht* was also based in the Town Hall at the latest once the new building was complete.

This political and spatial centralisation of council rule, which was manifested in the sequence of spaces used for the council election, as well as the concentration of the court premises and the controlled public reading of the city statutes, can be understood as a consequence of, or reaction to, competition within the city community. The council's legal authority was, of course, contested by the bishop and the cathedral chapter. And, as of 1348, the construction of a new town hall in the Neustadt had created a political counterweight to the Altstadt within the city. Indeed, this new building was actually larger than the then Altstadt Town Hall, so documenting the growing confidence of the Neustadt, which flourished in the fourteenth century. Furthermore, with its own cloth hall, the Neustadt was competing for revenues from across the whole city, especially as the very significant wool weaving trade was centred there.[81] By this time, the relative numerical strengths on the council, which was made up of twelve councillors from the Altstadt ranged against four councillors from the Neustadt, hardly corresponded any longer to the relative sizes of the populations of the two parts of the city, even if the Neustadt was probably always less populous. However, the balance of power on the council in favour of the Altstadt, which also continued in the Great Council created around 1400, ultimately remained decisive: the four fundamental decisions of the council and representatives of the citizenry that founded the polity of the united city curtailed key rights and revenues enjoyed by the Neustadt in favour of the Altstadt. The function of the Altstadt's market and Town Hall as the political and economic centre of the city was therefore firmly consolidated.[82] The Neustadt town hall remained the venue for meetings of the four-member Neustadt council, which was able to preserve a certain autonomy with regard to internal matters up until the beginning of the nineteenth century; the Neustadt's lower court also met in the town hall, and it remained the eco-

---

[79] Karsten Igel, "Die Heilige Katharina, das Rad, die Bürger und der Bischof: Das Osnabrücker Stadtsiegel und die Katharinenkirche — auch in Osnabrück war Jerusalem," *Osnabrücker Mitteilungen* 111 (2006): 27–60, here 42–45; Thomas Vogtherr, "Osnabrück im frühen und hohen Mittelalter," in *Geschichte der Stadt Osnabrück*, ed. Gerd Steinwascher (Osnabrück: Meinders & Elstermann, 2006), 61–86, esp. 81–83.

[80] Igel, "Vom Gewerberaum zum Repräsentationsraum," 210.

[81] Igel, "Von der vorkommunalen zur kommunalen Stadt," 60.

[82] *Das älteste Stadtbuch von Osnabrück*, Nos. 45, 47, 49, and 127.

nomic centre of the Neustadt, even if a proportion of the revenues collected there flowed into the coffers of the Altstadt.[83] At the same time, the Neustadt council lists that have been preserved from the early fourteenth century indicate that changes were becoming evident within the ruling group. From the end of the fourteenth century, for instance, the Dumpstorp family, which had originated from the Altstadt, began to play a significant role in the affairs of the Neustadt council.[84] During the fifteenth century, it is possible to locate the homes of the Neustadt councillors primarily in St Catherine's parish, which extended across the south-west of the Altstadt and the north-west of the Neustadt and was also favoured as a place of residence by the principal families represented on the Altstadt council.[85] Despite the internal conflicts that flared up again and again between the two parts of the city, their ruling groups were closely connected by family ties and their membership of a single parish from the fifteenth century at the latest.[86] The creation of the Great Council that numbered more than sixty or seventy members, probably towards the end of the fourteenth century, put in place a body much bigger than the sixteen-member ruling council. The larger amount of space required by the Great Council, which probably met in the cloth hall at first, may have been one reason for the building of the new Town Hall. At the same time, however, its establishment also increased the pressure on the smaller ruling council, and most of all on the individuals and families who dominated it, to document, consolidate, and legitimise their own status within the society of the city. In this connection, it is particularly notable that five leading members of the council had themselves immortalised with their coats of arms in consoles on the Town Hall façade while it was being built, practically as if they were the patrons responsible for its construction.[87] Should the prevalent interpretation of the sculptural programme of the main façade as the Nine Good Heroes be correct, this also allowed them to link themselves with its symbolism and so underline the status within the society of the city to which they laid claim. In itself, the construction of the new Town Hall and the square extending in front of it illuminates the position of the city's governing elite, which may have been contested repeatedly, but never genuinely came under threat.

---

[83] Karsten Igel, "Zwei Städte in einer Stadt: Zum Verhältnis von Alt- und Neustadt Osnabrück im Mittelalter," in *Zwei Städte in einer Stadt: 700 Jahre Vereinigung von Alt- und Neustadt Osnabrück (1307–2007), Beiträge zur Osnabrücker Stadtgeschichte*, ed. idem and Nicolas Rugge (Osnabrück: Verein für Geschichte und Landeskunde von Osnabrück, forthcoming).

[84] Olaf Spechter, *Die Osnabrücker Oberschicht im 17. und 18. Jahrhundert: Eine sozial- und verfassungsgeschichtliche Untersuchung* (Osnabrück: Wenner, 1975), 137–40.

[85] Karsten Igel, "Möglichkeiten einer Sozialtopographie des spätmittelalterlichen Osnabrück," *Osnabrücker Mitteilungen* 109 (2004): 69–85, esp. 80–85.

[86] Igel, "Rat und Raum," 211–13.

[87] Igel, "Rat und Raum," 204–6.

Discord in the Public Arena:
Processes and Meanings of the
St Bartholomew's Day Festivities in
Early Sixteenth-Century Sandwich

Sheila Sweetinburgh

English society during the reign of Henry VIII witnessed considerable religious, political, and cultural changes. Nevertheless, the chronology of these changes at differing levels within society is contested by historians, and even though the Reformation debate is apparently moving on from what Patrick Collinson and John Craig called the 'sterile argument' of 'top down' or 'bottom up,' 'fast' or 'slow', the whole century, but the early decades especially, remains hotly debated.[1] In response to A. G. Dickens' *The English Reformation*, revisionist ideas regarding the state of the church in late medieval England have highlighted what seems to be a robust spirituality based on the parish community where individual parishioners could exercise a degree of choice within the confines of the collective.[2] As a consequence, any tensions could generally be contained and the

---

[1] Patrick Collinson and John Craig, "Introduction," in *The Reformation in English Towns, 1500–1640*, ed. eidem (Basingstoke: Macmillan, 1998), 2.

[2] A. G. Dickens, *The English Reformation*, 2nd ed. (London: Batsford, 1989). This literature is extensive, though not always in agreement, and includes Eamon Duffy, *The Stripping of the Altars: Traditional Religion in England 1400–1540* (New Haven and London: Yale University Press, 1992); idem, *The Voices of Morebath: Reformation and Rebellion in an English Village* (New Haven and London: Yale University Press, 2001); Clive Burgess, "The Benefactions of Mortality: The Lay Response in the Late Medieval Urban Parish," in *Studies in Clergy and Ministry in Medieval England*, ed. D. Smith (York: University of York, 1991), 65–86; idem, "London Parishioners in Times of Change: St Andrew Hubbard, Eastcheap, c. 1450–1470," *Journal of Ecclesiastical History* 53 (2002): 38–63; idem and Beat Kümin, "Penitential Bequests and Parish Regimes in Late Medieval England," *Journal of Ecclesiastical History* 44 (1993): 610–30; Beat Kümin, *The Shaping of a*

Negotiating the Political in Northern European Urban Society, c.1400–c.1600, ed. Sheila Sweetinburgh, MRTS 434 (Tempe: ACMRS, 2013). [ISBN 978-0-86698-482-9]

variation within orthodox piety was in a sense one of its main strengths.[3] In turn this scenario has been challenged by those who believe that they have found evidence of heterodoxy in pre-Reformation England, that is, fissures within collective religion which in certain cases became radical divergences.[4] Other historians have looked elsewhere in their search for greater understanding of this period, seeing popular politics, the dynamic relationship between the regime and the locality through 'points of contact', as a major contributory factor.[5] Of particular significance in these investigations are lay–clerical relations, the points of conflict traditionally labelled 'anticlericalism' though more recently this term has been either rejected as anachronistic and unhelpful or modified to signify a more complex situation.[6] Some of those adopting the latter approach have sought to

Community: The Rise and Reformation of the English Parish (Aldershot: Scolar Press, 1996); Christopher Haigh, "The Recent Historiography of the English Reformation," *Historical Journal* 25 (1982): 995–1007; idem, ed., *The English Reformation Revised* (Cambridge: Cambridge University Press, 1987); idem, *English Reformations: Religion, Politics, and Society under the Tudors* (Oxford: Clarendon Press, 1993); Ronald Hutton, *The Rise and Fall of Merry England: The Ritual Year 1400–1700* (Oxford: Oxford University Press, 1994).

  [3] Gervase Rosser is among those who have published on this; see "Communities of Parish and Guild in the Late Middle Ages," in *Parish, Church and People: Local Studies in Lay Religion, 1350–1750*, ed. S. J. Wright (London: Hutchinson, 1988), 29–55; idem, "Parochial Conformity and Voluntary Religion in Late-Medieval England," *Transactions of the Royal Historical Society*, 6th ser., 1 (1991): 173–79.

  [4] For example, Margaret Aston, "Iconoclasm at Rickmansworth, 1522: Troubles of Churchwardens," *Journal of Ecclesiastical History* 40 (1989): 524–52; J. F. Davis, *Heresy and Reformation in the South-East of England, 1520–1559* (London: Royal Historical Society, 1983); Anthony Hope, "The Lady and the Bailiff: Lollardy among the Gentry in Yorkist and Early Tudor England," in *Lollardy and the Gentry in the Later Middle Ages*, ed. Margaret Aston and Colin Richmond (Stroud: Sutton, 1997), 250–77; Robert Lutton, *Lollardy and Orthodox Religion in Pre-Reformation England* (Woodbridge: Boydell Press, 2006).

  [5] Among these are Tim Harris, ed., *The Politics of the Excluded, c. 1500–1850* (Basingstoke: Macmillan, 2001); Ethan H. Shagan, *Popular Politics and the English Reformation*, Cambridge Studies in Early Modern British History (Cambridge: Cambridge University Press, 2003); David Lamburn, "Politics and Religion in Early Modern Beverley," in Collinson and Craig, *The Reformation in English Towns*, 63–78; Anthony Hope, "Martyrs of the Marsh: Elizabeth Barton, Joan Bocher and Trajectories of Martyrdom in Reformation Kent," in *Pieties in Transition: Religious Practices and Experiences, c. 1400–1640*, ed. R. Lutton and E. Salter (Aldershot: Ashgate, 2007), 41–55.

  [6] Whereas Christopher Haigh has been particularly scathing as part of his attack on Dickens' interpretation of the Reformation and especially his use of the term, others have looked again and consider that a more nuanced use of the term can be helpful: Haigh, *English Reformations*, 40–55; Shagan, *Popular Politics*, 131–61; Collinson and Craig, "Introduction," 6–7; Peter Marshall, *The Catholic Priesthood and the English Reformation* (Oxford: Clarendon Press, 1994), 211–32; Robert N. Swanson, "Problems of the Priesthood in Pre-Reformation England," *English Historical Review* 417 (1990): 845–89. More

show that there were different, yet sometimes linked forms of antagonistic relations between members of the laity and certain clerics, and that at different times during the sixteenth century either side might employ evangelical views or language. Also significant in these disputes was the use of ritual—the symbolism of the taking of a chalice from its owner, the placing of contested tithe offerings on the altar, or the detailing of specific forms that parishioners expected the clergy should adhere to—actions that were understood by participants and by onlookers, though interpretations might differ, being dependent on complex and often shifting beliefs and values.[7]

Such ideas are useful in the context of this essay, but it is also worth noting Patrick Collinson and John Craig's remarks regarding the diversity of experiences towns had in the Reformation. Rather than finding regional patterns of common ground, the essays provided by their contributors to *The Reformation in English Towns* highlighted the individual experiences of the chosen towns.[8] Many of these were moderate-sized urban centres, not dissimilar to Sandwich, where the factors that seemed to have greatest bearing on how the town fared during the sixteenth century were the structure of power relations and the personnel involved. Also important was the destabilising of religion, certainly through the Reformation but also, as noted above, in some places as a result of divergence from orthodoxy during the earlier period. Taking such notions together, it would seem fruitful to examine English urban society more fully, including studying certain towns afresh using the more nuanced approaches that have developed over the last few decades.

Consequently, this essay explores the history of early sixteenth-century Sandwich, taking as its entry point the events of 1532 and their aftermath. Writing in 1979, Peter Clark noted that "anticlericalism prepared much of the ground for the emergence of Protestant groups at [. . .] Sandwich in the 1530s," and in particular he cites what he calls "a bitter dispute in 1532 between the magistrates and the curate and chantry priests of St Peters" as setting the scene "for major religious change."[9] This is an interesting reading of the situation which might be developed

---

recently the concept has been revisited again: Peter Marshall, "Anticlericalism Revested? Expressions of Discontent in Early Tudor England," in *The Parish in Late Medieval England*, ed. Clive Burgess and Eamon Duffy (Donington: Shaun Tyas, 2006), 365–80.

[7] Shagan, *Popular Politics*, 137–38. Paula Simpson, "Custom and Conflict: Disputes over Tithe in the Diocese of Canterbury, 1501–1600" (Ph.D. diss., University of Kent, 1997), 40.

[8] Collinson and Craig, "Introduction," 15.

[9] Peter Clark, "Reformation and Radicalism in Kentish Towns c. 1500–1553," in *Stadtbürgertum und Adel in der Reformation: Studien zur Sozialgeschichte der Reformation in England und Deutschland [The Urban Classes, the Nobility and the Reformation: Studies on the Social History of the Reformation in England and Germany]*, ed. Wolfgang J. Mommsen with Peter Alter and Robert W. Scribner (Stuttgart: Klett-Cotta, 1979), 107–27, at

further by looking more closely at the participants involved in the dispute within a contextual framework. Before looking in detail at this dispute, the first two sections below will consider the origins of the procession at the centre of the disagreement and the nature of the town in the early sixteenth century.

The Early History of the Procession

For many English towns the struggle for autonomy against outside lordship began during the late twelfth and thirteenth centuries, and Sandwich was no exception. Furthermore, on 24 August 1217 the special nature of the town became even more apparent to the townsmen following their success at the battle of Sandwich, and subsequently the myth surrounding the events of that day became part of the local civic ideology.[10] The main components of the myth are as follows: the French forces were commanded by the renegade and traitor Eustace the monk, who used diabolical powers to make himself invisible. The English forces were primarily drawn from the Cinque Ports and included Crabbe, a locally well-known seaman, who was immortalised as the slayer of Eustace. However, Crabbe was also killed in the fray, which thoroughly demoralised the portsmen; they were rallied only by the intervention of St Bartholomew, whose appearance established divine approval for their cause. As a mark of gratitude the portsmen donated most of the booty to the founding of a town hospital dedicated to their saintly saviour, and to commemorate their deliverance they agreed to process annually to the hospital where they would deliver a gift in thanksgiving.[11]

114–15. See also idem, *English Provincial Society from the Reformation to the Revolution: Religion, Politics, and Society in Kent 1500–1640* (Hassocks: Harvester Press, 1977), 37.

[10] The first near contemporary reference is in the poem *L'Histoire de Guilaume le Marechal*, which states that after the decisive battle of Sandwich on 24 August 1217, William Marshal ordered the extensive booty from the French ships to be divided among the portsmen. Some of the spoils were to used to found a hospital for the care of God's poor, in honour of St Bartholomew who had given them victory: H. Cannon, "The Battle of Sandwich and Eustace the Monk," *English Historical Review* 108 (1912): 649–70, at 667 n. 144, citing the editor's paraphrase *L'Histoire de Guillaume le Marechal*, ed. P. Meyer (1901), for the text, ii, lines 17501–68. For a recent new edition with full translation, see *History of William Marshal*, ed. A. J. Holden, Anglo-Norman Text Society, 3 vols. (Woodbridge: Boydell Press, 2002–2006). Matthew Paris provides an illustrated account of the battle: Cambridge, Corpus Christi College, MS. 16, fol. 56. See Sheila Sweetinburgh, *The Role of the Hospital in Medieval England: Gift Giving and the Spiritual Economy* (Dublin: Four Courts Press, 2004), 189–90.

[11] It seems that at some point in the thirteenth century the initiative for founding the hospital shifted from William Marshal to the portsmen. Unfortunately apart from *L'Histoire*, there are no other extant thirteenth-century English accounts of the battle and the hospital's foundation, which means that the first known version is the early

The creation of the myth, including the initiation of the procession as a town ritual, during the thirteenth century by the leading men of Sandwich needs to be set against the conflict over sovereignty. This three-way power struggle among Christ Church Priory, the Crown, and the town saw, for example, the townsmen supporting Simon de Montfort in the baronial wars of the 1260s, and in the last decade of the century they were again engaged in an even more protracted struggle against the king. According to Justin Croft, the production of the town custumal in 1301 was a further attempt to curb the expansion of royal authority over the town.[12] He sees the custumal as representing the writing up of the social memory of the town, whereby the rights and duties of the civic officers and the place of the town's institutions, including the hospitals, were established, providing precedents for subsequent actions. The description of the St Bartholomew's day procession is the first entry in the hospital custumal, suggesting that it may represent similar ideas, its inclusion highlighting for the leading citizens their role as patrons, who, like their ancestors and successors, had a continuing moral and spiritual relationship with the town's saint in his hospital.[13]

Perhaps significantly, the custumal refers neither to the battle nor to any of the other elements within the myth. Instead it is the procession that takes centre stage. Thus it appears that the mayor and jurats, as the legitimate authority in Sandwich through the foundation and maintenance of a hospital for the local poor, were seeking to demonstrate their moral worth, their charitable actions endorsed by divine authority. Yet Eustace, and so the battle, did not disappear completely, because in the late fifteenth century 'Stace the monk', or at least his head, was apparently still paraded through the town, presumably as part of the procession, an official but popular re-enactment and reminder of what had happened to the town's enemy in 1217.[14]

---

fourteenth-century Christchurch Priory chronicle, the *Polistorie de Jean de Canterbury*: London, British Library, MS. Harley 636, fols. 201^v–202^v. Burgess notes that in addition to the Latin chronicles of Roger of Wendover and Matthew Paris, which recount the activities of Eustace and the battle of Sandwich, there is the chronicle of Walter of Guisborough (probably early fourteenth century but maybe as early as 1270), none of which mentions the hospital: G. Burgess, *Two Medieval Outlaws: Eustace the Monk and Fouke FitzWaryn* (Cambridge: D. S. Brewer, 1997), 5.

[12] Justin P. Croft, "An Assault on the Royal Justices at Ash and the Making of the Sandwich Custumal," *Archaeologia Cantiana* 117 (1997): 13–36.

[13] Whitfield, East Kent Archives, SA/LC 1, fol. 15^v. William Boys, *Collections for an History of Sandwich in Kent, with Notices of the Other Cinque Ports and Members and of Richborough* (Canterbury, 1792), 309, 431.

[14] Whitfield, East Kent Archives, Sa/FAt 9. 'Giants' or giant puppets were part of the civic Becket festivities at Canterbury in the early sixteenth century, and there are also examples from London and Norwich: Canterbury, Canterbury Cathedral Archives and Library, CC/AB 1, fols. 5^v–6; *Historical Manuscript Commission: Canterbury*, 241;

FIG. 3.1: Sandwich, north aisle, St Peter's church. *Photograph by Sarah Pearson.*

Nonetheless, for the civic authorities one of the most powerful themes within the ritual may have been the linking of church, civic governance, and charity by beginning the procession at St Peter's church (see Fig. 3.1) and ending at St Bartholomew's Hospital (see Fig. 3.2). The choice of St Peter's rested on a number of factors: it was used for the election of certain civic officers, it was the central parish church, and the town court was held there (until the building of a court hall nearby in the early fifteenth century or perhaps slightly earlier).[15] Moreover, the advowson was held jointly by the town and the abbot of St Augustine's, Canterbury, which may have meant that the leading citizens felt they had a right to appropriate and extend the use of the church to include the St Bartholomew's day procession.[16] Thus the mayor would be departing from a sacred

Gervase Rosser, "Myth, Image and Social Process in the English Medieval Town," *Urban History* 23 (1996): 5–25, at 22–23.

[15] Boys, *Sandwich*, 443; Croft, "Making of the Sandwich Custumal," 17–18; Helen Clarke, Sarah Pearson, and Mavis E. Mate, *Sandwich: 'The Completest Medieval Town in England'. A Study of the Town and Port from its Origins to 1600* (Oxford: Oxbow, 2010), 33, 49, 76, 78–79, 81, and esp. 86–88.

[16] *The Register of St Augustine's Abbey, Canterbury*, ed. G. J. Turner and H. E. Salter, 2 vols. (London: Oxford University Press, 1915–1924), 2: 543.

FIG. 3.2: Sandwich, chapel at St Bartholomew's Hospital. *Photograph by Sarah Pearson.*

space near the town centre, a site of ecclesiastical jurisdiction but one where he had previously dispensed justice at the town court in his role as moral guardian of Sandwich. Even though the route of the procession is not recorded, it went from the central area of Sandwich to the edge of the urban area where the hospital was sited. Physically and symbolically, by bridging the gap between the centre and the margins, the town officers, as pilgrims, were underlining the nature of the relationship between St Bartholomew's and the town, both in terms of the myth of the first gift exchange and the ongoing process of reciprocity. Furthermore, the asymmetrical relationship between the mayor and jurats, and St Bartholomew's, highlighted the hospital's charitable function and its subordinate role in the exchange process as the grateful receiver of civic generosity. Such ideas were exemplified by the corporation's control of the high Mass at the hospital chapel: the authorities gave the unlit tapers and chose the priest who presided at the Mass. Concerning the gift-giving of the tapers, the town officers, as patrons of the hospital, performed the dual role of supplicants and recipients. They gave the tapers to St Bartholomew, perhaps laying them on the high altar, and thereafter one of the jurats controlled their use at the chapel (he held the key to the chest where they were kept).[17]

This description suggests that the civic authorities saw the procession as a symbolic demonstration of their role as moral guardians of the whole community, where the linking of ritual and myth was part of the town's sacred knowledge. Yet even in this account 'others' were involved. The mayor and jurats were said to lead the procession, but accompanying them were other civic officers, including the town waites, and the freemen.[18] The town clergy were also present, and members of certain local knightly families, particularly the Sandwich family (early hospital benefactors), might join the procession and donate tapers at St Bartholomew's Hospital chapel. As honoured guests of the corporation, their presence might have enhanced the status and reputation of the other participants and the procession itself, but may also have been viewed with a degree of ambivalence. Such men were outsiders and some had served the Crown, their participation perhaps seen as undermining the civic authorities' own relationship with the hospital.[19] Finally there were those from outside the freeman body who witnessed the procession, whose presence might have been viewed by the authorities as endorsing the procession's place in the town's history. This apparent interplay among the various participants seems to fit Gerd Baumann's hypothesis that rituals are undertaken by "competing constituencies" where the performances, symbols, and meanings are directed at others beyond the core 'community'.[20] Under these circumstances such potential diversity does not of necessity lead to a breakdown of the ritual, but may instead provide opportunities for those involved

---

[17] Sheila Sweetinburgh, "Mayor-making and Other Ceremonies: Shared Uses of Sacred Space among the Kentish Cinque Ports," in *The Use and Abuse of Sacred Places in Late Medieval Towns*, ed. Paul Trio and Majan de Smet (Leuven: Leuven University Press, 2006), 165–87, at 180–84.

[18] Interestingly, the custumal seems to imply that the lights (candles) were carried by the laity, though this may refer just to the candles which were to be left at the hospital, not those for the procession (the order may have been thurifer, lights, cross). Otherwise the order of the procession apparently follows the expected format: the people preceding the corporation followed by the clergy (Imogen Corrigan, pers. comm.).

[19] Even though the tomb effigy of a knight, reputed to be Sir Henry de Sandwich, may not be in its original location, it is now close to the high altar in St Bartholomew's chapel, the presence of such a tomb may still provide a further example of the way sacred space was negotiated.

[20] Baumann's work explores the notion that rituals are performed by "competing constituencies," that they do not "celebrate the perpetuation of social values and self-knowledge," but rather "speak to aspirations towards cultural change." Consequently it is important to recognise the "frequency of outsider participation," thereby highlighting "how rituals can be addressed" to "Others": Gerd Baumann, "Ritual Implicates 'Others': Rereading Durkheim in a Plural Society," in *Understanding Rituals*, ed. Daniel de Coppet (London: Routledge, 1992), 97–116, at 98–99, 110–11.

to adapt particular aspects for their own ideological purposes. Furthermore, as David Parkin has argued, participants may deny the meanings of others by "colluding collectively" through their own involvement in the ritual process.[21] These ideas would seem to indicate that there was a degree of flexibility and ambiguity within the performance of the procession, which presumably meant that over the next three centuries its meanings remained open to negotiation.

Sandwich in the Early Sixteenth Century

Even though the town had by the early sixteenth century shrunk to a population of about 2,700 from its height of c. 5,000 in the high Middle Ages, its ancient importance as a head port among the Cinque Ports meant that the civic authorities were acutely aware of its heritage.[22] Its position on the east Kent coast at the mouth of the River Stour and at the southern end of the Wansum Channel had provided the early portsmen with a sheltered anchorage and a safer passage to the Thames Estuary and London than the notorious voyage around the Isle of Thanet and the shifting sandbanks of the Goodwin Sands. This had provided considerable opportunities for overseas trade, both long distance and across the English Channel, though much of it was in the hands of Londoners and other foreigners. Nevertheless, the architectural evidence does indicate the presence of a wealthy minority during the twelfth and thirteenth centuries, and later developments, such as the annual arrival of Italian shipping in the fifteenth century, continued to sustain the port after the devastation of the Black Death.[23]

By the late fifteenth century, however, those involved in the town's maritime economy had had to adapt to the loss of the Venetian galleys and other long-distance traders.[24] Also by this time there seems to have been a major reduction in the town's involvement in the North Sea herring fleet and in military expeditions to France, Sandwich mariners apparently primarily engaging in coastal trade both with other English ports and those across the Channel. Among the commodities traded were fish, malt, and hops, and in the early sixteenth century the brewing of beer and ale was a major component of the town's

---

[21] David Parkin, "Ritual as Spatial Direction and Bodily Division," in *Understanding Rituals*, ed. de Coppet, 11–25, at 23.

[22] This assessment of the later population is based on a detailed tax return dated 1513: London, British Library, MS. Add. 33511, fols. 33–44; Clarke, Pearson, and Mate, *Sandwich*, 137.

[23] Clarke, Pearson, and Mate, *Sandwich*, 73–75, 121–27.

[24] J. Wallace, "The Overseas Trade of Sandwich, 1400–1520" (M.Phil. thesis, University of London, 1974); Clarke, Pearson, and Mate, *Sandwich*, 126–27, 130.

economy.[25] Another aspect of the town's economy was the supplying of livestock and grain to the garrison at Calais and its environs.[26] For certain individuals such growth areas provided significant commercial opportunities, but as well as this tiny wealthy minority the town accommodated an increasing number of poorer people and those classed as paupers.[27] Moreover, few families could trace their ancestry in Sandwich beyond a couple of generations, and even though some migrants settled in the town, others were transitory.[28] Most, but not all, were men, perhaps generally young or younger adults from other parts of Kent, the neighbouring county of Essex, and other places in the British Isles, northern France, and the Low Countries, the town becoming a melting pot of people and ideas (the early arrival of the Jesus Mass is perhaps indicative of this, see below).[29] Even if many stayed for only a short period, this influx of people (possibly coupled with an increase in the young natal population) may have altered the age-distribution pattern in Sandwich. Though not unusual in urban society at this period, such a socio-economic structure had implications with respect to the governance and well-being of the town.

Having gained the right in the thirteenth century to elect their own mayor, the men of Sandwich had sought to extend and consolidate their civic authority

---

[25] Mavis E. Mate, *Trade and Economic Developments, 1450–1550: The Experience of Kent, Surrey and Sussex* (Woodbridge: Boydell Press, 2006); Clarke, Pearson, and Mate, *Sandwich*, 133, 140–42.

[26] For example, in December 1531 a licence was granted to the lieutenant of Calais castle to export annually from the ports of Sandwich, Dover, and Hythe to the soldiers at the castle forty-four oxen and 250 sheep; a similar licence was also granted for 500 quarters of malt from Dover or Sandwich, and in the following January considerably more livestock and malt were required: *Letters and Papers, Foreign and Domestic, of the Reign of Henry VIII, preserved in the Public Record Office, the British Museum, and elsewhere in England* [subsequently cited as *L.P. Hen. VIII*], 23 vols in 38 (London: HMSO, 1862–1932), 5: 286, 365–66.

[27] The 1513 tax assessment provides a valuable picture of the social structure of the town: London, British Library, MS. Add. 33511, fols. 33–44. Clarke, Pearson, and Mate, *Sandwich*, 137.

[28] As well as the 1513 list, there is another detailed locally-compiled tax list for c. 1471 which provides 523 names. Though not specifically stated in the town book, the assessment may be that granted by the commons of a whole "maltote, howserent and frerent" in that year to pay for bringing back Queen Margaret and Prince Edward from France: Whitfield, East Kent Archives, Sa/AC 1, fols. 199–199ᵛ.

[29] Amongst several Scotsmen, Frenchmen, and Flemings listed as aliens having shops in Sandwich in 1533/4 were Patrick Hutchenson (Scotsman), Peter Marten (Frenchman), and John Peterson (Fleming); Whitfield, East Kent Archives, Sa/FAt 30. Two years later Henry Spicket from Ludlow in the Welsh Marches, Robert Gowght from south Wales, and Robert Faier and Elizabeth his wife from Bury St Edmunds, Suffolk, all suffered banishment from the town for various misdemeanours: Whitfield, East Kent Archives, Sa/AC 3, fol. 74.

over the town which had brought them into conflict at various times with Christ Church Priory and later the Crown. Moreover, certain townsmen became involved in dynastic royal politics in the fifteenth century, leading on occasion to severe divisions among the town officers.[30] Thus the demarcation between particular factions within the town was vertical as well as horizontal, and such divisions in Sandwich may have been instrumental in the decision by the mayor and jurats in the mid-1450s to extend the governing body to include a common council.[31] Modifications to this new structure were implemented about a decade later, but the move towards greater accountability survived for barely more than a generation. In 1526 the Cinque Ports' own court stipulated that at each port the right to choose the mayor and jurats would lie with a group of twenty-four local men, and that at Sandwich the freemen would no longer elect the mayor, the jurats succeeding each other in order of seniority.[32] In addition, the common council was to be reduced from thirty-six men to twenty-four who would be appointed by the mayor and jurats.

These changes came at a difficult period in the town's history. The problem of the overall decline in Sandwich's economy was linked to such factors as falling population, dilapidated buildings, and the growing number of poorer people, especially migrants, at a time when civic revenue was falling and there was an increasing need to safeguard the prices and availability of staple commodities for the benefit of the townspeople.[33] Whether this resulted in a 'flight from office' is a moot point, but certain leading townsmen did seek to excuse themselves from civic office, the treasurership being seen as an especially unwelcome position.[34] In addition, from the mid-1520s the civic authorities were engaged in an acrimonious dispute with the town's bailiff, a royal appointee who sought to regain the revenues associated with the bailiwick (see below).[35] Matters were made worse

---

[30] Certain leading townsmen supported Warwick and Fauconberg during the crisis period of 1469–1471: Whitfield, East Kent Archives, Sa/AC 1, fols. 196, 199, 201. Dorothy Gardiner, *Historic Haven: The Story of Sandwich* (Derby: Pilgrim Press, 1954), 49–50.

[31] Whitfield, East Kent Archives, Sa/AC 1, fol. 96v. Clarke, Pearson, and Mate, *Sandwich*, 131–32.

[32] Whitfield, East Kent Archives, Sa/ZB4/14; *A Calendar of The White and Black Books of the Cinque Ports, 1432–1955*, ed. Felix Hull, Kent Records 19 (London: HMSO, 1966), 201–2; Gardiner, *Sandwich*, 156.

[33] Clarke, Pearson, and Mate, *Sandwich*, 137–38. On attitudes to the poor and poorer people, see Sweetinburgh, *Role of the Hospital*, 206, 208–13.

[34] In 1500, for example, both candidates sought exemption: Thomas Bigge stated that he was aged and impotent and William Morgan said that he was intending to go on pilgrimage to St James of Compostela: Whitfield, East Kent Archives, Sa/AC 2, fol. 75.

[35] There are numerous entries in the town books, and in a suit brought by the king and his bailiff in 1526–1527 many of the details regarding the dispute are restated: *Kent: Diocese of Canterbury*, ed. James M. Gibson, Records of Early English Drama, 3 vols. (Toronto and London: University of Toronto Press and British Library Publishing Division,

by the state of the haven, the civic authorities frequently seeking to find remedies to the problem of silting which were exacerbated owing to the unwillingness of some individuals and institutions to co-operate.[36] As a result, the recruitment of new freemen apparently declined, though a few of the local gentry did join the franchise (to take advantage of the ancient privileges pertaining to the town), but that in itself may have added to the tensions within Sandwich society.[37] The town court records illustrate such tensions, partly through the ordinances enacted against itinerant beggars and the cases involving various petty offences, but also those brought before the court for slandering members of the town government, some of whom were their peers.[38]

The church was an integral part of the town, three parish churches having perhaps been established soon after the Conquest. St Clement's, probably the oldest, has traditionally been linked to the town's maritime community, and it, like the much smaller parish of St Mary's, was under the patronage of the archdeacon.[39] As already noted, the central parish of St Peter's was at least partly under the control of the civic authorities, sharing the right of appointment of the rector with the abbot of St Augustine's Abbey, who had also from an early date held the settlement of Stonar across the river. In addition to the parish churches, there was a chapel dedicated to St James and a hermitage close to St Mary's church, four hospitals, and a Carmelite friary.

The architectural evidence indicates that considerable building work in terms of extensions and other modifications had taken place at all the churches during

---

2002), 2:839–46 citing London, British Library, MS. Lansdowne 276, fols. 187–95; Gardiner, *Sandwich*, 152–55.

[36] Among those resisting such efforts were the master, brothers and sisters at St Bartholomew's Hospital. Initially they refused to pay their contribution to repair the wharf at Davygate in 1528: Whitfield, East Kent Archives, Sa/AC 3, fol. 10ᵛ; Gardiner, *Sandwich*, 195–201.

[37] Symptomatic of such problems is an ordinance of 1519 where it was agreed by the town that anyone who had been made a freeman but had not paid the necessary fine and now refused to pay it should be dismissed as a freeman unless he had paid by the next meeting of the town: Whitfield, East Kent Archives, Sa/AC 2, fol. 267ᵛ.

[38] For example, in 1523 when the mayor and two senior jurats were present in the corn market, they were verbally abused by two of the other jurats, John Worme and John Pynnok. Both men were committed to gaol; and in an attempt to put a stop to such altercations the mayor and jurats the same day brought in an ordinance that henceforth any jurat who openly rebuked another would automatically be fined 21*d*: Whitfield, East Kent Archives, Sa/AC 2, fol. 281. Five years later John Pynnok refused to be sworn in as a jurat saying that he feared for his life: Whitfield, East Kent Archives, Sa/AC 3, fol. 6. Attacks also came from those outside the jurats: in the same year John Master was denounced as a "hedgecreper" by a barber called Robert Kenny: Sa/AC 3, fols. 14–14ᵛ.

[39] For a discussion of the development of the Sandwich parishes, see Clarke, Pearson, and Mate, *Sandwich*, 32–34, 38.

the Middle Ages, probably the last of these being the new steeple or tower at St Clement's, perhaps completed by about 1530, and supported through subscriptions and testamentary bequests.[40] As well as the high altar, each church housed a considerable number of images, altars, and lights, some of which are known to have had fraternities. Furthermore, the cult of the Name of Jesus had arrived at St Mary's by the mid-1460s, and testamentary giving to the Jesus Mass indicates that it received support from the middling sort as well as from certain leading families.[41] There was at least one chantry at each church, Thomas Elys' late fourteenth-century foundation at St Peter's being exceptionally large for Kent, having three chantry priests. Of the two chantries at St Clement's church, the second established in 1492 by Nicholas Burton was at St George's altar, the fraternity of the same altar receiving 6*s* 8*d* annually from the town treasurers towards the annual St George procession.[42]

Looking at the parish clergy, longevity was probably instrumental in the greater level of involvement of Sir William Merryman, the vicar at St Mary's church, in the wills of his parishioners compared to Master Leonard Eglisfelde (rector of St Peter's) and Sir Thomas Cogayne and Sir John Oxley (vicars of St Clement's).[43] This pattern was reversed in terms of the chantry chaplains at the three parishes. Nonetheless, other issues may also have been influential because some incumbents were apparently ignored by local testators, suggesting that it is important to consider a range of factors. Similarly, testamentary support for the various chantry priests in the town may reflect several considerations, and it is worth noting that Sir John Stephynson of Elys' chantry was the most widely recorded cleric, followed by Sir William Kene of Burton's chantry at St Clement's church.[44]

---

[40] For a detailed architectural history of the churches, see Clarke, Pearson, and Mate, *Sandwich*, 199–205. Probably as a result of this expensive building project the church plate had to be used as collateral, being redeemed through Nicholas Orpath's testamentary bequest in 1533: Maidstone, Centre for Kentish Studies, PRC 17/20, fol. 3.

[41] The first reference is in the will of Richard Bilton dated 1466: Maidstone, Centre for Kentish Studies, PRC 17/1, fol. 256; Sweetinburgh, *Role of the Hospital*, 222–23. On the Jesus Mass see Clarke, Pearson, and Mate, *Sandwich*, 203–4. For the possible implications of such Christocentric devotion in terms of heterodoxy, see Lutton, *Lollardy and Orthodox Religion*, 71–80.

[42] Nicholas Burton's will: Maidstone, Centre for Kentish Studies, PRC 32/3, fol. 368.

[43] Though a crude measurement of 'popularity', Sir William is recorded seventeen times under various headings in Sandwich wills, Master Eglisfelde twelve times, Sir Thomas nine times, and Sir John twice.

[44] Sir John was listed twenty-three times and Sir William fourteen times.

Although some historians have questioned the value of testamentary provisions as indicators of lay piety, they remain the most widely used source.[45] The records from Sandwich seem to indicate moderate levels of support for the parish churches.[46] As the figures suggest, Sandwich testators were not dissimilar to their peers at the other Cinque Ports, and this pattern is comparable to the findings from much of east Kent but not those from some other English towns where levels of support appear to have been significantly higher. Yet in comparison to the Wealden parish of Tenterden the townspeople of Sandwich were not parsimonious. This is important because Robert Lutton believes his detailed study of this Wealden parish offers a pattern of testamentary piety that indicates that a significant proportion of families there were frugal in such matters, which may in part reflect "long-standing traditions of heterodoxy."[47] Moreover, he considers that the changing pattern he saw in testamentary giving during the early sixteenth century—a decline in the provision of temporary or perpetual chantries and bequests to church fabric but a marked increase in the desire for obsequies and a slight increase in bequests to lights (though never above 21 per cent)—is suggestive of a parish where there was "a general drift towards [. . .] a moderate reformist strand [. . .] that was in part inspired by Erasmian humanism" but also perhaps by heretical or at least heterodox ideas.[48] Looking comparably at the Sandwich figures for the same period, temporary chantry provision similarly fell to about 10 per cent of testators, though this was even lower in the 1510s, and as at Tenterden the wish for obsequies also rose to over 70 per cent of testators by the 1530s.[49] However, bequests to lights were far more popular throughout

---

[45] Clive Burgess has written extensively on this topic: for example, "Late Medieval Wills and Pious Convention: Testamentary Evidence Reconsidered," in *Profit, Piety and the Professions in Later Medieval England*, ed. Michael Hicks (Gloucester: Sutton, 1990), 14–33; idem, "The Benefactions of Mortality," 65–86. For a recent critical assessment of such views, see Lutton, *Lollardy and Orthodox Religion*, 11–26. On Sandwich wills see Clarke, Pearson, and Mate, *Sandwich*, 207–9.

[46] For the period 1470–1500 comparing Sandwich to the other Kentish Cinque Ports: bequests to own church fabric: Sandwich 42 %, Dover 23.5 %, Hythe 63 %, New Romney 30 %; own special church fabric: Sandwich 24.5 %, Dover 18 %, Hythe 21.5 %, New Romney 24 %; own named lights: Sandwich 31 %, Dover 67 %, Hythe 32 %, New Romney 51 % ; own unnamed lights: Sandwich 19 %, Dover 23.5 %, Hythe 1.5 %, New Romney 3.5 %. For the period 1500–1530: bequests to own church fabric: Sandwich 19 %, Dover 50 %, Hythe 41.7 %, New Romney 43.8 %; own special church fabric: Sandwich 22 %, Dover 27.6 %, Hythe 14.4 %, New Romney 26 %; own named lights: Sandwich 27 %, Dover 60 %, Hythe 28.8 %, New Romney 68.4 %; own unnamed lights: Sandwich 10 %, Dover 30 %, Hythe 11.4 %, New Romney 10.5 % (includes reversionary bequests).

[47] Lutton, *Lollardy and Orthodox Religion*, 101.

[48] Lutton, *Lollardy and Orthodox Religion*, 101.

[49] Lutton, *Lollardy and Orthodox Religion*, 56.

the period and barely showed any decline (except among testators in the 1510s, though generally as a group they were less likely to make pious bequests). Similarly, Sandwich testators were far more likely to support religious houses, though primarily this may reflect the local presence of the Carmelite friars rather than a more general interest in the various religious orders.[50] Yet it is perhaps significant that the friars continued to receive bequests until the dissolution of their house, and they were also the recipients of certain civic largesse, the town officers maintaining such links until at least the early 1530s, and the king similarly providing gifts when he stayed there in 1532.[51] Considered as a whole, therefore, the testamentary evidence does seem to indicate that parish religion in Sandwich should be seen as predominantly orthodox, and included those whose piety can be characterised as conservative.[52] Yet even within this apparent parochial orthodoxy there may have been certain families who tended towards the parsimonious.[53] For at least two generations before the 1530s members of the prosperous Cok and Butler families had made few pious provisions in their wills.[54] How far this may be envisaged as evidence of heterodoxy is open to question, but Richard Butler, in particular, was a major supporter of religious reform in the late 1530s (see below). Nonetheless, during the early decades of the sixteenth century, even though religious views may have played a part in the various disputes, socio-economic and political issues were probably of greater concern to those living in Sandwich. Consequently, it is against this background that the events of 1532 and beyond need to be assessed.

A Time of Conflict

In 'The Old Red Book' of Sandwich there is a record of what took place in St Peter's church on 24 August 1532. The entry states:

> And that wheras the Mayor, Jurats and Commonalty of the said town wher personallie in the cherche of St Peter on the feast day of St Bartholomew

---

[50] Sweetinburgh, *Role of the Hospital*, 118.

[51] *LP Hen. VIII*, 5: 761; Sweetinburgh, *Role of the Hospital*, 218–19.

[52] For an assessment of the Rochester diocese which seems not dissimilar see Paul Lee, "Monastic and Secular Religion and Devotional Reading in Late Medieval Dartford and West Kent" (Ph.D. diss., University of Kent, 1998), 144–97. Lutton has examined the evidence regarding the incidence of heresy and heterodoxy for this period: "Heresy and Heterodoxy in Late Medieval Kent," in *Late Medieval Kent, 1220–1540*, ed. Sheila Sweetinburgh (Woodbridge: Boydell Press, 2010), 167–89.

[53] Lutton, *Lollardy and Orthodox Religion*, 130–33.

[54] Thomas Cok (1472), Henry Cok (1505), John Botelere (1452), and Thomas Butler (1494): Maidstone, Centre for Kentish Studies, PRC 17/2, fol. 81; 17/10, fol. 229; 32/1, fol. 61; 17/6, fol. 39.

last past accordige to the ancent usannce of our custumal ever accustumned there redie with tapers to go in procession to the hospital of St Bartholomew, whereof the said Mayor and Jurats and Commonalty as founders and in the apperith be sinistre meanes of diverse of the parish of St Peter and inespeciall that the curat Sir John Yonge of the same cherche myght not have preemynce ther to execute the high mass ther, withdrewe the selve from the fulfillinge of ther duties ever of auncient and time out of mind used. In breche wherof the said Mayor and Jurats have commanded the said curat and chantry prestes and cherche wardens of the same cherche to warde [gaol].[55]

Although it is not possible to ascertain the names of the churchwardens, nor their fate, the records do provide some information regarding the clergy. Sir John, who seems to have been a relatively recent incumbent, apparently left Sandwich within two years of the incident, because his successor was listed among the beneficiaries of a local will dated 1534. He may have taken the parish of St Lawrence in Thanet, which was also held by St Augustine's Abbey, because a priest of that name made his will there in 1538, dying soon after.[56] The chantry priests involved were the three priests at Thomas Elys' chantry in St Peter's church, a foundation established in 1392. Sir John Stephynson was possibly the most senior. He had served at the chantry for twenty years in 1532, and he seems to have been an active and well-respected member of the local community. His death in December 1533 (he was found drowned at the bottom of his own well) may not be linked to the events of the previous year, but he had suffered official censure in the intervening period.[57] The other long-serving chantry priest, Sir William Ussher, was replaced in 1534, while the third, Sir Thomas Philipp, had been removed a year earlier (June 1533) and sent to the Poor Priests' hospital in Canterbury.[58] In the Sandwich Year Book, the mayor and jurats justified Philipp's removal and replacement by Sir Edmund Grene, a chaplain "of good conversation," by saying that Philipp's fellow chantry priests had acted wrongfully in allowing

[55] Whitfield, East Kent Archives, Sa/AC 3, fol. 36ᵛ. See also Clarke, Pearson, and Mate, *Sandwich*, 208.

[56] Maidstone, Centre for Kentish Studies, PRC 17/21, fol. 147.

[57] Whitfield, East Kent Archives, Sa/AC 3, fol. 51.

[58] According to Archbishop Cranmer's register, William Lott replaced John Stephynson and Edmund Grene replaced Thomas Philipp in 1533, and Thomas Lawney replaced William Ussher in 1534. However, according to the chantry certificates Ussher and Philipp were still serving the chantry when Lott was appointed to replace Stephynson, but by the following year (1534) the commissioners in the *Valor* noted the three chantry priests were William Lotte, Edmund Grene, and Thomas Launde. Launde or Lawney does not appear to have held his place for more than a matter of months because John Newman joined Lotte and Grene in 1534: *Kent Chantries*, ed. Arthur Hussey, Kent Records 12 (Ashford: n.p., 1932), 266–67.

him to keep the position because he was a beneficed priest.[59] Before taking this action the mayor and jurats had had the chantry foundation charter read to them, thereby publicly confirming their legitimacy to act as patrons, first because the other chaplains had been at fault and second because the civic authorities saw the chantry chaplains as 'theirs' from 'ancient times', the process made legally binding through the use of the town's seal.[60] As a consequence, the leading town officers had publicly re-established their control over the chantry and the procession, and in the process had penalised the clergy at St Peter's by replacing them with more malleable priests.

William Stokes, the rector in 1532, who might have been expected to officiate at the high Mass in St Bartholomew's chapel, is not mentioned at all in these proceedings.[61] Nor is he recorded in any capacity in any Sandwich wills, a situation apparently shared by his predecessor and successor. As far as these latter men are concerned this may be because they were nominated by the abbot of St Augustine's, and it is possible they had little involvement in the parish, their pastoral and other duties being undertaken by the curate. However, in terms of Stokes this seems strange because the mayor's previous nominee, Master Leonard Eglisfelde, seems, as might be expected in such circumstances, to have been an active parish priest.[62]

Although the year of Stokes' appointment as rector is unknown, the evidence from the town books points to 1528, that is, five years after Sir Henry Guldeford, of the powerful west Kent family, first sought the position for his chaplain, the mayor and jurats agreeing to his request for the next nomination on the grounds that Sir Henry had previously aided the town and the Cinque Ports more generally.[63] This was not the first time the mayor and jurats had given the right of nomination to a third party, Cecily Duchess of York having chosen the new rector in 1465.[64] Presumably the earlier occasion was a political decision, the civic authorities being predominantly supporters of the Yorkist regime, and it is possible that their successors' decision in 1523 was similarly motivated, especially because it was not the only favour they granted the Guldefords. Two years later

---

[59] According to the foundation charter, at six months after their induction the chaplains were not allowed to hold any other benefice: Whitfield, East Kent Archives, Sa/AC 3, fol. 46ᵛ; Boys, *Sandwich*, 185.

[60] The foundation charter had been copied into the town book in 1509: Whitfield, East Kent Archives, Sa/AC 2, fols. 166ᵛ–67.

[61] The Rev. Thomas Frampton compiled a list of the rectors and their patrons, tracing the incumbents back to 1174. A copy is in St Peter's church.

[62] His appointment is recorded in the town book: Whitfield, East Kent Archives, Sa/AC 2, fol. 79.

[63] Sir Henry's request is recorded in some detail in the town book: Whitfield, East Kent Archives, Sa/AC 2, fol. 324ᵛ.

[64] Frampton's list.

Sir Edward Guldeford's man was given the office of sergeant of the mace.[65] Sir Edward, as warden of the Cinque Ports, was an even more powerful figure than his half-brother, and both men were important courtiers and favourites of the king. Nevertheless, there seems to have been a degree of unease on this second occasion, the mayor and jurats deciding that their actions should not set a precedent and in future no other town offices were to be granted as favours, yet when Sir Henry and Sir Edward presented their candidate in 1528 he appears to have been approved without any difficulty.[66] However, the proviso of 1525 may suggest that the earlier service to Sir Henry was not an endorsement of his humanist ideas (or those of his brother), nor a desire to appoint a cleric who perhaps held reformist ideas. Circumstances may have changed by the time the Guldefords presented their candidate in 1528, but even though the evidence is limited there is little to indicate that Stokes was active at St Peter's, and instead the curate seems to have been the principal parish priest. Nonetheless, this seems somewhat strange assuming the brothers were followers of Erasmian humanism, and may imply that Sir Henry was more of a courtier than a serious reformer.[67]

In these circumstances Sir John Yonge's expectations in August 1532 seem wholly justified. Consequently it would have been useful to know whether the churchwardens had wanted to give the honour at St Bartholomew's chapel to one of the Elys chantry chaplains, though the actions of the mayor and jurats appear to point to this conclusion. In terms of longevity there was relatively little to choose between Stephynson and Ussher: the latter was an Oxford university graduate, but it is feasible that Philipp was too.[68] Furthermore, the latter's recent appointment to the chantry in 1529–1530 may suggest that he is the most likely candidate. Whether the upstaging of Yonge by the churchwardens related to the curate's religious views is very difficult to know. Neither Philipp nor Yonge had had much time to be involved in the wills of those from St Peter's parish, but it is interesting that one of the very few wills Yonge had witnessed, and in the leading role of first witness, was that of Alexander Alday, gentleman.[69] Alday was a relatively young, prosperous jurat and member of a substantial landholding family in east Kent, who made his will in the spring of 1532, possibly during his last

[65] Whitfield, East Kent Archives, Sa/AC 2, fol. 359.

[66] Whitfield, East Kent Archives, Sa/AC 3, fol. 6ᵛ.

[67] Lutton, *Lollardy and Orthodox Religion*, 189; S. Lehmberg, "Guildford, Sir Edward," and K. Dockray, "Guildford, Sir Henry," in *Oxford Dictionary of National Biography* (hereafter *ODNB*) (Oxford: Oxford University Press, 2004), 24: 186–87, 187–90 respectively.

[68] A. Emden, ed., *A Biographical Register of the University of Oxford, AD 1501–1540* (Oxford: Clarendon Press, 1974), p. 589.

[69] Maidstone, Centre for Kentish Studies, PRC 17/19, fol. 207.

illness because he died in May, three months before the date of the procession.[70] Unusually, his testament is almost devoid of any references to his funeral or commemoration. He made no pious bequests beyond sums of money to the high altar and for church repairs, the remainder of his will being devoted to gifts to his pregnant wife, two daughters, and his overseer. His extensive property was in the hands of his feoffees, including his fellow jurat Richard Butler. Even though such evidence is notoriously difficult to use to assess personal religious convictions, it is conceivable that Alday's instructions indicate that he, and perhaps also Butler and Yonge, were interested in the ideas of men such as Erasmus and Colet or possibly even more radical ideas.[71] Alday's death, therefore, may have robbed Yonge of much needed support and protection in August 1532 and may imply that the churchwardens were not sympathetic to his views.

Nor do the mayor and jurats appear to have been any more sympathetic: rather the entry in the town book suggests that they envisaged what they saw as a serious disruption of this ancient quasi-religious civic ritual in other terms. The stress placed on such phrases and words as "ancient usage of our custumal," "ever accustomed," "sinister means," "fulfilling of their duties ever of ancient and time out of mind," and "in breach" indicates certain key points for the civic authorities. The first of these is the antiquity of the ritual which could be vouchsafed through the written record of the custumal and equally the oral testimony of the town's memory—time out of mind. Antiquity provided authenticity, as did the idea of bringing together "usage" and the custumal, the written word and the annual performance, and, in addition, each reinforced the authority of the mayor and jurats: it was "our" custumal.[72] The concept of authority was important: it was part of the civic identity of Sandwich which drew on ancient rights and privileges, and responsibilities that included oversight of the town's charitable institutions. Of these St Bartholomew's Hospital was of greatest consequence, not least because the saintly saviour of the town was commemorated there, and the refusal of the St Peter's clergy to fulfil their duty not only meant the mayor

---

[70] Assuming it is the same man, he was admitted as a freeman by birth in 1525: Whitfield, East Kent Archives, Sa/AC 2, fol. 359.

[71] On the broad range of views within Catholicism in Henry VIII's reign, see Shagan, *Popular Politics*, 36–59. Equally on the diversity within religious dissent (and orthodoxy): Lutton, *Lollardy and Orthodox Religion*, 154–210; idem, "Heresy and Heterodoxy," 181–87.

[72] Justin P. Croft, "The Custumals of the Cinque Ports, c. 1290–c. 1500: Studies in the Cultural Production of the Written Record" (Ph.D. diss., University of Kent, 1997), 24, 37–38.

and jurats could not fulfil theirs either but meant the whole town risked divine as well as mortal censure.[73]

The use of the word "sinister" in the account is significant because it denotes the idea of the devil's hand in the affair, as well as ideas about dissent, strife, and even anarchy within St Peter's, and especially respecting lay–clerical relationships there.[74] As upholders of the king's royal authority and justice in Sandwich, the mayor and jurats were confronted by a situation that required them to act quickly to regain authority. Their need may have been especially pressing for two reasons. First, the king and a large entourage were due to pass through east Kent in September en route to a meeting with the French king in Calais, and even though this was not due to take place immediately, preparations had already begun.[75] Second, the civic authorities, and particularly certain jurats, were still involved in the affair over the disputed rights of the Crown's bailiwick in the town, thereby heightening their sensitivity to those matters which came under their own authority. In 1532 the senior jurats who were particularly implicated in the at times violent dispute with the king's bailiff, Sir Edward Ringley, were Henry Boll, Roger Manwood, and Vincent Engeham, and it may have been these men (and others), with the mayor John Boys, who took the lead in the imprisoning of the various parties from St Peter's.[76]

Of the four, Boll's family may have had the longest links to Sandwich, Henry's grandfather having been a successful brewer (like his grandson) in the town in the mid-fifteenth century.[77] Notwithstanding that for all four self-interest may have played a part in some of their dealings, Manwood and Engeham also seem to have seen themselves as staunch supporters of the town's interests in the preceding decades, and Boys, as a local gentleman who purchased the freedom in 1528 and became a jurat the same year, may have been similarly motivated.[78]

---

[73] The essential role of the priest in the Mass as 'Christmaker', a salvific force that was for the benefit of the people of Sandwich, meant that without the cleric's co-operation the mayor and jurats were left powerless: Swanson, "Problems of the Priesthood," 855–56.

[74] Marshall, "Anticlericalism Revested?" 380.

[75] The king and his train of between 3,000 and 4,000 people were expected in Canterbury: *L.P. Hen. VIII*, 5: 537, 545.

[76] It may be significant that Ringley had links to the Neville family, the rival magnate family of the Guldefords (see above): Clark, *English Provincial Society*, 14. He discusses the rivalry between the two families for influence and so supremacy in the region in some detail (14–17, 32–34, 37).

[77] As well as leaving gifts to all of the lights in St Peter's church, Henry's grandfather wanted to give his parish an antiphoner costing 20 marks: Maidstone, Centre for Kentish Studies, PRC 17/1, fol. 126. It was to Henry Boll that his kinsman from Deal turned when he heard that the bailiff was intending to lead a hundred armed men against Sandwich: Whitfield, East Kent Archives, Sa/AC 2, fol. 368v.

[78] As mayor, Roger Manwood had been the target of verbal abuse in 1528: Whitfield, East Kent Archives, Sa/AC 3, fol. 9ᵛ. Several months later that year John Boys

Thus, assuming this assessment of the entry in the town books is correct, it seems that ideas concerning civic authority and identity were uppermost in the minds of these men.

Moreover, it was the priests as individuals rather than the clergy per se who were seen as having broken the divinely sanctioned, ancient agreement between civic and clergy, and it was, therefore, the town officers' duty to punish them.[79] This was right not just in what might be termed secular terms but probably equally, if not more importantly, in spiritual terms because of the evil that was now active at St Peter's church. Even though there is nothing in the records to indicate that the civic officers had had to deal with such a situation before, they had in the past certainly seen it as part of their responsibility to censure certain clerics. In 1500 the two chantry chaplains at Elys' chantry were called before the town court for unlawfully appointing a chaplain to the vacancy, and four years later the vicar at St Mary's was condemned for dereliction of duty.[80] Furthermore, returning to the likely prime civic officers in 1532, the testaments of all four men contain pious bequests that indicate strongly held orthodox Catholic beliefs. For example, Boll and Manwood left bequests to a considerable numbers of lights in their respective parish churches; Manwood intended that the traditionally-conservative vicar at St Mary's should receive an annuity of 20*s*; Boll and Boys gave generous gifts to several friaries and both wanted numerous masses, included specific ones, Boys leaving particularly detailed instructions.[81] Engeham too wanted an orthodox Catholic funeral, which is especially revealing because he made his will in May 1547; though probably equally informative is Manwood's instruction concerning his tomb.[82] He wanted to be buried next to his late wife in St Laurence's chancel in St Mary's church, the grave covered by a stone on which there was to be a brass showing himself, his two wives and six children; at the corners were to be four shields, two having the arms of the Cinque Ports, one showing the cross of St George, and the fourth having "a token of deth on it." Age may have been a critical factor: Boll, Boys (in 1533), and Manwood (in 1534) were elderly men when they died, and even though they, like others in Sandwich, would have been well aware of the parliamentary and royal decisions

---

became a freeman and was sworn in as a jurat (fol. 13). Engeham was especially involved when the town was allowed to purchase the bailiwick: Whitfield, East Kent Archives, Sa/FAt 29; 30; 32.

[79] For the wider implications of such ideas see Shagan, *Popular Politics*, 138–39.

[80] Whitfield, East Kent Archives, Sa/AC 2, fols. 77, 120ᵛ.

[81] Henry Boll, Roger Manwood, and John Boys: Maidstone, East Kent Archives, PRC 17/20, fol. 25; 17/20, fol. 73; London, The National Archives, PCC PROB 11/25, fol. 2.

[82] Vincent Engeham: Maidstone, East Kent Archives, PRC 17/26, fol. 136.

emanating from Westminster, there is nothing to indicate that they would have taken a lead from them beyond their traditional stance on lay–clerical matters.[83]

So did this change in 1533 and 1534 when first Philipp and then Ussher were replaced by Grene and Lawney respectively? In 1532/3 the mayor was John Pyham, another prosperous brewer whose father had been a major benefactor of the St George altar and guild in the late fifteenth century.[84] John's will, made eight years after his mayoralty, does not reveal deep religious convictions of any form, and perhaps more indicative of his stance is an order in the town book made during his mayoralty to revive certain annual payments due to the town that were recalled as being part of its ancient customs.[85] As mayor he may, therefore, have been perfectly at ease with the idea of upholding the civic dignity of Sandwich against those seen as malefactors, and may even have initiated later that year the similar recalling of the Elys chantry charter and the subsequent injunctions against the serving chantry priests. As noted above, this was not without precedent, and as well as Elys' chantry the mayor and jurats had on several occasions appointed the priest of Condy's chantry at St Mary's church.[86] Moreover, with respect to Elys' chantry they had, in 1509, required the chantry priests to produce the papal bull and royal patent of the grant in mortmain so that copies could be made in the town book, the documentation relating to the chantry henceforth to be stored in a chest in the vestry at St Peter's church, the keys for the three locks held by the chantry priests.[87] Consequently the decision to replace Philipp and the process involved appear to have been in keeping with the ideas and concerns expressed the previous year.

What happened in 1534 is more problematic because it is not clear exactly what process was used to remove Ussher, or what happened with respect to Lawney and Newman. As a result the role of the mayor and jurats in the events of 1534 is difficult to assess, especially the degree to which the deaths of several senior jurats and Alexander Alday had affected the town's governing body, but in broad terms the magistracy remained conservative in outlook. Nevertheless, it is worth noting that in 1534 two cases were brought before the town courts relating to property disputes involving two local men and chaplains from Elys' chantry and from Jenkyn Grene's chantry at St Clement's church respectively.[88] Though

---

[83] On the impression such legislation must have made, see Marshall, *Catholic Priesthood*, 223–24. The town sent two barons to Parliament. In 1529 they were John Boys and Vincent Engeham who, therefore, had first-hand knowledge of all the religious and political changes: Whitfield, East Kent Archives, Sa/AC 3, fol. 18.

[84] Henry Pyham: Maidstone, East Kent Archives, PRC 17/6, fol. 291.

[85] Maidstone, East Kent Archives, PRC 17/16, fol. 16. Whitfield, East Kent Archives, Sa/AC 3, fol. 44ᵛ.

[86] *Kent Chantries*, 259.

[87] Whitfield, East Kent Archives, Sa/AC 2, fol. 166.

[88] Whitfield, East Kent Archives, Sa/AC 3, fol. 55ᵛ.

overtly there is nothing to suggest that either the townsmen's or the priests' religious views were factors in these cases, the change in personnel at Elys' chantry added a further dimension to the probably increasingly complex divisions within the town.[89]

Returning to the appointments of Grene in 1533 and of Lawney the following year, it is the act of recommending these particular men, not the civic authorities' action of replacing a priest they disapproved of with another, that may indicate an important ideological shift, and may as a result have influenced the course of the history of the Reformation at Sandwich. The town book does not record who nominated the Oxford graduate and reformist cleric Sir Edmund Grene to the mayor and jurats, but the most likely member of the magistracy is Richard Butler (see above).[90] Yet it is also possible that the proposal was endorsed by John Master because Master was mayor in 1528 (having replaced Roger Manwood who had initially been elected three months earlier for the year 1527/8) when the Guldefords received the right to nominate the new rector at St Peter's. As a wealthy merchant Master had overseas contacts that may have influenced his religious affiliations, and his involvement in the provisioning of Calais may also have contributed to his support of the regime's standpoint. Familial rather than overseas connections may have been the main contributory factor regarding Richard Butler's reformist views, and like Holy (see n. 89) he may have been an early convert. His later activities in the reformist cause included aiding Sir John Crofte, Merryman's successor, to pull down the images at St Mary's church, and among the witnesses of his will made in 1545 was the locally very active reformer William Norris.[91]

However, when Grene arrived to take up his office, such destruction was almost ten years in the future and the mayor and jurats may have believed they had just appointed a cleric "of good conversation." How outspoken he was initially is unknown, and similarly the activities in Sandwich of Thomas Lawney, another Oxford man who arrived in 1534 at Grene's invitation, are unrecorded.[92]

---

[89] The difficulties of allocating motive are illustrated by Thomas Holy's verbal abuse and refusal to pay Sir William Merryman, the vicar at St Mary's, the tithe payment due for the town crane in 1526. A decade later Holy was strongly espousing new religious ideas and he probably was an early convert: *L.P. Hen.* 18. 2: 311. Yet his dispute with the elderly vicar may also have involved a clash of personalities and financial considerations. The sum of 6*s* 8*d* in tithes was a major burden on the farmer of the crane, especially because it was due regardless of the fees received: Whitfield, East Kent Archives, Sa/AC 2, fols. 371–371ᵛ.

[90] Emden, *Biographical Register*, 244.

[91] *L.P. Hen.* 18. 2: 311. Maidstone, East Kent Archives, PRC 17/24, fol. 97.

[92] At the foundation of Cardinal's College, Oxford, in 1525, Lawney left Cambridge for a chaplaincy there, and three years later he may have been involved in some form of heresy. By 1540 he was a vicar in Sussex, having received that year a dispensation to hold additional livings: Emden, *Biographical Register*, 345.

Lawney's almost immediate replacement by John Newman is puzzling.[93] It may reflect a local desire to remove at least one reformist priest from the town, though equally it may indicate a move by the reformists to provide greater preaching opportunities for him in east Kent.[94] Nonetheless, for the probably tiny number of townspeople interested in reform Grene's arrival offered support for the only other known clerical reformist in Sandwich, Sir John Crofte, the curate at St Mary's. For this group Grene's continuing presence in the town and the dynamic relationship between the government and the country, especially during Cromwell's ascendancy, may have provided a spur to greater action: Crofte attacked both the parish service books and his conservative superior Sir William Merryman, the aged vicar, in September 1534 and in the year following.[95]

Thereafter Grene and Crofte presumably headed this small but seemingly increasingly vocal reformist enclave, Grene becoming the rector of St Peter's church in 1539 as the nominee of Archbishop Cranmer, and Crofte vicar at St Mary's church after the death of Merryman in 1537. Of the very few known supporters of evangelical ideas in the late 1530s and early 1540s, several were neither natives of Sandwich nor leading townsmen, and it is possible such men were attracted to the town through their knowledge of these two clerics. Thus, as a senior jurat from a long-resident family, Richard Butler was a significant exception, and to a lesser extent so were John Sarys, the town clerk, and William Crispe and Thomas Iden, Iden calling Crispe his "well-beloved friend" in his will dated 1541.[96] Rather William Norris, probably from London, who received the freedom of Sandwich through marriage in 1538, may be more typical in this respect, especially because he was a man of moderate wealth, judging by

---

[93] Newman's religious stance at this time is unclear, and even though there are several potential graduates from Cambridge who may be this man the evidence remains circumstantial: *Alumni Cantabrigienses from Earliest Times to 1751*, 4 vols. (Cambridge: Cambridge University Press, 1922–1927), 3.1: 250.

[94] According to Clark, Lawney was preaching in the Sandwich area: "Reformation and Radicalism," 115. One of the conservative clergy who preached in Sandwich was Edmund Shelter, a Six Preacher of Canterbury Cathedral, who was accused of preaching Catholic theology: *L.P. Hen. VIII*, 18. 2: 305. The importance of preaching is illustrated in the depositions concerning Archbishop Cranmer and the Prebendaries' Plot, each side accusing the other of the dangers of those who preached the 'wrong' doctrine: Shagan, *Popular Politics*, 197–232; Brian M. Hogben, "Preaching and the Reformation in Henrician Kent," *Archaeologia Cantiana* 101 (1984): 169–85. Newman's stance on doctrinal issues is uncertain, but he did remain at St Peter's until the chantry was dissolved: *Kent Chantries*, 266–67.

[95] It was reported in the court that Crofte had said that if Merryman "will not leve his jargyng att him he would make Sandwich and Caunterbury too hot for him and that all his frends ther should not help him": Whitfield, East Kent Archives, Sa/AC 3, fols. 69ᵛ–70.

[96] Maidstone, Centre for Kentish Studies, PRC 17/22, fol. 160.

his will made in 1546.[97] His activities in the cause of reform were more extreme than most, however, because not only was he called a "well-beloved friend" by several testators but he also helped Thomas Holy, another outspoken opponent of the traditional church, to destroy images at St Clement's church. Nor did Norris confine his iconoclasm to Sandwich, bearing witness against the curate at nearby Sholden for re-setting the images in the parish church and against a parishioner at North Mongeham for trying to retain the images in that parish church.[98] Yet even though this small group of evangelicals appear to have become more outspoken by the early 1540s, it seems likely that Vincent Engeham would have believed he still spoke for the majority, and certainly the righteous, when he commanded that nobody was to read the Bible nor hear it read, and those who disobeyed were to be imprisoned.[99]

Nonetheless, Engeham must have been acutely aware that his stance brought him into conflict with the Crown and with those within Sandwich who were prepared to engage with royal policy in what were increasingly difficult socio-economic conditions during the 1540s (and 1550s).[100] Yet he did retain his conservative religious beliefs throughout the remainder of his life (he died in 1547), and these and his outlook with regard to the centrality of civic rituals such as the St Bartholomew's day procession in the town's identity may still have been shared by many among the magistracy. For though Clark may be correct that "there was no concerted magisterial resistance to Reform, nor any outbreak of conflict within the corporation over religion"[101] at this time, the mayor and jurats during Edward VI's reign did continue to negotiate civic–clerical relations in the context of the locale and the nation. Two examples would seem to illustrate this. The St Bartholomew's day procession was not the only civic ritual that had to be negotiated, because the mayor and jurats sought to mediate the royal prohibition of the midsummer bonfires.[102] In 1550 they continued the civic, quasi-religious

---

[97] Whitfield, East Kent Archives, Sa/AC 3, fol. 98ᵛ. Maidstone, Centre for Kentish Studies, PRC 17/24, fol. 241.

[98] *L.P. Hen. VIII* 18. 2: 299, 311.

[99] *L.P. Hen. VIII* 18. 2: 299.

[100] Clark considers that "the Reform movement at Sandwich enjoyed considerable popular support [and] also relied on powerful outside allies": "Reform and Radicalism," 125. Shagan provides an interesting discussion on the meanings of the term 'popular' in the context of the Reformation and on the idea of collaboration: *Popular Politics*, 13–18, 22–23.

[101] Clark, "Reform and Radicalism," 124.

[102] Though it is difficult to trace exactly what happened with regard to the St Bartholomew's day proceedings in the 1550s as far as the civic authorities and the clergy's involvement were concerned, the procession probably disappeared. For the mayor and jurats, from Elizabeth's reign their public involvement seems to have centred as much on the day the accounts were presented as on St Bartholomew's day when the master was chosen: Whitfield, East Kent Archives, Sa/CH10B F3/16. However, by the early

celebration of the midsummer saints by replacing the bonfires with a beating of the bounds, which was concluded as in previous years by communal merrymaking.[103] By so doing they were also able to record in their town book a declaration that they, representing the town, deplored the removal of the stone crosses (as boundary markers). In the following year the rectory at St Peter's was vacant, and in an attempt to appoint a cleric who was acceptable to the parish (and presumably the civic authorities), the mayor and jurats opened negotiations with Cranmer because the king wanted the post for his nominee.[104]

In conclusion, it would seem useful to draw out the main threads regarding the role of civic–clerical relations in early Reformation Sandwich, and the implications of such relationships in the ways the mayor and jurats seem to have viewed their town and their place within it. In terms of the reformist ideas emanating from Westminster and the ideological antagonism between Crown and Church, which would have been common knowledge in Sandwich, it was the nomination of Sir Edmund Grene to be a chaplain at Elys' chantry that may mark a shift in civic–clerical relations, though how far this was ideologically motivated rather than personal remains unclear. Yet if it was a criticism of the clergy it is important because not only did it mean that there were at least two reformist priests in the town, perhaps acting as a catalyst for the Reformation there, but also the appointment of such a cleric (whether unwittingly or not) had been made for the benefit of the town by those representing the town, not by an outsider such as the archdeacon. In contrast, and even though it occurred only in the previous year, the violent censure of the clergy and others by the mayor and jurats after 24 August 1532 seems to reflect disapproval of particular individuals, not of the clergy per se. This difference is important with respect to the ways the people of Sandwich experienced the Reformation, but also because it opens up ideas about why civic ritual was valued and by whom, how "competing constituencies" were prepared to negotiate their places/roles in it and society more broadly, and what happened when conflict occurred. The resulting analysis has shown that the annual procession to the hospital chapel was an integral aspect of the town's identity as espoused by the civic authorities, but that others, such as the St Peter's churchwardens and the parish clergy, also envisaged it as 'theirs' (perhaps jointly and severally). Consequently, the processes through which the mayor and jurats attempted to resolve the dispute to their satisfaction involved a suppression of those 'competing' against them and the highlighting of the value placed on the reciprocal relationship between themselves and the town (St Bartholomew's

---

seventeenth century the mayor was again feasting at the hospital on St Bartholomew's day, perhaps after an edifying sermon in the hospital's chapel: Whitfield, East Kent Archives, Sa/CH10B F3/35.

[103] Whitfield, East Kent Archives, Sa/AC 3, fol. 236ᵛ.

[104] Sa/AC 3, fol. 239ᵛ.

Hospital as a town charity), its antiquity and authenticity. For men such as Boll, Manwood, and Engeham the damage to the civic–clerical relationship in 1532 was considerable but not beyond repair, and, as their predecessors had done in times past, they took it upon themselves to put right the situation for the common good—the commonweal—by ridding the town of those whom they believed were no longer willing to undertake their designated responsibilities. Thus the events of 1532 provide valuable insights on the complex negotiations those of the town and others (both individuals and groups) engaged in as they sought to mediate the political and religious dynamics of the Reformation in Sandwich. Returning to Collinson and Craig's observation, Sandwich's experience appears to underline their point about diversity, yet the important role of the civic authorities and their relationships with the town's clergy and others has been seen elsewhere, which suggests that the ongoing process of negotiation at various levels was one of the defining features of sixteenth-century urban experience.

The Skin of the Unjust Judge: 'Negotiating the Political' in Early Modern Canterbury[1]

Paula Simpson

Modern scholarship considering the work of the church courts has sought to redress the balance in response to earlier assessments of the corrupt and inefficient nature of ecclesiastical jurisdiction.[2] Historians such as Ingram,[3] Houlbrooke,[4] and Marchant[5] in their studies of the dioceses of Winchester, Norwich, and York have reached the broad consensus that while inefficiency, high costs, and malpractice were known in the work of the courts, this was very much a matter which varied from year to year and from diocese to diocese.[6] Events at Canterbury in the closing years of the sixteenth century, to be considered in this chapter, offer an opportunity to test broad judgements on the operation of ecclesiastical justice through detailed local study. This analysis will contribute to the debate concerning the effectiveness of ecclesiastical justice by a consideration of contemporary perceptions of its operation at a local level.

---

[1] This chapter is dedicated to my father, Canon John B. Simpson.

[2] For early work see, for example, Christopher Hill, *Society and Puritanism in Pre-revolutionary England* (London: Secker and Warburg, 1964), 298–343; F. D. Price, "The Abuses of Excommunication and the Decline of Ecclesiastical Discipline under Queen Elizabeth," *English Historical Review* 57 (1942): 106–15.

[3] Martin Ingram, *Church Courts, Sex and Marriage in England, 1570–1640* (Cambridge: Cambridge University Press, 1987).

[4] Ralph A. Houlbrooke, *Church Courts and the People during the English Reformation 1520–1570* (Oxford: Oxford University Press, 1979).

[5] R. A. Marchant, *The Church under the Law: Justice, Administration and Discipline in the Diocese of York, 1560–1640* (Cambridge: Cambridge University Press, 1969).

[6] The work of Price, "The Abuses of Excommunication," is now understood to describe an extreme situation.

Negotiating the Political in Northern European Urban Society, c.1400–c.1600, ed. Sheila Sweetinburgh, MRTS 434 (Tempe: ACMRS, 2013).   [ISBN 978-0-86698-482-9]

The discussion takes as its starting point a sermon preached in February 1593 by a Kentish clergyman in the Chapter House of Canterbury Cathedral. In the course of this sermon the preacher denounced the conduct of the ecclesiastical courts at Canterbury and, more particularly, the judge of those courts, Dr Stephen Lakes. The preacher, Anthony Kingsmill, subsequently became the subject of a disciplinary case heard in the very same courts that he had maligned. Kingsmill had criticised ecclesiastical justice and hinted at the pervasiveness of corruption at Canterbury[7] before recommending, by a classical allusion, that the judge should be flayed. One witness recalled that Kingsmill "then and there cyted the storie of the wicked iudge whose skyn beeing pulled of was hanged on or aboute the judgment seate wherin living he used to syt."[8] The sermon gave great offence and was clearly regarded by many who heard it as a political act: one which criticised ecclesiastical justice as well as challenging contemporary notions of appropriateness, decorum, and respect for office-holding.

These events of 1593 have an interesting and significant follow-up in that the maligned judge, Stephen Lakes, later testified concerning the alleged corrupt practices of his successor, Sir George Newman. In a Star Chamber case, which will also be considered, and which occurred just ten years later, it is apparent that the personnel of the ecclesiastical courts at Canterbury were peculiarly sensitive to accusations of corruption. It will be argued that this sensitivity had its foundation in the extremity of the attack orchestrated by Kingsmill in the early 1590s. This reveals that grievance with the courts in Canterbury had perhaps never entirely been laid to rest. Old complaints and injured sensibilities often resurfaced calling for reappraisal and re-examination. 'Negotiating the political' was, therefore, in many ways a constant and ongoing process; one which was, at a micro level, an integral part of negotiating everyday social and economic relationships and which, at a point of crisis, could result in the more formal appraisal provided by a court case.

1.

The events preceding the sermon are of significance. All of the evidence is drawn from testimony given in the disciplinary case against Kingsmill. Around 1590, about three years before the occasion of the sermon, one of Kingsmill's parishioners was declared excommunicate by the ecclesiastical courts. The whole case against him, though, was attended by accusations of malpractice. Around the same time, after another protracted case in the Canterbury courts, one Thomas Hayward, also of Kingsmill's parish of Milton, was declared to have died

[7] Canterbury, Canterbury Cathedral Archives and Library [henceforth cited as CCAL], PRC 39/16, fol. 5.

[8] CCAL, PRC 39/16, fol. 9.

intestate. The exact details of the case are unclear, but it seems that the document supported by Kingsmill as Hayward's last will and testament had been rejected by the ecclesiastical court. Again there were hints of malpractice and even bribery. It was alleged that some of the deponents (witnesses) had lied on oath,[9] and there was contention over the effect on the case of a failure to administer cross-examining questions.[10]

Kingsmill was clearly outraged by the decision of the courts with regard to Hayward's will, and his anger focused on their personnel: Dr Stephen Lakes, the judge; Mr Baker, a proctor (advocate) of the court; and Christopher Crammer, one of the apparitors (or court messengers) who happened to live in Milton. Kingsmill nursed his grudge for three years. In February 1593, while at the Crown inn in Canterbury, he came across one of the ecclesiastical court officers and complained to him about his treatment over the matter of Hayward's will. Time, it seems, had not lessened Kingsmill's sense of grievance, but by 1593 the sole surviving focus of his anger against the ecclesiastical courts was the judge, Dr Stephen Lakes, whom he characterised as an enemy of Christ.[11] The deaths in the intervening period of the proctor and the apparitor he ascribed to divine vengeance.[12]

This background reveals some of the tensions which influenced the sermon. Kingsmill's friend and fellow clergyman, Christopher Pashley, had been asked to preach at the cathedral on an appointed day in February 1593. Hearing that Pashley intended to preach on the gospel set for that date, Kingsmill declared "I am excellent at that text" and asked if he might take his place.[13] Discussion later will show that Kingsmill was alive to the possibilities that this opportunity presented for expressing his dissatisfaction with the local ecclesiastical administration.

Kingsmill's sermon began innocuously enough with exposition on the set text.[14] He discussed the etymology of the word 'Jerusalem' as signifying peace, but noted that Jerusalem had nonetheless been a city at war with God. Likewise, he declared, many were called Christians but behaved otherwise, and finally (observing that he was taking an example near at hand) that the spiritual courts did not live up to their name. Thus he swiftly escalated into a denunciation of the corrupt practices he perceived in the work of the ecclesiastical courts. As already noted, the sermon culminated with the shocking proposal that the Canterbury judge should be flayed. The events were summarised by a number of witnesses during the subsequent disciplinary case against Kingsmill. Most described how, after railing against the ecclesiastical courts as being "without equitie or

---

[9] CCAL, PRC 39/16, fols. 3ᵛ–4.
[10] CCAL, PRC 39/16, fol. 8ᵛ.
[11] CCAL, PRC 39/16, fol. 3.
[12] CCAL, PRC 39/16, fol. 13.
[13] CCAL, PRC 39/16, fol. 5.
[14] Luke 18:31.

conscience"[15] and recommending caution to those involved in testamentary matters, Kingsmill had retold the story of the punishment of the unjust judge who was flayed and whose skin was then stretched over his successor's chair to serve as a constant reminder of the consequences of corruption (Herodotus, *Histories* 5. 25). According to one witness Kingsmill's implication was obvious:

> [that] the like punishment might be shewed upon the judge of the courte about rehersed, and ther withall continually turning with his body towardes the seate of the right worshipfull the judge of this courte of Canterbury Mr Doctor Lakes, which was almost at his backe, with most unseemely gesture both of his head, armes and handes, unworthie of so reverend a place, signifieng therby . . . that he the said Mr Kingesmill meant no other courte to be the same, but this Court of Canterbury; and no other Judge to be him against whom he wished such a punishment, but Mr Doctor Lakes Judge of the Courte of Canterbury afforesaid . . .[16]

The sermon upset and offended those present in many ways. Not only was Kingsmill's criticism of the courts pointed and his recommendation of the judge's punishment shocking, but also his gestures left them in no doubt that he was referring, in particular, to the Canterbury courts. In the depositions relating to this case much attention was paid to Kingsmill's demeanour as he had preached. The comment regarding his "unseemely gesture [. . .] unworthie of so reverend a place" helps to locate Kingsmill's behaviour within the context of what was perceived to be appropriate or usual. His use of gesture was represented as having violated these codes in its lack of propriety, in relation both to his audience and to his surroundings. His outburst had offended convention and his use of gesture was generally perceived to have been an "unadvised usage of him self."[17] His performance was regarded as having reflected badly on all concerned: the personnel of the courts and in particular the judge, those implicated in the acceptance of Kingsmill as the preacher for that day, and on Kingsmill himself.

Kingsmill's use of word and gesture had combined to make a very explicit and presumably unexpected attack. While emphasising Kingsmill's vehemence, these depositions also draw attention to elements of what might be termed his 'over-acting'. He was described, for example, as having "thundered out the torments of hell."[18] Perceptions of anger were related to ideas about an imbalance of the humours, and the witness, Christopher Pashley, excused an earlier outburst by Kingsmill against the ecclesiastical courts which had taken place in a Canterbury alehouse as having "proceded of choler & heate."[19] Another witness

---

[15] CCAL, PRC 39/16, fol. 161ᵛ.
[16] CCAL, PRC 39/16, fol. 161ᵛ.
[17] CCAL, PRC 39/16, fol. 14.
[18] CCAL, PRC 39/16, fol. 12.
[19] CCAL, PRC 39/16, fol. 15.

expressed concern that Kingsmill had in his preaching "so overpassed him self"[20] and Kingsmill himself had declared after the event that "if I might have seene his [Lakes's] face [. . .] I would not have gone so farr, but he would not looke up."[21] This comment makes clear Lakes' own anger and embarrassment. In summary, the descriptions of Kingsmill's gestures and the interpretation and evaluation of their meaning are manifest within the deposition evidence. Witnesses emphasised the excessiveness of his performance and the sense that his presentation had violated the understood norms of appropriate behaviour.

Emphasis was not confined to attention to the detail of Kingsmill's words and gestures and the meaning attached to them. All of the witnesses also stressed the sense of occasion by stating that the sermon took place on the Sunday before Ash Wednesday (one identifying it as Quinquagesima).[22] Furthermore, it would seem that this was not simply an important date in the liturgical calendar, but an occasion on which many of the officers of the ecclesiastical court were present, sitting in specially appointed seats.[23] Their presence may mean that this was an important occasion in the legal year. Indeed, it was customary for the start of a legal session to be marked by the preaching of a sermon before assembled judges and gentry.[24] Kingsmill's performance and choice of exemplum gain a further significance if his sermon did indeed mark the opening session of the court. His lack of deference and open criticism would have been deeply offensive.

The venue in which the sermon was delivered was also of particular significance. Since the 1540s the cathedral had been a centre for reformed preaching. Archbishop Cranmer had ruled that each member of the Chapter preach at least once a quarter and established the 'Six Preachers': six clerics who were to provide sermons in the cathedral, as well as an itinerant preaching ministry. By 1547, the Chapter House had become the location for these sermons and was commonly known as the 'Sermon House'.[25] It seems likely then that by the 1590s the Sermon House was a well-attended and even prestigious place for the delivery of

---

[20] CCAL, PRC 39/16, fol. 14.

[21] CCAL, PRC 39/16, fol. 19.

[22] 25 February 1593. The gospel of Quinquagesima is the healing of the blind beggar, from Luke 18.

[23] CCAL, PRC 39/16, fol. 1.

[24] See, for example, A. Fager Herr, *The Elizabethan Sermon, a Survey and a Bibliography* (New York: Octagon, 1969), 43, who comments that "These sermons, as might be expected, were mostly conventional exhortations to truth, justice, and mercy, and to the punishment of wickedness and vice, calculated to open no controversial issue, and to offend nobody except the wicked and vicious."

[25] Patrick Collinson, "The Protestant Cathedral," in *A History of Canterbury Cathedral*, ed. idem, Nigel Ramsay and Margaret Sparks (Oxford: Oxford University Press, 1995), 179–80.

sermons.[26] According to contemporary descriptions, extra space was provided through the provision of galleries on the north and west sides, the north gallery having at its east end a royal closet or pew. Below were numerous pews and the pulpit. By 1635 (and perhaps somewhat earlier) "handsome seats" had been installed for senior clerics, members of the corporation, and the local gentry.[27] Thus the importance of this venue suggests again that the occasion was likely to have been defined by notions of particular recognised and established ways of preaching, notions which Kingsmill's sermon clearly contravened.

The Chapter House was, furthermore, certainly situated close to the venue for certain sessions of the ecclesiastical court and may even have been used for this purpose.[28] As such, the sermon would have been given especial resonance by the fact that it was preached in or close to the very same room in which the maligned court sometimes convened. It was preached, furthermore, before at least five of the ecclesiastical court officials. Thus we might interpret Kingsmill's performance as a symbolic inversion, his criticism coming from the heart of the cathedral, on a ritual occasion, and before the courts' personnel. If indeed this was an important ceremonial occasion, the prominent members of Canterbury's lay judiciary—the mayor and aldermen—would also have attended Kingsmill's sermon.[29] Furthermore, as leading figures they would have been prominently placed within the Sermon House, their presumed discomfort at Kingmill's performance and accusations of corruption being witnessed by their peers and other Canterbury citizens. Consequently, the venue, occasion, and audience combined to heighten the resonance of his performance, implying that Kingsmill was aware

---

[26] Consider, for example, the declaration of William Swift to the parishioners of St George's parish in 1621: "You have on every side such as are both able and willing to instruct you; you are well neighboured also by the cathedrall Church adioyning to you, whether you do often resort, and receive instructions from divers very learned Divines": W. Swift, *A Sermon Preached at the Funerall of that Painfull and faithfull servant of Jesus Christ, Mr Thomas Wilson, in his owne Church at St Georges, in Canterbury the 25 day of January. In the yeare of our Lord God 1621* (London, 1622), fol. 21.

[27] Margaret Sparks, *Canterbury Cathedral Precincts: A Historical Survey* (Canterbury: Dean and Chapter of Canterbury, 2007), 99.

[28] Study of the Act Books of the ecclesiastical courts reveals that the court often convened in the cathedral, especially in the latter part of the century. It is not clear where exactly the sessions took place, however, since the statement of venue was simply '*in loco consistorum*'. It has been suggested that from the early thirteenth century, the consistory court sat in the cathedral under the north-west tower of the nave: B. L. Woodcock, *Medieval Ecclesiastical Courts in the Diocese of Canterbury* (London: Oxford University Press, 1952), 31. For discussion of the venues of the ecclesiastical courts throughout the century see Paula Simpson, "Custom and Conflict: Disputes over Tithe in the Diocese of Canterbury, 1501–1600" (Ph.D. diss., University of Kent, 1997), 10–12.

[29] In 1567 certain aldermen were rebuked for failing to attend sermons there: CCAL, CC/J/Q/367.

of the existing structures and modes of observance and could envisage ways in which to take advantage of these in expressing his anger.

2.

The milieu in which recall of this event circulated was that of a provincial society in which much attention was paid to honour, shame, and reputation. These were matters which were regularly negotiated in the local community through gossip and hearsay, as well as in the more formal surroundings of the courtroom.[30] Many of those present at the sermon would have been well known to one another, united by bonds of marriage, friendship, neighbourhood, business, and religious adherence. Certainly the deponents in the disciplinary case are distinguished by the fact that they were drawn from among the local clergy, minor gentry, and ecclesiastical court officials. Eight people who were in the congregation that heard Kingsmill's sermon later deposed to the court.[31] All of these men had strong connections with the city of Canterbury and six of them were living there at the time of the sermon. Probate evidence reveals that these men were almost certainly literate: they were book-owners[32] and five were graduates from either Oxford or Cambridge.[33] As members of the clergy and officers of the ecclesiastical courts, they shared various working relationships. They were relatively wealthy men,[34] with the exceptions of Aldrich and Norwood roughly of an age (born in the mid-1550s) and generally of comparable social status.

---

[30] For discussion see Andrew F. Butcher's introduction to William Urry, *Christopher Marlowe and Canterbury* (London: Faber and Faber, 1988), esp. 15–40.

[31] Francis Aldrich; Theodore Beacon, doctor of physic; Marcus Culling; Joshua Hutton, clergyman; Alexander Norwood, notary public; Christopher Pashley, clergyman; Christopher Reitinger, doctor of physic; and Thomas Wilson, clergyman. Richard Walleys, proctor of the court, was also present, though he did not appear as a witness.

[32] Aldrich, Beacon, and Pashley all bequeathed unspecified books in their wills. Reitinger bequeathed a Latin text, *Josephus de antiquitate Iudaica*, and other books (including a Latin herbal) valued at £5. Wilson bequeathed Latin and Greek texts, as well as two English Bibles, to his son Samuel, and the remainder of his English books to his wife.

[33] Aldrich, Beacon, Hutton, Pashley, and Wilson. Kingsmill was also a Cambridge graduate. All information from J. Foster, *Alumni Oxonienses*, 1–4 (Nendeln: Kraus Reprints, 1968) and J. Venn, *Alumni Cantabrigienses*, 1–4 (Cambridge: Cambridge University Press, 1922–1927).

[34] Total inventoried wealth was as follows: Theodore Beacon, £736 15*s* (Maidstone, Centre for Kentish Studies [henceforth cited as CKS], PRC 10/47, fol. 223); Alexander Norwood, £570 7*s* 1*d* (CKS, PRC 10/49, fol. 177); Christopher Pashley, £133 15*s* 6*d* (CKS, PRC 10/34, fol. 178); Christopher Reitinger, £215 3*s* (CKS, PRC 10/52, fol. 276);

It is also likely that they shared religious convictions, and this is certainly revealed to varying degrees by their later testamentary evidence. The Protestant credentials of certain witnesses were impressive. Theodore Beacon was the son of the Marian exile and prolific author Thomas Beacon. The elder Beacon's many works would, without doubt, have been familiar to the audience attending Kingsmill's sermon.[35] Another witness, Thomas Wilson, the rector of St George's parish in Canterbury, was himself to become a distinguished Protestant divine, the author of a number of books[36] as well as a renowned preacher. Indeed, it is significant that many members of the audience were probably themselves experienced preachers. Both Thomas Wilson and Christopher Pashley were shortly to be appointed to the Six Preachers.[37] Wilson, in particular, was reputed at the time of his death to have preached three or four times a week.[38] In the eulogy delivered as part of Wilson's funeral sermon, the rector of nearby St Andrew's parish praised him as "both an eloquent, and a powerful dispenser of the Word."[39]

The lay witnesses were probably also frequent attendees at the cathedral. Christopher Reitinger, gentleman, was born in Hungary, but had lived in the nearby parish of St Mary Bredin for the previous seventeen years.[40] Theodore Beacon lodged in the precincts with one of the prebendaries. His brother, the rector of Warehorne in Kent, had also been examined on the matter of his preaching style in the Canterbury courts in 1589.[41] Given the scholarly, Protestant character of many in the congregation, a fairly sober style of preaching was probably the expectation.[42] It seems likely that the use of exaggerated gesture would not have

---

Thomas Wilson, £204 4s 11d (CKS, PRC 10/53, fol. 211); Anthony Kingsmill, £124 4s 8d (CKS, PRC 10/48, fol. 393).

[35] See A. W. Pollard and G. R. Redgrave, *A Short-Title Catalogue of Books Printed in England, Scotland, and Ireland 1475–1640* [henceforth cited as STC], 2nd ed. (London: Bibliographic Society, 1976), nos. 1710–1776. For discussion of the career of Thomas Beacon see S.B. House, "Becon, Thomas," *ODNB* 4: 748–50; H. Thomas, "Thomas Becon, Canon of Canterbury," *Archaeologia Cantiana* 69 (1955): 159–70; D. S. Bailey, *Thomas Becon and the Reformation of the Church in England* (Edinburgh: Oliver and Boyd, 1952).

[36] STC nos. 25786–25798.

[37] Derek Ingram Hill, *The Six Preachers of Canterbury Cathedral, 1541–1982: Clerical Lives from Tudor Times to the Present Day* (Ramsgate: K. H. McIntosh, 1982), 5.

[38] Swift, *Sermon*, 17.

[39] Swift, *Sermon*, 18.

[40] He later went to Russia to act as physician to the Tsar: John H. Appleby, "Doctor Christopher Reitinger and a Seal of Tsar Boris Godunov," *Oxford Slavonic Papers*, 2nd ser., 12 (1979): 32–39.

[41] Basil Beacon referred in a sermon to the one hundred eyes of Argus and to subjects which were denounced by a deponent to the court as "profane historyes and not to bee mentyoned or rehearsed in a sermon": CCAL, PRC 39/13 fol. 39ᵛ.

[42] Fager Herr, *Elizabethan Sermon*, 89–91.

been considered a proper accompaniment to this favoured plain style of preaching. Kingsmill's violation of the customary norms of standard sermon delivery must then have been felt all the more acutely by these experienced preachers and sermon-attenders.

As discussed earlier, the depositions were structured in such a way as to make the aspects of display within Kingsmill's performance paramount: his speech, demeanour, and use of gesture. The language used to describe his preaching style was typically unequivocal. Deponents referred to his "rayling termes," "thundering," "bitter invective," and "great vehemencye." These terms were probably part of a shared and understood discourse with regard to transgression and were chosen, perhaps, to impress and persuade the court officials. Audiences were clearly sensitive to particularising sermons, those which denounced individual sinners using hellfire terminology, often also expressing confidence in divine retribution. It is not thought that these kinds of sermons were commonplace, but people were certainly conscious of their use.[43] Much later Samuel Hieron, writing in the 1630s, declared "God forbid the pulpit should be made a place of rayling, or a Theater for invectives, and for bitterness of spirit to shew it selfe on."[44]

Those members of the audience who testified to the court were then learned, godly, and articulate men. However, there must have been an element of self-interest in their relation of events. Office (disciplinary) cases were usually instigated by the judge of the ecclesiastical court, in this case the very man whom Kingsmill had criticised. As already noted, officers of the ecclesiastical courts also testified in the case. The closeness of their working relationships, strengthened by bonds of apprenticeship,[45] marriage, and household, is particularly noteworthy and perhaps goes some way towards explaining the 'closing of ranks' which took place in relation to Kingsmill's proscecution. Indeed there is some indication that the other officers of the court perceived themselves to have been held up to ridicule. One of the court officials testified that on the day following the sermon, at a friend's house, one of the company

> presentlie towlde him this deponent in freendlie or iesting manner hee this
> deponent had a lesson or that hee was spoken to yesterdaye meaning that
> becawse hee this deponent was one of the procurators of the spirituall courte
> where Mr Doctor Lakes was judge and bycawse the said Mr Kingsmill did

---

[43] Eric Josef Carlson, "Good Pastors or Careless Shepherds? Parish Ministers and the English Reformation," *History* 88 (2003): 423–36.

[44] Quoted in Carlson, "Good Pastors," 426.

[45] Alexander Norwood, for example, had been a servant of Richard Walleys and later married Elizabeth Cranmer, almost certainly the daughter of a previous registrar of the court: *Canterbury Marriage Licences*, ed. J. Meadows Cowper (Canterbury: Cross & Jackman, 1892), 306.

soe expressly and plainlie note and signifie the saide Judge and cowrte that therfore this deponent was therby towched.[46]

Here we have insight into the repercussive effects of Kingsmill's actions beyond the immediate audience. The ramifications of his sermon undoubtedly extended far beyond those who later deposed to the court and, as already noted, details of the sermon and its circumstances would have been circulated around the city, the subject of learned interpretation, as well as laughter and local gossip.

It is clear then that to an erudite audience the exemplum of the unjust judge provided ample opportunity for 'political' interpretation. A study of Kingsmill's sermon and its ramifications provides a means of understanding the way in which those involved attempted to manipulate and control 'political' events through the medium of the courtroom. It has been shown that the sermon and its performance gained an immediate notoriety and that it was discussed within the city and beyond. That information was circulating about these events and being debated is very likely and this in itself implies a certain element of 'story-telling'. Although it has been argued that the sermon may have had a very particular resonance for certain scholarly, Protestant members of the congregation, the percolation of the 'story' throughout the town and countryside must have tapped into common beliefs regarding gesture and display, and a familiarity with certain methods of discourse and the manipulation of ideas.

The case reveals well the way in which testimony before the ecclesiastical courts was subject to continual reworking and reinterpretation. Natalie Davis has drawn attention to the importance of understanding the 'crafting' of the narrative: the way in which the shaping choices of language, detail, and order served to present a description of events which seemed meaningful or explanatory.[47] This was perhaps especially important in a case such as this which had so offended and upset those present at the sermon. An arresting and disturbing performance had clearly taken place, and yet the depositions were made over five months after the occasion: time for reflection, conference, and even rehearsal amongst witnesses. A number of factors combined to ensure that the event was presented in a very particular way, focusing on its transgressive nature. There is evidence that, even on the day the sermon was preached, it was being interpreted as a 'political' act, and this was certainly the assessment by the time the case reached court.

The court material reveals that the sermon was discussed on at least two subsequent festive occasions soon after the event: during a supper at the house in the Precincts of one of the prebendaries and at a gathering at another house in Canterbury later in the same week. These gatherings gave rise to interesting reappraisal of the sermon. Thomas Beacon, who was concerned that he may have

---

[46] CCAL, PRC 39/16, fol. 9ᵛ.

[47] Natalie Z. Davis, *Fiction in the Archives: Pardon Tales and Their Tellers in Sixteenth-Century France* (Stanford: Stanford University Press, 1987), passim.

been implicated in Kingsmill's invitation to preach, invited him to supper on the evening of the same day and described to the court how "as they sate at supper this deponent fabling into some remembrance of his sermon [. . .] expostulated with him the said Mr Kingsmill."[48] It was on this occasion that Kingsmill admitted that he may have gone too far. The use of the word 'fabling' itself suggests elements of dissembling and fiction.[49] Kingsmill's performance would have been subject to much re-imagining in the assessment of the meaning attached to his performance.

Witnesses drew attention, also, to Kingsmill's drinking habits. On the evening before the sermon, Kingsmill was at the Crown inn at Canterbury. His speech on that occasion his colleague, Christopher Pashley, was anxious to excuse as having "proceded of choler & heate." Although no one suggests that Kingsmill was himself drunk when preaching, the juxtaposition of references to drinking and preaching is too close to ignore. This association also feeds into the ideas about instability and lack of control and the implicit relationship between rhetorics of drunkenness (again a transgressive act) and Kingsmill's "overpassing" performance in his sermon. A disapproval of drunkeness was, of course, also typically Protestant.

Although Kingsmill had clearly undertaken some preparation, declaring when asking to act as substitute preacher, "I am excellent at that text," the spontaneous and improvisatory nature of his preaching comes across very strongly in the depositions. Kingsmill's opportunist and self-declared intent had been to "rattle up the judge," and the implication here would seem to be that he had been attempting to goad him into a response. It seems, however, that there was some attempt to play down the premeditated aspects of Kingsmill's performance and represent it as a less conscious act. This was perhaps a way of excusing the shock of the proposed punishment for the judge.

3.

This section will focus on the learned interpretation applied to the sermon in an attempt to understand some of the ways in which the 'political' act was understood and negotiated. Kingsmill's use of the exemplum of the unjust judge was drawn from the life of Cambyses, king of Persia (530–522 BC) and conqueror of Egypt. The life of Cambyses was a familiar theme in classical sources, and the punishment imposed on the unjust judge was described by Valerius Maximus

---

[48] Office versus Kingsmill (1593): CCAL, PRC39/16, fol. 14ᵛ.

[49] Fager Herr, *Elizabethan Sermon*, 77–84, suggests that it was common for members of congregations to make notes during sermons. Many prefaces to printed editions of sermons suggest that they were compiled both from the preacher's notes as well as from those of his congregation.

in his moral compendium, *Facta et Dicta Memorabilia*. [50] It was also recorded by Herodotus:

> Sisamnes [. . . whom] King Cambyses slew and flayed, because that he, being of the number of royal judges, had taken money to give an unrighteous sentence. Therefore Cambyses slew and flayed Sisamnes, and cutting his skin into strips, stretched them across the seat of the throne whereon he had been wont to sit when he heard causes. Having so done Cambyses appointed the son of Sisamnes to be judge in his father's room, and bade him never forget in what way his seat was cushioned. [51]

The exemplum of the unjust judge was also included in the fifteenth-century treatise *Secreta Secretorum* and by Hoccleve in *The Regiment of Princes*. In the sixteenth century, John Taverner included the life of Cambyses in his *Second Booke of the Garden of Wysedome*. [52] Especial resonance was given to Kingsmill's choice of the exemplum by Thomas Preston's play *Cambises*, which had been printed by John Allde in London in 1570. [53] A second edition of the play was published around 1585 and a third before 1589, and so it is likely that the play was enjoying renewed success around the time of Kingsmill's sermon. This gives the exemplum a more immediate context. Within Preston's play the punishment of the unjust judge, Sisamnes, was intended as a grisly scene. The execution took place on stage and a stage direction was given to the protagonists to "flea him with a false skin." [54] The life of Cambyses and, in particular, the punishment of the unjust judge would therefore have been familiar to Elizabethan audiences, and the contemporary popularity of Thomas Preston's play is perhaps confirmed by Shakespeare's reference to it in *Henry IV, Part 1* (Act 2, Scene iv).

Taverner's *Garden of Wisdom* is believed to have been the direct source for Preston's play. If so, this is just one of the factors which lend the play a peculiarly Protestant resonance. Taverner had been in the service of Cromwell, who had secured his appointment as clerk of the Privy Seal and had encouraged him to produce works to encourage the official Reformation in England. [55] W. A. Armstrong regards the focus on kingship within Preston's play as following in the tradition of the *speculum principis*, including works such as Erasmus's *Institutio*

---

[50] The following information is drawn from W. A. Armstrong, "The Background and Sources of Preston's *Cambises*," *English Studies* 31 (1950): 129–35. See also idem, "The Authorship and Political Meaning of *Cambises*," *English Studies* 35 (1955): 289–99.

[51] G. Rawlinson, trans., *History of Herodotus* (London: J. Murray, 1862), 3: 191.

[52] It was also well known in continental sources: Valentin Groebner, *Liquid Assets, Dangerous Gifts: Presents and Politics at the End of the Middle Ages*, trans. Pamela E. Selwyn (Philadelphia: University of Pennsylvania Press, 2002), 78–79.

[53] STC 20287, 20287.5, and 20288.

[54] *Cambises*, Act 1, Scene iv.

[55] See A. W. Taylor, "Taverner, Richard," *ODNB* 53: 840–42, at 841.

Principis Christiani (1516) and Thomas Elyot's *The Gouvernour* (1531).[56] He also noted that the play emphasised obedience to a legitimate king, again a Protestant doctrine explored in such works as Tyndale's *The Obedience of a Christian Man* (1528) and Cranmer's *Notes for a Homily Against Rebellion* (1549).[57] This particular doctrine of passive obedience was reiterated in sixteenth-century sermons by Latimer, Hooper, Cranmer, and Lever.[58] Finally, the play explored the nature of divine intervention as exemplified by the death of Cambyses.

Aspects of Anglican doctrine form, therefore, a major influence on the play's themes. The punishment of the unjust judge had been used as a sermon illustration before, most notably by two early reformers who later became Marian martyrs, Bishops Hugh Latimer and John Hooper.[59] The former, in particular, used the exemplum a number of times by referring to the punishment of the unjust judge with a degree of approval: "Surely it was a goodly sign, a goodly monument, the sign of the judge's skin. I pray God we may once see the sign of the skin in England!"[60] Almost certainly an echo of this sermon can be detected in Kingsmill's alleged declaration: "Oh what a goodly thinge were it if the old iudges skin might be flaine of and nayled to the seat of iustice; that all the yonge iudges that followe after might be warned by his example."[61] The life of Cambyses was then one strongly identified with Protestant preoccupations with obedience, justice, and authority. It is perhaps not surprising, given the Protestant character of the audience who heard Kingsmill, that the sermon's substance was explored in such depth in their depositions to the court.

As shown, the judgement of Cambyses was undoubtedly a powerful exemplum in the late medieval and early modern period, in literature, in sermons, and in drama. It also, furthermore, featured in late medieval art. The artist Gerard David (c. 1460–1523) was commissioned by the Magistrature of Bruges to provide a series of paintings to hang in the Hall of Justice of the Hotel de Ville.[62] Two paintings form the group known as "The Judgement of Cambyses" and were painted between 1487 and 1498. The paintings were probably based on the account of Herodotus, but David set the events against the background of the

---

[56] Armstrong, "The Authorship of *Cambises*," 292.

[57] Armstrong, "The Authorship of *Cambises*," 295.

[58] Armstrong, "The Authorship of *Cambises*," 296.

[59] *The Early Writings of Bishop Hooper* (Cambridge: Cambridge University Press, 1843), 483.

[60] *Sermons of Hugh Latimer* (Cambridge: Cambridge University Press, 1843), 146, 181, 260.

[61] CCAL, PRC 39/16, fol. 12ᵛ. This may reflect either Kingsmill's knowledge of Latimer's work, or more likely that of the deponent (Joshua Hutton) who recalled (or interpreted) his words.

[62] *Gerard David and His Followers* (London: Wildenstein Gallery/Arts Council of Great Britain, 1949).

medieval city of Bruges. The first painting depicts the arrest of the corrupt judge and the second shows, in gruesome detail, his punishment.

The commissioning of "The Judgement of Cambyses" is just one of a number of such commissions made by town authorities to civic painters. The paintings produced usually explored the themes of injustice and retribution. Other examples are Dirk Bouts' "Justice of the Emperor Otto III" for the magistrature of Louvain and Roger van der Weyden's works depicting the "Legend of Trajan and Herkinbald" for the town hall in Brussels.[63] The prominent display of works such as these, in important civic buildings and close to local courts, provided an unequivocal message emphasising the insistence on justice and the punishment of corruption.

4.

So how did Kingsmill's accusations of corruption relate more generally to perceptions of ecclesiastical justice in the diocese of Canterbury? The sermon and the events leading up to it occurred during a period of dissatisfaction with the work of the ecclesiastical courts. It is apparent that the courts were subject to contemporary criticism from the beginning of the sixteenth century, and it has been argued that their authority was significantly weakened during the years of the official Reformation.[64] By the later years of the century the ecclesiastical courts were subject to strenuous and sustained criticism from Puritans who were unhappy that the pursuit of 'godly discipline' was overseen by lay bureaucrats. Puritans were also sceptical of the tendency they perceived amongst court officers to regard judicial business as a lucrative source of income.[65] Additionally, concern was voiced over the ineffectiveness of methods of punishment, in particular penance, and the habitual use of excommunication.[66] Furthermore, the work of the ecclesiastical courts had long been subject to tension arising from a conflict of interest with lay jurisdiction, and another conflict arose through the use of prohibition which prevented judgement in a case by an ecclesiastical judge through removal to common law.[67]

---

[63] R. Mills, *Suspended Animation: Pain, Pleasure and Punishment in Medieval Culture* (London: Reaktion Books, 2005), 61. Other extant depictions of the punishment are also described by Mills (69).

[64] Ralph A. Houlbrooke, "The Decline of Ecclesiastical Jurisdiction under the Tudors," in *Continuity and Change: Personnel and Administration of the Church of England 1500–1642*, ed. R. O'Day and Felicity Heal (Leicester: The University Press, 1976), 241–46.

[65] Houlbrooke, "Decline," 251; Ingram, *Church Courts*, 4.

[66] Ingram, *Church Courts*, 4.

[67] Houlbrooke, "Decline," 239–43; Ingram, *Church Courts*, 5–7.

Testimony reflecting many of the criticisms outlined above can be found in the Canterbury archive. These included scepticism about the use of excommunication and objections to high fees. In February 1597, for example, Solomon Boxer, vicar of Marden in Kent, similarly chose to use the pulpit to voice his criticisms of the ecclesiastical courts. At the time Boxer was the subject of a disciplinary case and was accused of pursuing vexatious litigation.[68] After complaining about the use of excommunication which he likened to a fool's dagger — "alwaies redie to be hurled at those which stand nerest unto him" — he exclaimed

> against the officers of the courte ecclesiastical for or about the takinge of fees for wills and administrations recitinge in a most exclaiminge manner the statute provided in that behalfe and how that not withstandinge the said statute the officers of the courtes ecclesiasticall did use to take far more [. . .] [69]

Members of the laity were, it seems, equally virulent. One declared in 1592 that "The popes Courte and the devilles courte and the comissaries courte [. . .] are all one, and a plage on them all, for it hath cost me [. . .] mony there this weeke [. . .]."[70] Resentment of the activities of court officials most often focused on apparitors of the court such as Christopher Crammer who had been so despised by Kingsmill. Often these court messengers bore the brunt of the anger expressed by those summoned to appear or testify.[71] Indeed, it may have been these court officials who were most tempted to take bribes and certainly they were unpopular figures in local communities.[72] There are, of course, difficult distinctions to be made between gifts and bribes, but some testimony does reveal that contemporaries believed the bribery of court officials to be a distinct possibility. A court case in 1598, for example, included discussion as to whether the gift of a sheep presented to the archdeacon of Canterbury had constituted a bribe.[73]

It is against this background that the accusations of corruption levelled at the beginning of the seventeenth century against George Newman, Lakes' successor as Commissary, must be considered. In February 1605, seven officers of the ecclesiastical courts at Canterbury travelled to London to testify in the

---

[68] CCAL, PRC 39/18, fols. 260–70.

[69] CCAL, PRC 39/20, fol. 22. For discussion of Whitgift's Standard (1597), which established a standard table of fees, see Ingram, *Church Courts*, 55–56.

[70] CCAL, PRC 39/14, fol. 110.

[71] See, for example, CCAL, PRC 39/22, fol. 120ᵛ and CCAL, PRC 39/21, fol. 69.

[72] For discussion of the qualifications and conduct of courtroom personnel, including apparitors, see Ingram, *Church Courts*, 54–64. It seems that apparitors may have been popularly perceived as informers or as promoters of disharmony. For discussion of the legislation by Whitgift in 1597 which sought to remedy this situation see Houlbrooke, "Decline of Ecclesiastical Jurisdiction," 252.

[73] CCAL, PRC 39/21, fol. 91.

Star Chamber in a case brought by Sir Thomas Baker against George Newman. Though the case was ostensibly concerned with contested claims to rights in the parsonage of Staplehurst in Kent, the conduct of George Newman since he had been judge of the court was also explored. Accusations of malpractice and of accepting bribes had been made against him.

Of especial interest is the fact that Stephen Lakes (by now living in London and a master in Chancery) also testified in this case.[74] He claimed that he had earlier, in the Easter term of 1601, drawn up a list of fifty articles concerning the conduct of Newman since his appointment.[75] These he had presented to the archbishop who had agreed that he would address the complaints during the course of the summer which he was spending in Kent. However, no subsequent examination or judicial proceedings took place. Lakes believed that the matter had been resolved following the mediation of the dean and the archdeacon of Canterbury at the solicitation of Newman. Lakes alleged that the archdeacon later expressed regret to him that he had intervened on Newman's behalf.[76] Likewise, Lakes testified that the archbishop had often commented that "he thought the defendent was as corrupt a person as ever came into such an Office."[77]

Lakes' remarks, and his concern that he may have been implicated in the choice of Newman as his successor, reveal his own sensitivity. Lakes had told the archbishop that Newman had been "recommended unto him for a man of better condicion than he proved in his place."[78] This sensitivity was probably a legacy of the attack made against Lakes himself just over ten years earlier. Furthermore, it was a sensitivity shared by Francis Aldrich and Richard Walleys, court officials, both of whom had been present at Kingsmill's sermon. Lakes described how, since his own resignation, they had both complained to him many times concerning the implementation of fees by Newman. After rehearsing a number of examples of raised fees in his testimony to the Star Chamber, Lakes commented that

> these and such like fees did theis twoo auncient Officers of these Cortes affirme and certifie to the deponent to have bene newlie raysed and usuallie receyved by the said defendant and [they] did greatly complayne therof

---

[74] London, The National Archives [henceforth cited as TNA], STAC 8/252/26, fols. 50, 51, 54.

[75] Lakes also claimed that about a year before he drew up his own list, various other articles were presented to the Dean of the Arches by another party: TNA, STAC 8/252/26, fol. 50. See also Peter Clark, *English Provincial Society from the Reformation to the Revolution: Religion, Politics and Society in Kent 1500–1640* (Hassocks: Harvester Press, 1977), 182.

[76] TNA, STAC 8/252/26, fol. 50.

[77] TNA, STAC 8/252/26, fol. 51.

[78] TNA, STAC 8/252/26, fol. 51.

aswell for the iniurie of the Subiectes, as also to the slandre of those Cortes wherin they had so long served.[79]

The emphasis here on longevity is important. It implies the particular pride of the "auncient officers" in their association with the work of the courts, as well as revealing still further the repercussive effects of the personal attack on Lakes himself. It suggests that, as a consequence, Lakes and those who had served with him were peculiarly defensive and sensitive with regard to the work of the ecclesiastical courts. Lakes' accusations against Newman, largely based on hearsay, were seemingly unsupported by many of the newer serving officers of the court, and Newman appears to have enjoyed the loyalty of the men who served under him.[80]

5.

It remains to consider, finally, whether the accusations regarding corruption were justified. It is of significance that these events took place in Canterbury, a city which was a centre for ecclesiastical jurisdiction as well as for civic justice. As both city and county officials, Canterbury's mayor and aldermen presided over the court of quarter sessions at the guildhall, having received this recognition from Edward IV in the late fifteenth century. Moreover, the cases brought before these civic magistrates included matters relating to public reputation and moral standards.[81] Accusations of corruption, therefore, would have had widespread ramifications amongst all sectors of the judiciary. In addition, by the time of Kingsmill's sermon in 1593, Lakes was probably a well-known and perhaps even notorious figure within the local community at Canterbury. He was born in Smarden in the Weald of Kent and had been serving as judge of the ecclesiastical courts at Canterbury for the preceding ten years. Prior to that, he had attended King's College in Cambridge.[82] While there he was embroiled in controversy focusing on the provost and had been involved in the drawing up of articles criticising the provost's management of the college. After a hearing before the chancellor, the provost was cleared and his accusers were censured. Lakes was

---

[79] TNA, STAC 8/252/26, fol. 51.

[80] TNA, STAC 8/252/26, fols 14, 18, 20, 22, 25. Alexander Norwood remembered him in his will as "my worshipfull good frend" and bequeathed him 40 shillings "as a token of my love and duty to him": CKS, PRC 17/56, fol. 42. For an assessment of Newman as a competent and effective judge, see J. M. Potter, "The Ecclesiastical Courts in the Diocese of Canterbury" (M.Phil. thesis, University of London, 1973), 133–34.

[81] Though outside what may be seen as the official arena, certain morris dancers were brought before the civic magistrates for dancing outside the mayor's house, which seems to have been some sort of social protest: CCAL, CC/J/Q/388.

[82] *Alumni Cantabrigienses*, s.n.

imprisoned briefly in the gatehouse at Westminster. These events were recorded by John Strype who believed that Lakes had been motivated by a sense of grievance against the provost, who had earlier rebuked him for wearing inappropriate clothing. Strype commented that "this had ever after stuck in his stomach [. . .] such was his stout nature and impenitency to be reproved."[83] This comment is revealing of Lakes' peculiar sensitivity to criticism.

Furthermore, his earlier career at Canterbury was also attended by controversy. In 1590 he was accused of the unfair prosecution of the minister of Westwell in Kent and on this occasion he had again drawn up articles of accusation.[84] Kingsmill's sermon would almost certainly have been delivered with the knowledge of these controversial aspects of Lakes' career, and it seems likely, then, that discussion and gossip in Canterbury in the spring of 1593 might well have re-explored some of these earlier events. There was perhaps an element of 'saving face' in Lakes' decision to prosecute Kingsmill. It seems unlikely that Lakes presided over an inherently corrupt administration, and it is probable that his decision to pursue Kingsmill in the courts was a way of defending both his own honour and that of local justice.

Kingsmill's vehement and personal attack on Stephen Lakes appears to have been motivated by personal slight. In the course of his sermon, warming to his theme, he may have spontaneously introduced the story of the unjust judge. As shown, this prompted a reaction which notably came from scholarly and devout members of the local community, but which also had ramifications which extended far beyond this select group. The disciplinary case against Kingsmill demonstrates the important role which the ecclesiastical courts played in providing a forum for the articulation of complaint and for the exploration of matters of honour, shame, and reputation.

Similarly, Lakes' own accusations against his successor, George Newman, appear to have been essentially unsubstantiated. The complaints of the long-serving court officials discussed above simply objected to the raised fees. It is also significant that the only allegation explored in depth by Lakes — that Newman had accepted a bribe in order to facilitate a marriage between two persons related within prohibited degree — also involved Solomon Boxer, the same cleric who had earlier denounced ecclesiastical justice from the pulpit of his church in Marden. Clearly this was a society which operated a culture of favour, and it has been suggested that it is unlikely that officials, other than in isolated cases, would have been involved in activities which contemporaries would have regarded as inherently and seriously dishonest. Indeed it has been argued for the

---

[83] J. Strype, *Annals of the Reformation and Establishment of Religion* (Oxford: Clarendon Press, 1829, repr. 1922), 2.2: 38–41.

[84] B. Levack, *The Civil Lawyers in England 1603–1641* (Oxford: Clarendon Press, 1973), 246.

early seventeenth century that the diocese of Canterbury provided more effective, honest, and competent administration than most.[85]

It is significant, then, that in both cases the accusations of corruption seem to have been unfounded. As far as can be deduced, Kingsmill escaped censure. He remained as vicar of Milton near Sittingbourne in Kent until his death in 1616. Lakes remained as judge of the courts at Canterbury in the years after the sermon until his appointment as master in Chancery probably around 1597. George Newman (Lakes' successor) pursued an illustrious career which included a period as parliamentary representative for Dover and later for Canterbury. He was knighted in 1616.[86]

Though it might then be concluded that the accusations against both Lakes and Newman lacked real substance, it is at the same time clear that the 1590s saw the beginnings of a growing climate of dissatisfaction with the workings of ecclesiastical justice. Criticisms were probably expressed relatively frequently within everyday parlance, though often these would have been remarks and attitudes which failed to reach the attention of local parish officials or court officers. Kingsmill's attack was noteworthy in that it was made in a public arena, and the other denunciations discussed above were certainly special in that they were reiterated in court. The concentration in the 1590s of these criticisms of local ecclesiastical justice is quite remarkable. It should be noted, furthermore, that it was in this decade that the two main foci of opposition, that is, Puritan criticism and common law encroachment, found shared ground in the controversy over the *ex officio* oath, by which defendants might incriminate themselves.[87] Although criticisms of the courts may have been more common, they were still utilised frequently in the resolution of conflict. This chapter has drawn attention to the processes involved in upholding the accepted norms of local society through judicial and more informal procedures. The rising use of the ecclesiastical courts in the sixteenth century and in particular in the 1590s demonstrates that, despite criticism, they were valued and utilised as a forum for 'negotiating the political.'

---

[85] For a generally favourable assessment of the efficiency of the ecclesiastical courts in the diocese of Canterbury in the seventeenth century see Potter, "Ecclesiastical Courts," esp. 133 and 207–13.

[86] For biographical details of Lakes, see Levack, *Civil Lawyers*, 246 and of Newman, see Levack, *Civil Lawyers*, 258 and Potter, "Ecclesiastical Courts," 133–34. Note, however, that Levack records that Newman was commissary of the archbishop by 1587. This is certainly a misprint for 1597.

[87] For further discussion see Ingram, *Church Courts*, 4–6, 329–31.

'With the consent of the towne, and other skillfull marryners and gentlemen': An Examination of Textual Negotiations in the Elizabethan Restoration of Dover Harbour 1582–1605

Claire Bartram and Mary Dixon

This article examines relations between town and Crown in late sixteenth-century Dover. Using a manuscript written by John Tooke, who was "one of the Jurattes of the town and port of Dovor," the article argues that Tooke presents a specifically 'Dovorian' perspective on the processes of negotiation undertaken in relation to the essential repairs to Dover harbour.[1] The article explores the ways in which Tooke depicts the establishment of consensus between different parties in Dover town concerning the procedure for the repairs and how members of the Dover elite negotiated with external power and patronage networks as a Cinque Port and at county and state level. By exploring Tooke's representation of social relations in some detail, the article engages with ongoing debates about the nature of relations between the state and the provinces and sees this very much as a dynamic relationship, open to negotiation to protect interests on both sides.[2] As well as the specific instances recorded by Tooke, the manuscript is also placed in the broader context of power relations between town and Crown. Adopting an interdisciplinary approach, the article employs both literary and social-historical analysis of Tooke's manuscript to draw out the significance of the complex pro-

---

[1] London, British Library, MS. Add. 12514, fol. 33.

[2] For further discussion of these issues see S. Hindle, *The State and Social Change in Early Modern England, c. 1550–1640* (Basingstoke: Macmillan, 2000) and M. Braddick, *State Formation in Early Modern England c. 1550–1700* (Cambridge: Cambridge University Press, 2000).

Negotiating the Political in Northern European Urban Society, c.1400–c.1600, ed. Sheila Sweetinburgh, MRTS 434 (Tempe: ACMRS, 2013). [ISBN 978-0-86698-482-9]

cesses of negotiation that Tooke recounts. Reconstructing Tooke's life in Dover and his place in the ruling oligarchy, the article argues that Tooke was representative of a gradual change in the nature of oligarchic rule in Dover. The article also draws attention to the literary merits of the manuscript, and its deliberate use of particular rhetorical and generic forms, and suggestively reconstructs Tooke's coterie both within Dover society and within patronage networks in the county more widely.

1.

At the beginning of the sixteenth century Dover had established customs and traditions of liberty that it perceived as ancient, and that were expressed in its custumal. The freeing of church lands after 1538 brought new men into the town, nudging the church's lay administrators into the service of new landowners and ultimately into the service of the town. Dixon argues that the beginnings of more pronounced legalism can be observed from this point when laymen began to use the law to justify their actions in taking the tithes that had formerly been a matter of custom.[3] Certain men came to the town to take advantage of the more open land market after the dissolution of church lands, and in the 1550s a new group of merchants appeared, some of whom formed a bank or stock together in 1551, and they, together with some entrepreneurial landowners, established themselves, forming kinship links that led to the formation of a markedly Protestant ruling group in the Elizabethan period. State influence on local government was apparent in this period in the common council's more impersonal methods of dealing with the poor, with market regulation, and with hygiene, measures undertaken often in response to Tudor Statutes. The acceptance of Crown intervention in the town's affairs perhaps began to seem more normal, and increased oversight by the Privy Council from the Marian period ironically encouraged the establishment of this educated Protestant ruling elite by giving it more power and making it more professional.[4] The first man to claim 'merchant' as his main occupation became part of the ruling body of the town in the early 1550s at a time when there was an unusual concentration of mariners in the oligarchy.[5] It was in this decade too that membership of the common council became more prescribed and increasingly separate from the commonality. Membership was limited to thirty-seven from 1556, with the jurats elected by vote and not by

---

[3] Mary Dixon, "Economy and Society in Dover 1509–1640" (Ph.D. diss., University of Kent, 1992), chap. 4.iii, 430–33.

[4] London, British Library, MS. Egerton 2094, fols 154, 205.

[5] London, British Library, MS. Egerton 2016, fol. 34 for an indenture with Edmund Michell, 'merchant'; London, British Library, MS. Egerton 2094, fol. 42ᵛ for his juratship.

common acclaim, accepting the post for life. It was in this decade also that a Crown officer, a Customer, became a jurat.[6]

When in 1581 Queen Elizabeth acted to finance the new harbour, the ruling group was predominantly made up of merchants, but it also included brewers and lawyers. The mayoralty of Thomas Andrewes in the early 1580s brought with it a period of factionalism within the town and visible resistance to the Crown's intervention in the town's affairs as Andrewes rejected Privy Council rulings and sought to control Crown-nominated appointments within the town. For example, in 1582, Richard Barry wrote to the Privy Council in his capacity as the Lieutenant of the Castle, reporting that after the mariner William Tiddyman had been taken before the Privy Council to answer certain lewd speeches he had made against them, the action taken by the mayor, Thomas Andrewes, on his return was so slight that Tiddyman did not modify his behaviour but instead "Challenged Captain Ward at Dover in the market place that he had certified untruly against him to the Lords of the Council."[7] In January 1584, the Privy Council insisted that Mr Thomas Andrewes should be removed from the mayoralty. He was sent to the Marshalsea that year, charged, among other things, with "wasting the town's treasure."[8] Articles exhibited against him show that his most serious fault was that he had taken the office of bailiff—a Crown appointment—upon himself while he was mayor so that he was both "judge and minister to one self court where all warrants, precepts and processes are by him awarded as mayor, executed by himself as bailiff and returnable before him as judge."[9] It was perhaps his perceived flouting of custom and the removal of the just exercise of authority by the town's officers that led to a gradual movement by those officers towards the authority offered by the Lieutenant of the Castle and his staff. By the early seventeenth century, when Tooke was an active jurat, the ruling group sought to further emphasise the difference between themselves and the commonalty, establishing a godly exercise in St James's parish every Wednesday forenoon and enforcing Sabbatarianism.[10]

The significance of Crown intervention was perhaps more pronounced in Dover owing to its status within the Cinque Ports as a head port.[11] The Lord

---

[6] London, British Library, MS. Egerton 2094, fols 154, 205; London, British Library, MS. Add. 28530; London, British Library, MS. Egerton 2094, fol. 107 (1554) William Burden, jurat, fol. 176 William Burden 'Controller of Dover.'

[7] London, The National Archives, SP 12/157, fol. 43 No. 16. Tiddyman also appears in London, British Library, MS. Add. 12514 as 'Tydeman'.

[8] London, British Library, MS. Egerton 2095, fol. 289.

[9] London, The National Archives, SP 12/157, fol. 17.

[10] See for example Whitfield, East Kent Archives, Dp/FCa 4. Expenses 1607–1608.

[11] For details of Dover's changing relationship with the Cinque Ports see Dixon, "Economy and Society in Dover," 210–24.

Warden, a post dominated in the sixteenth century by the Kentish Lords Cobham, was nominally resident at Dover Castle and acted as an obligatory conduit of information between the Crown and the Ports and between the Ports themselves. As the warden seldom lived in the castle by this period, his duties fell largely upon his deputy, the Lieutenant of the Castle, and a permanent staff of legal officials. Although the mayor and jurats would occasionally reward this secretariat with gifts for their help in communicating with the Crown, there were also times when the castle came into direct conflict with the oligarchy, particularly during the factious years of the 1580s. In one instance Mayor Andrewes openly challenged the authority of the castle by displacing William Vanwylder from his position as town clerk, replacing him with his own close friend, the lawyer John Goodwin. Vanwylder, the son-in-law of Richard Barry, then Lieutenant of the Castle, was subsequently reinstated.[12] Significantly, by the early seventeenth century Sir Thomas Fane, who was the then Lieutenant of the Castle, chose to live in the town rather than the castle, and it was also in this period that the post of Lord Warden was transferred out of Kentish hands into those of the Catholic Henry Howard, earl of Northampton.[13]

Dover had a dual economy derived from its market and its harbour. The town's accounts show that dues exacted at the harbour provided its chief source of income for most years from the early 1560s until at least 1640.[14] Like many small towns in this period, its economy was vulnerable to pressures from outside, but the corporate life of the town normally survived because it was in the hands of intrinsically opportunistic men who were nevertheless dedicated to the interests of the town and its inhabitants. The town corporation of Dover was accustomed to financing its own projects with credit rather than with large capital resources. The development of a sizeable project, like a port, was necessarily checked by problems that could be solved only by greater capital investment than local authorities could find. The town had not had sufficient resources to prevent the rapid deterioration of the harbour since an injection of money by the Crown in 1535, when, in response to a petition from the town, King Henry VIII had funded the start of a major reconstruction that was never completed.[15] In

---

[12] London, The National Archives, SP 12/157, fols. 19–21.

[13] Whitfield, East Kent Archives, Do/AAm 2, fol. 16, 1605 and fol. 24ᵛ, 1606.

[14] See Dixon, "Economy and Society in Dover," 56–67 for income derived from shipping and port dues.

[15] See London, British Library, MS. Egerton 2093, fols. 44–45; London, British Library, MS. Add. 26618, Expenses 1531–32; London, The National Archives, PRO, E 101/58/13; London, British Library, MS. Add. 12514, fol. 37; *Letters and Papers, Foreign and Domestic, of the Reign of Henry VIII, preserved in the Public Record Office, the British Museum, and elsewhere in England* [subsequently cited as *L.P. Hen. VIII*], 23 vols. in 38 (London: 1862–1932), 10: 102; 8: 826; London, British Library, MS. Titus B.1 425; *L.P. Hen. VIII*, 11: 45, 150, 151, 184; H. M. Colvin, "Dover Harbour," in *The History of the*

the mid-1550s responsibility for the maintenance of the harbour was transferred from the Crown to the mayor and chamberlains of Dover, and it was this body which appealed to the Privy Council in 1559 and to Lord Cobham in the mid-1560s to take action to preserve the harbour.[16] In 1576 Sir Francis Walsingham sent William Borough, comptroller of the Navy, to view the state of the harbour, and by 1579 a commission headed by Lord Cobham, Lord Warden of the Cinque Ports, was consulting on the various options for the maintenance of the harbour.[17] The town accounts and minutes of the common council in the 1560s and 1570s record many suits made at London for a "new haven." Possibly more influential were the complaints made to the queen by ambassadors who had experienced difficulties at the harbour, but it was not until 1581 that the Statute of Tonnage finally brought sufficient funds to renovate the harbour.[18]

In 1582 a newly commissioned board of harbour commissioners comprising mainly gentry of Kentish birth[19] suggested a plan to reinforce the shingle bank, then dam up the river water into a pent or pool by building a cross-wall from the land to a point midway along the shingle bank. The River Dour would then feed the pent where it would be dammed up and could then be controlled by a sluice to provide a head of water that would flush the channel and clear the entry to the harbour. From the years 1584–1585 Dover at last had a viable harbour with a good depth of water. Although it was still threatened by the entry of 'beach' and maintenance such as the rebuilding of the sluice was ongoing, the harbour was of such strategic value to the Crown that it received support when other Cinque Ports were left to decay. However, the proceedings of the common council of Dover on 4 August 1605 show that its members had already realised that the only way to keep their harbour viable was to surrender their rights to some of the duties they took from it to the Crown "considering the same is meant to be procured to the benefit of the haven, without which the town will decay."[20]

King's Works, 6 vols. (London: HMSO, 1963–1982), 4.2: 729–68, at 736; London, British Library, MS. Egerton 2093, fol. 134ᵛ.

[16] Colvin, "Dover Harbour," 4.2: 755–56. For a detailed account of the Elizabethan harbour works at Dover see also Eric H. Ash, "'A Perfect and an absolute work': Expertise, Authority and the Rebuilding of Dover Harbour, 1579–1583," *Technology and Culture* 41 (2000): 239–68; idem, *Power, Knowledge and Expertise in Elizabethan England* (Baltimore: John Hopkins University Press, 2004), 55–86.

[17] Colvin, "Dover Harbour," 4.2: 755–76.

[18] The act 23 Eliz. Cap. 6 passed by Parliament in 1581 levied a tax of 3*d* per ton on all ships above twenty tons entering English ports for the next seven years. The act was revised in 1589 and 1593 and modified in 1601.

[19] The commission included Lord Cobham, Sir Thomas Scott, Sir James Hales, Thomas Wotton, Edward Boyes, the mayor of Dover, Richard Barry, the Lieutenant of Dover Castle, Henry Palmer, Thomas Digges, Thomas Wilford, and William Partridge who oversaw the day-to-day running of the project.

[20] Whitfield, East Kent Archives, Do/AAm 2, fol. 17ᵛ.

At this point the relationship between town and Crown concerning the harbour underwent considerable change as the town negotiated the erosion of their local customs and liberties to enable Crown intervention in the long-term maintenance of the harbour. Returning the harbour to the Crown was an essential strategy in maintaining the economic survival and prosperity of the town, just as seeking its support for the harbour works had been two decades previously. The common assembly agreed at a meeting in November 1605, in the mayoralty of George Binge, that their rights in the harbour must be surrendered to the Crown "for and towards the perpetual reparations of the same harbour" and in return for a new grant of money.[21] The royal charter of July 1606 granted the "oversight and government" of the Port and Harbour at Dover to a body of eleven men which would include the Lord Warden of the Cinque Ports, the Lieutenant of the Castle, and the mayor. The charter granted this body the whole of the harbour, the pent, and significant reclaimed land nearby as a free gift providing that this estate be used for the benefit of the harbour. Both the town of Dover and the Crown benefited from this arrangement, reinforcing the findings of other historians that relations between town and Crown were not of necessity "adversarial or oppositional" but could instead be "co-operative, reciprocal and flexible" and were subject to change "according to the specific needs of the town's inhabitants and the king's government."[22] At this date, the common council also agreed that an already projected new market cross "upon better consideration shall be enacted meet for a court hall."[23] The building was probably needed for increased commercial and legal activity in the town, and its construction presumably began, as the new edifying of the town hall had been in 1581, in expectation of increased revenue for the harbour. The new building of 1606 might have served the ruling group as a reminder of their commercial and legal power in the town and therefore as some compensation for their loss of control over the harbour. In its windows were worked the arms of the king, the Cinque Ports, and the burgess to parliament, Sir Thomas Waller. Thus the building had built into it the emblems of the town's new dependence upon the Crown and its agents.[24]

---

[21] Do/AAm 2, fol. 19.

[22] Jeffery R. Hankins, "Crown, Country and Corporation in Early Seventeenth Century Essex," *Sixteenth Century Journal* 38 (2007): 27–47, at 46–47.

[23] Whitfield, East Kent Archives, Do/AAm 2, fols. 16, 17v.

[24] For further discussion of the significance of town halls see Robert Tittler, *Architecture and Power: The Town Hall and the English Urban Community c.1500–1640* (Oxford: Clarendon Press, 1991).

2.

Tooke's biography glimpsed in the town records for Dover points to a number of occasions on which he represented the town's interests to external parties; and his career as a whole exhibits a tireless interest in the harbour and its maintenance. He arrived in Dover from Hythe in about 1574 and obtained his freedom by purchase of a freehold in 1586, presumably by then having resources of his own. Tooke's first public appointment was as one of the council's cessors for ship cess in 1588, although he was not actually elected to the common council until 1590. He took his first step onto the oligarchic ladder by the customary method of being appointed one of the four chamberlains, responsible for the town's finances, in 1590–1591. His subsequent appointments were usually connected with work at the harbour, as an auditor of the ship, bench, and dike cess in 1592 and one of the directors of the "beach work" in 1593. He was also sent as a representative to the Brotherhood meeting of the Cinque Ports in 1595.[25]

By the early 1600s, when it is likely this manuscript was compiled, Tooke was a substantial member of an educated Protestant ruling elite in Dover. He was first elected jurat, or magistrate, of the town in May 1603, in time to be one of the men sent to plead with the Lord Warden for the renewal of the Statute of Tonnage. He was elected bailiff to Yarmouth in 1604, a largely ceremonial post which would have brought him into touch with officers of similar rank in the other Cinque Ports and which usually presaged election to the mayoralty. He became master of the almshouse in 1605, was appointed one of the overseers of work on the new court hall in June 1606, and was elected mayor in September of that year but never again despite being twice nominated. He continued to act in the interests of the harbour, and was given £5 in 1613 for his "great care and pains" in serving for a second year as Surveyor of the Harbour, which was by then a gratis appointment. He died in 1617 having already disposed of his boats. His will testifies to his relative wealth, recording his many leases in Dover including a storehouse and a herring hanger, and his goods totalled over £472.[26]

Tooke's probably incomplete manuscript, now British Library, MS. Add. 12514, "A Discourse of Dovor Harbor since the tyme that Julius Ceaser first entred this realme until the raigne of our late soveraigne Queene Elizabeth of Famous memory," is a first-person narrative which discursively explores the history of the port. As will be discussed in more detail, Tooke uses a wide range of sources in the compilation of his "Discourse." When he addresses the more recent history of the port his style and his sources change from discursive engagement with chronicles to the kind of personal testimony seen in witness depositions,

---

[25] Canterbury, Canterbury Cathedral Archives and Library, X.11.7, fol. 142; London, British Library, MS. Egerton 2095, fols. 326, 380ᵛ, 384, 394, 401, 403.

[26] Whitfield, East Kent Archives, Do/AAm 2, fols. 6, 214, 23, 55; Maidstone, Centre for Kentish Studies, PRC 32/44, fol. 365ᵛ.

and he gives eyewitness accounts of meetings between the Kent Commission-
ers and members of the Privy Council in London and then in Dover in 1584.
Tooke then continues his history of the port by presenting four distinct pieces:
"The Conference had betweene John Tooke and William Gilbert touching the
sayed harborowe before the mayor and jurattes of the sayed towne and other
marryners ther before the meeting of the commissioners"; "A Dialogue betwene
Opynion and Reasone concerning the openinge and keeping open of Dovor
Harbor"; "Certayne Arguementes made by John Tooke betweene the Master and
wardens of the Trynitye house of London and the wardens of the fellowshipe of
Loadmandage of Dovor concerninge the tonnage of Dovor Harbor" formatted
as a dialogue between 'London' and 'Dovor'; and "John Tookes petitione to Sir
Thomas Fane Leutenant of Dovor castle for the setting of the stone sluce in the
best place," presented in a question-and-answer format.[27] These latter pieces are
linked together with a bridging narrative by Tooke except for the last "Petitione"
which is separated from the rest of the work by a single blank folio and which
may mark the beginning of a new section, although the verso of this final folio
is considerably discoloured suggesting that it had served as the back of the pamphlet for a time. Tooke's rhetorical range is that of an educated man with some
knowledge of the classics.[28] He is well versed in the political life of Dover and is
able to negotiate a range of genres and modes of address to suit particular situations, from historical discourse to deposition, to dialogue between social equals
and across social distinctions.

Taken individually, the sections of the manuscript can be seen to correspond
with Tooke's own involvement in the negotiations for the harbour works. As well
as his attendance at meetings in London and Dover, Tooke was one of the men
chosen to petition the Lord Warden of the Cinque Ports in 1603 for renewal of
the Statute of Tonnage and, in 1605, he was a member of the party sent to negotiate the future of the harbour with the new king.[29] It is entirely possible that
pieces within the manuscript such as his dialogue "Certayne Arguementes [. . .]
concerninge the tonnage of Dovor Harbor" were presented at these meetings and
that the work as a whole was compiled for presentation to the new monarch in
1605.[30] It perhaps also indicates that Tooke was influenced by classical humanist and specifically Ciceronian ideals concerning the active role of the citizen in
processes of governance through the provision of written advice.[31] This pragmatic context for texts within the collection links it to the many other documents

---

[27] London, British Library, MS. Add. 12514, fols. 33–45ᵛ.

[28] See Tooke's reference to "the beach of Oblivion," London, British Library, MS.
Add. 12514, fol. 37.

[29] Whitfield, East Kent Archives, Do/AAm 2, fol. 16.

[30] We are grateful to Dr Astrid Stilma for confirming this practice.

[31] Q. Skinner, *The Foundations of Modern Political Thought*, 2 vols. (Cambridge:
Cambridge University Press, 1978), 1: 81.

reporting on or petitioning for the harbour works, such as Thomas Digges' 1582 work, "A briefe discourse declaringe how honorable and profitable to youre most excellent majestie and howe necessary and commodiouse for your realme, the making of Dover Haven shalbe", and it is entirely possible that Tooke initially composed the "Dialogue", "Arguementes", and "Petitione" for circulation with a view to presenting them to a particular local patron, perhaps the mayor, but more likely to the Lieutenant of the Castle or to a gentry commissioner.[32]

This initial context for production is made more compelling when we consider Tooke's use of the dialogue form, which closely resembles the format adopted by many of the other harbour-related pieces written in this period.[33] Burke recognises the dialogue as a Renaissance "phenomenon."[34] Commenting on its ubiquity, he also highlights some very relevant motivations for its popularity. He states that "its immediacy made the dialogue an appropriate medium for the presentation of controversial issues." He argues that it was a format that facilitated oral dissemination and highlights the existence of formal discussion groups which could comprise "a social base" or "stimulus" for the texts.[35] Furthermore, it can be argued that Tooke's choice of dialogue form is a natural extension of the climate of dispute and debate that surrounded the harbour works and which characterises other pieces in the manuscript. In employing what Burke characterises as the "disputation" form in which "different points of view are expressed but one speaker is allowed to win, more or less subtly," Tooke perhaps sought to educate and persuade his audience of readers and listeners in Dover and beyond.[36] Other contemporary authors testified to the accessibility of this format: "I haue done it in waye of a Dialogue, to make the fitter for the capacity of the simpler sort" claimed one author in 1593.[37]

One of the rarer 'gentlemen' mariners, John Tooke had connections in the town with the educated Protestant elite, but in his will he also named a "loving kinsman," John Tooke of London, to whom he left his gold seal ring.[38] John Pringle, a Dover baker and merchant who frequently acted as overseer to the wills of seamen, was one of Tooke's witnesses. Pringle was elected mayor in 1626, stood as burgess to Parliament, and was reportedly "well acquainted with proceedings in

---

[32] "A briefe discourse declaringe how honorable and profitable to youre most excellent majestie and howe necessary and commodiouse for your realme, the making of Dover Haven shalbe and in what sorte, with leaste charge in greateste perfection the same may be accomplished," *Archaeologia* 11 (1794): 212–54.

[33] See for example London, The National Archives, SP12/170, fol. 158, May 1584.

[34] Peter Burke, "The Renaisssance Dialogue," *Renaissance Studies* 3 (1989): 1–12, at 2.

[35] Burke, "The Renaissance Dialogue," 7–8.

[36] Burke, "The Renaissance Dialogue," 2–3.

[37] George Gifford, *A Dialogue concerning Witches and Witchcrafts* (1593), fol. A3.

[38] Maidstone, Centre for Kentish Studies, PRC 32/44, fol. 365ᵛ.

Parliament."[39] It is perhaps a significant indicator of Tooke's status in the town that Pringle, together with two other well-educated men, Francis Raworth and Randolph Partridge, stood as witnesses of his will. Francis Raworth, gentleman, was appointed as town clerk in 1601. Born in Dovebridge in Derby, he had been resident in Chart-next-Sutton for twelve years and had only recently settled in Dover.[40] He was a frequent witness to wills of men of substance in the town and to those of a Protestant inclination. His own will, with its fervent assurance of salvation, asked that "his loving friend" John Reading the Calvinist preacher at St Mary's should preach at his funeral.[41] When William Fulbeck, minister of Waldershare, died in 1616, he left four "divinity books in English" to Raworth and "all my books of civil law, canon law or common law" to Raworth's son. He also left "four of my divinity books in English which shall be the most meet for his understanding" to Randolph Partridge of Dover, and "four small books of humanity" to his younger son Randolph or Randell Partridge.[42] Such educated associates, together with the suggestive bequeathing of books, are also perhaps indicative of one level of the coterie context in which BL MS. Add. 12514 was compiled.

While it is possible to assert an initial pragmatic context in which to consider the compilation of sections of this manuscript, it is also possible to conceive a secondary quasi-literary context which the writings assume as a collection. The formatting of the manuscript suggests that Tooke might have been preparing it for circulation in printed or manuscript form and that it should be read in its entirety rather than as a series of unconnected individual items. The manuscript's final resting-place in a "volume of heraldic and historical treatises" directly alongside other pieces related to the Lords Cobham, the jurisdiction of the Lord Warden of the Cinque Ports, and the constables of Dover castle written by Francis Thynne reflect the interests of at least one "Gentle reader."[43] In this context perhaps, Tooke's figuring of the collection of texts as a "Discourse" is a significant act. This transformation of a series of distinct stand-alone pieces into a history of the harbour locates the manuscript in a potentially very interesting coterie environment that corresponded with the literary interests of the gentry commissioners and with conventions of textual production and circulation in elite society in Kent.

Literary patronage proliferated in the county during Elizabeth's reign. William Brooke, Lord Cobham, for example was patron of the second edition of

---

[39] *Calendar of State Papers, Domestic Series, Preserved in the Public Record Office: Coverage 1547–1704*, 66 vols. (London: HMSO, 1856–), *1628–29*: 130/73.

[40] Canterbury, Canterbury Cathedral Archives and Library, X.11.8.

[41] Maidstone, Centre for Kentish Studies, PRC 32/46, fol. 188.

[42] Maidstone, Centre for Kentish Studies, PRC 32/44, fol. 249ᵛ.

[43] London, British Library, MS. Add. 12514, fol. 36; see David Carlson, "The Writings and Manuscript Collections of the Elizabethan Alchemist, Antiquary and Herald Francis Thynne," *Huntington Library Quarterly* 52 (1989): 203–72.

Holinshed's *Chronicle*, which included an extensive account of the recent harbour works by Reginald Scot.[44] Significantly, the association of BL MS. Add. 12514 with other texts concerning the Cinque Ports and Dover Castle either written or annotated by Francis Thynne provides a further link to this family, as Thynne presented a manuscript copy of his history of the Lords Cobham to Sir Henry Brooke, Lord Cobham, in 1598.[45] Tooke's verbatim copying of William Lambarde's *Perambulation of Kent* is also suggestive, as the second edition of this work (1596) included new material on the building of the harbour and the work as a whole was dedicated initially to the Kentish gentleman Thomas Wotton who subsequently dedicated the work to the Kentish gentry as a whole. Finally, Tooke's reference to the viewing of a book "written by Parsone Dorrell, as the owner of the book tould me" may provide a suggestive link to the antiquarian activities of Archbishop Parker's circle if this work was William Darrell's treatise on Kentish castles.[46]

Tooke demonstrates an awareness of printed works circulating on Kentish history and of the kinds of texts that would appeal to influential Kentish patrons. Recent trends, it could be argued, existed in terms of both precedent and patronage for the successful circulation of a history of Dover harbour, and it is possible that the collected writings were compiled for a particular Kentish patron such as Sir Thomas Fane. However, what is perhaps most striking about the manuscript is the central and essential voice of Tooke himself. Tooke's narrative of the negotiation of relations between town and Crown in the 1580s and 1590s places him not only at the centre of events but also as a recorder of the town's history and as the compiler of pragmatic and purposeful texts used to promote the interests of the town. In his retelling of events, Tooke creates a new narrative which places his own skills and expertise at its centre.

---

[44] For further details see Claire Bartram, "The Reading and Writing Practices of the Kentish Gentry: The Emergence of a Protestant Identity in Elizabethan Kent" (Ph.D. diss., University of Kent, 2004). Scot championed his kinsman Sir Thomas Scott in his narrative and is one example of a writer who consistently sought Kentish patronage for his works.

[45] London, British Library, MS. Add. 39184, "The hystorye, lyves, descentes and successions of the howse and Barons of Cobham" (1598).

[46] London, British Library, Ms. Add. 12514, fol. 33; Patrick Collinson, "The Protestant Cathedral, 1541–1660," in *A History of Canterbury Cathedral*, ed. idem, Nigel Ramsey, and Margaret Sparks (Oxford: Oxford University Press, 1995), 153–203, at 169; May McKisack, *Medieval History in the Tudor Age* (Oxford: Oxford University Press, 1971), 20, 29–30, 49.

3.

The community of Dover was formed from a changing population that probably tripled between 1500 and 1640. At any given time there were a number of dynamic and overlapping sub-communities. The family, in the sense both of blood-kin and of wider groups based on friendship and mutual obligation, played a significant role in the maintenance of these communities, particularly among those whose trade depended on the ownership of capital resources in ships, buildings, and equipment or land—notably therefore among mariners, innkeepers, brewers, and butchers. The largest occupational group in the town was formed by the mariners, whose families bonded most closely together and who exhibited the most apparent clan-like identity from intermarriage and a territorial distinction in the town through continuous residence in St James's parish. The inventories of seafarers show that most of them owned very few goods, and their limited financial means, together with the frequent absences from the town that their occupation demanded, meant that they were the least likely sector of society to enter the ruling elite. Of the 107 men to hold the office of mayor between 1500 and 1606, only eight were mariners, and they were men who were primarily wealthy shipowners in their own right.[47]

Another significant group were the brewers, who had substantial capital invested in land and equipment, with strong familial ties in the rural hinterland and business links in the town. Like the mariners, they allied themselves by marriage and operated a system of mutual benefit and obligation. By the seventeenth century some of them became more dependent on selling and shipping grain than on brewing beer. A number of Dover's more distinguished mayors came from this group. A third significant group were the innkeepers and innholders. Probably more than any other group, they came to have connections outside the immediate area, developing an unusually close relationship with the castle and the Crown thanks to their provision of hospitality to the castle's visitors and to noblemen waiting to cross the Channel. In the late sixteenth and early seventeenth century immigrants from as far afield as London, Tadcaster, and Flanders seem to have used the ownership of inns to enter into clientage and office with men whose connections were with the Crown rather than the town of Dover.[48]

Evidence from the manuscript reinforces biographical evidence of John Tooke's activity in local town government as a representative of the town's interests. His ability to present evidence and to argue a cause, together with his ability, as he presents it, to negotiate with different parties across the social spectrum, are suggestive of an individual with a keen familiarity with the social complexities of Dover society. Tooke undertakes to record a series of negotiations in his

---

[47] Dixon, "Economy and Society in Dover," chap. 4, 376–88.
[48] Dixon, "Economy and Society in Dover," chap. 4, 398–402, and esp. 389–98.

historical discourse, the first between the recorded evidence of written histories and what might be termed 'Dovorian' knowledge and experience. In the subsequent 'eyewitness' sections concerning the position of the new harbour mouth, Tooke can be seen to be depicting the establishment of consensus as the experiential knowledge of the mariners is successfully challenged and the mayor's party is overruled by the Lieutenant of the Castle and the county gentry commissioners. Tooke is careful to counter this situation in his depiction of Lord Burghley as a fair-minded arbitrator of the two proposals who advocates further detailed hearings at Dover rather than overruling one party or the other. Tooke also seeks to further validate his party in his depiction of the mariners as obstinate in "The conference had betweene John Tooke and William Gilbert." The establishment of consensus is also apparent in the use of dialogue form in the final pieces in the work.

Seeking evidence for a working or purpose-built harbour at Dover at an early date, Tooke's opening pages of "A Discourse of Dovor Harbor" negotiate a range of sources. Tooke's report of what contemporary chroniclers and antiquarians William "Lambert" (*sic*; Lambarde), "Hollinshed", "Mr Stowe" and others "sayeth" about the Roman and Saxon history of the harbour is countered by his "owne poore judgement" based on an intimate knowledge of Dover, its people and geography. Tooke evaluates this printed evidence against what "I myself have seene" and "herd men saye" in Dover.[49] His evidence includes the town accounts for the repairs to the harbour completed under Henry VIII: the "bookes of the charges of worke within the wyke bearing the date in the second year of Henry viijth with the names of the officers and workmen."[50] Tooke's evidence extends beyond "those bookes" to the streets of Dover itself. "See my house in the Fyshmarkett" he asserts, "and that parte which standeth at the other syde of the brooke standeth uppon beach, see the very flowers of the sayd house at this day is beach mingled with earth." This material is bolstered by the anecdotal evidence of Dover men like "Thomas Chalice yett a lyve and borne in Dovor and brought up in the Masondue," and William Gyles and Thomas Watsone aged eighty-four and eighty-five years respectively when they died in 1599, and also by surmise from things he had *not* "herd." Concluding that the Henrician alterations to the harbour joined previous repairs undertaken by the townsfolk, Tooke clarifies, "I say by the towne because that I never herd that the Kinge of this realm nor any other did any work within the wyke before this tyme."[51]

The sense that Tooke is engaging with local opinion and debate about the history of the harbour is apparent in his conversational style. His question "But how I

---

[49] London, British Library, MS. Add. 12514, fols. 33, 33ᵛ, 34.

[50] London, British Library, MS. Add. 12514, fol. 36ᵛ, now London, British Library, MS. Egerton 2108.

[51] London, British Library, MS. Add. 12514, fols. 33, 35, 34, 35, 36ᵛ.

must answer some that say [. . .] [that] it was not likely that the Havins mouth was stopped with beach" is countered by evidence from the streets of Dover.

> But if any think the havins mouth was not choked with beach he is deceived [. . .] for I my selfe have seene one hole under the [town] wal agaynst the stable of The George wher you might playnly see that the foundacons of the wall was sett uppon the beach.[52]

Elsewhere he can be found to be in agreement with local consensus — "I agree with them that say the towne did stand uppon both sydes of the river" — or to be appealing to a shared sense of 'Dovorian' 'experience'. "Yet" he comments in rationalising his argument, "the freshwater which stood within would breake thorough the beach somtymes at one place and sometymes at another as wee by experience well knowe."[53] This sense of what "We knowe" reflects a very specific relationship with the coastal waterways around the town and their very real capacity to cause the economic and physical structure of the town to erode and evolve.

The authorities within Dover that Tooke uses to bolster his position, the town accounts, the remembrances of elderly townsfolk, and other things he had "herd saye" as well as evidence from the streets of Dover, transforms this into a 'Dover-centric' text that can be successfully navigated only by someone with a specialist knowledge of the town. Familiarity with the layout of the town, of where St James Street is or where Mr Elwoodes's lime kilns are or where "Goodman Tydeman" lives, is essential to comprehend Tooke's argument. The authority of Tydeman, Chalice, Gyles, Watsone, and indeed Tooke himself is dependent on an understanding of the communities and power structures within Dover itself.

The 'experience' of those who lived and worked in this coastal town becomes a powerful theme across subsequent sections of the work as Tooke dramatises the conflicting authorities who had an interest in the maintenance of the harbour at Dover. The two subsequent sections of the "Discourse" dramatise the dispute that arose concerning the site for the mouth of the new harbour. While Tooke's section on the ancient history of the port demonstrated his capacity for historical discourse, these subsequent two sections present Tooke as an eyewitness, a credible observer of event and personality. It is interesting to note that many of those local authorities appealed to in the construction of his narrative of the haven's history are from precisely that quarter within Dover society that, in the shift of style in these subsequent verbatim sections, appear to be jeopardising the harbour's future by disputing the site of the harbour entrance. If Tooke is prepared to engage with local debates about the history of the haven in the streets of Dover or in early printed accounts in "A Discourse", these subsequent verbatim sections are more concerned with demonstrating the establishment of consensus.

---

[52] MS. Add. 12514, fol. 34ᵛ.
[53] MS. Add. 12514, fol. 35.

Opinion was split between those who supported the platt of the proposed harbour initiated by the mayor and those who supported Richard Barry, Lieutenant of Dover Castle. The mayor's party included mariners such as William Tydeman and Thomas Watsone and the townsman William Gilbert. Sir William Winter, surveyor and master of ordinance of the Navy, and William Borough, the famed navigator and comptroller of the Navy, spoke out in defence of constructing the harbour entrance between the Black Bulwark and Stoneham's Head.[54] Richard Barry's party included Sir Richard Grynfeild, Mr Thomas Digges, and Tooke himself. On witnessing the water being drained from the harbour "close by the south Head" Barry argued that to set the harbour entrance here instead would "prove [. . .] better for the harbor and [be] fynished with the lesse charge." Barry's reasoning was presented to "Mr Secritary" Lord Burghley "if it stand with your good lykinge to here mee," at an initial meeting of the parties in London at which Tooke was present. However, Burghley determined that the mariners of Dover were not sufficiently represented at this meeting and announced that "It is the councalls plesure that the comissioners shall meet at Dovor very shortly to take the opyniones of the mareners and that ther opiniones shall be followed concerning the entrance or mouth of the harbor or any other worke about the harbour."[55]

Burghley's comments suggest that the mariners possessed a valuable specialist knowledge and experience of seafaring, but this is not borne out by Tooke's account. Tooke vividly depicts two altercations with the mariners. In the first untitled piece he contrasts the formal courtesies of the London meeting and the reasoned argument of Barry against the response of the Dover mariners to the Commission held at Dover:

> 'Mr Watsone,' sayed Mr Boyse, 'What say you, where is the best place [for the haven's entrance]?' 'In the Broad Bight', sayed hee. 'What is your reason that that is the beste place?' Sayed Mr Boyse. 'I have no reason but that that is the best place' Sayed Mr Watsone.[56]

Here the mariners are depicted as obstinate and argumentative, and the dispute is settled only when "Mr Barry caused one of his men to goe fetch him a compast and Sir Thomas Scott and hee with the rest of the comissioners went to the haven's mouth and all the marryners." In so doing, Barry was able to demonstrate that his choice of site would enable "the entrance or mouth [to] come norwest in and goe southest out." Challenging the mariners, "they could not deny but that it would" serve as well as their proposed harbour entrance. "Then, said Sir Thomas Scott, 'Lett there be a draught made in wrightinge and let them sett ther hande

---

[54] Colvin, "Dover Harbour," 4.2: 755, 758.
[55] London, British Library, MS. Add. 12514, fols. 39–39[v].
[56] MS. Add. 12514, fol. 39[v].

to it.' Which all the marryners did."[57] The defeat of the mariners was significant not least because of Burghley's assertion that their opinions would be sought and followed. The brandishing of the compass is perhaps a redolent symbol of conflicting forms of knowledge and authority within the town. Respect for the mariners as learned elders with direct experiential knowledge is diminished by the reasoned, quasi-scientific demonstration by Barry and by the fact that the mariners appear to have had no political leverage within the town.

"The Conference had betweene John Tooke and William Gilbert" offers a further snapshot of the opposing parties as the mariners accuse Tooke of telling a "fayre tale and nothing treue." Tooke responds:

> Then, sayed I, 'It was esier for you to say soo then to prove it so.' Then I tooke William Tydeman by the hand and sayed unto him, 'You are a man of reasone, I marvayle you will stand agaynst it, being so playne.' 'It is not playne to me,' Sayed he, 'and I have set my hand to the platt and I will not goo agaynst my hand.'[58]

Here Tooke reinforces the points he is making about the mariners and politics in Dover. Tooke's retort that the mariners cannot easily prove him wrong follows after their very visible humiliation at the harbour and the vindication of Tooke's stance. The mariners are depicted as slanderers of good men, are unable to reason their position (as Watsone demonstrates), and are obstinate in the extreme. Of course Tydeman (or Tiddyman as his name appears in other documents) was known by the Privy Council to be outspoken and, perhaps worse, was associated with the factionalism that had only very recently dominated Dover town government. Significantly, Tydeman's assertion that he could not break his allegiance to the platt that he signed could, in other circumstances, have been used positively to depict the loyalty of the mariners to the mayoral party. Sir Thomas Scott's assertion that all the mariners should "sett ther hande" to a new document breaks that allegiance and symbolises how consensus was achieved.

The rendering of the final three sections as "dialoge" or "arguement" appropriately continues the process of negotiation that characterised these earlier sections of the "Discourse". The three dialogues represent three further stages in the harbour repairs. The first, a "Dialoge betwene Opynione and Reason", was written in response to "some of the towne of the best and yet lyvinge" who disputed the efficacy of the sluice to drive out the beach from the harbour in neap tides and argued that the beach be allowed to block the harbour entrance so that a new mouth could be opened on the north side. The dialogue is spirited, with both Reason and Opinion calling each other "strange" for pursuing their lines of argument. As might be expected, Reason wins the debate, not by disputing

---

[57] MS. Add. 12514, fol. 40.
[58] MS. Add. 12514, fol. 41.

the inefficiency of the sluice in particular weather or tidal conditions but by emphasising that it were "better to have a reasonable harbour" in all but the most extreme conditions "than none at all." The second, a dialogue between London merchants and Dover lodesmen, debated whether the renewal of the Act of Tonnage in 1601 was beneficial to the realm or just to Dover.[59] Arguments about the strategic value of Dover as a harbour in times of war, in bad weather, or for quick passage and effective trade lead to the conclusion by 'Dovor' that "I hope none of discretion will denye but that a good harbor for shipping at Dovor is good both for the cittye of London and the whole realme."[60]

The final piece in the manuscript is addressed to Sir Thomas Fane, Lieutenant of Dover Castle, and concerns the "setting of the stone sluice in the best place," which can be linked to work undertaken on a replacement stone sluice in 1598. Formatted initially as a letter—"Right Worshipful Sir," begins Tooke—the piece becomes an interview between Fane and Tooke. "We are both friendes to Dovor harbour" begins 'Question,' "therefore let me here your opynione." The formal manner of Question's invitations to 'Answer', "I pray you let me here wher you think it best, that when all men's opynions be knowne the best way may be taken," recalls the formal interviewing by Burghley of Barry in London, whom he invited to "pray, speake." Furthermore, 'Question' is clearly a figure imbued with the status and authority to act on the information that he elicits from 'Answer'.[61] Tooke's role as 'Answer' is one which he would have frequently undertaken as a representative of the town.[62]

4.

Little attention has been given to Tooke's manuscript by historians. In Colvin's grand narrative of the harbour works, Tooke's text is used as a means of corroborating events and, strikingly, the events and the people that Tooke himself chooses to write about barely feature in Colvin's reconstruction.[63] Ash's recent article on "Expertise, Authority and the Rebuilding of Dover Harbour" also gives surprisingly scant attention to BL MS. Add. 12514, and instead it is the expertise of the gentry commissioners and specifically Thomas Digges that is

---

[59] The better class of sailors were lodesmen, and there was a Court of Lodemanage (or Lodemenage) to which men belonged and which operated in a strictly hierarchical order. It stipulated which ships could go out of the harbour and in what order, and the lodesmen were also responsible for surveying the coast and reporting on problems; probably the best modern equivalent would be 'pilotage.'

[60] MS. Add. 12514, fols. 41ᵛ, 44.

[61] MS. Add. 12514, fols. 45–45ᵛ.

[62] See for example Whitfield, East Kent Archives, Do/AAm 2, fols. 10ᵛ, 15ᵛ.

[63] Colvin, "Dover Harbour," 4.2: 729–68.

singled out for analysis.[64] Close analysis of this manuscript, however, highlights the important role that the people of Dover played in debating the form the harbour works should take and in negotiating the patronage and power structures at a county and state level. As such, Tooke's manuscript provides evidence of the "social depth" of engagement with matters concerning the harbour works.[65] Crucially, it also widens and rebalances Ash's depiction of events, for while there were indeed polymath gentlemen such as Thomas Digges on hand to act as expert "facilitators of knowledge" in liaising with the Privy Council, there were also men within Dover society who also had some claim to expertise.[66] Even brief literary analysis of the language and genres chosen by Tooke reveals his considerable ability to communicate that expertise and to represent the interests of the town.

Literary and social-historical analysis of this document also repositions discussion about the harbour works if not in their rightful, then in an appropriate context, that of relations between town and Crown in a period which witnessed an intensification of dialogue between the centre and the localities.[67] Tooke's narrative offers insight into how consensus was achieved within the town, and crucially how the local patronage of Crown appointees, such as the Lieutenant of the Castle, was instrumental in achieving this consensus. Equally striking is Tooke's depiction of the intervention of the Crown-appointed gentry commissioners, such as Sir Thomas Scott, who actively sought to consolidate that consensus. As such, this reading of Tooke's text reinforces the paradigm of the interactive nature of central and local relations in which, as Patterson has demonstrated, the civic governors played an active part in shaping patronage relations, enlisting aid to serve the purposes of themselves and their communities.[68]

When Tooke was elected as mayor in September of 1605 the nature of relations between Dover and the Crown had been significantly rebalanced, the pragmatic surrender of the harbour reinforcing a move by the ruling group towards the support of the Crown-appointed officials of the castle which the early 1580s

---

[64] Ash, "'A Perfect and an Absolute Work'," 266–67.

[65] For further discussion of the social range of individuals involved in early modern governance see Hindle, *The State and Social Change*, 12.

[66] For further discussion of such 'Facilitators' see Lisa Jardine and Anthony Grafton, "'Studied for Action': How Gabriel Harvey Read his Livy," *Past and Present* 129 (1990): 30–78; William H. Sherman, *John Dee: The Politics of Reading and Writing in the Renaissance* (Amherst: University of Massachusetts Press, 1995). See also C. Bartram, "Chronicling Dover: Reconstructing Book Culture in Elizabethan Kent," in *Book Culture in Provincial Communities: Contexts for Reading and Writing 1400–1700*, ed. eadem (forthcoming).

[67] Hindle, *The State and Social Change*, 12.

[68] C. Patterson, *Urban Patronage in Early Modern England: Corporate Boroughs, the Landed Elite and the Crown 1580–1640* (Stanford: Stanford University Press, 1999), 6–7.

factionalism had largely set in play. Equally, Tooke took on the mayoralty at a time when many of those gentry commissioners, pillars of Kentish society under Elizabeth I who had played such a key role in the 1580s harbour works, were now aging or deceased and a new generation of sometimes Crown-appointed non-Kentish personnel were assuming their place.[69] In the last decades of Elizabeth's reign, it seems likely that Tooke was seen by the representatives of the Crown as a man likely to save them money on their project and by the commonalty as a man well placed to press for the interests of the town. Moreover, in the early years of James I's reign, Tooke's manuscript projects his reputation as a man who was capable, educated, prudent, and indifferent (i.e. not prejudiced), effectively advertising his expertise in a changing political climate, where he could be the pivotal actor between the Crown and 'his' town.[70]

---

[69] For the history of the county in this period see Peter Clark, *English Provincial Society from the Reformation to the Revolution: Religion, Politics and Society in Kent 1500–1640* (Hassocks: Harvester Press, 1977), and Michael Zell, ed., *Early Modern Kent 1540–1640* (Woodbridge: Boydell Press, 2000).

[70] For further discussion of the balance between private interest and public responsibility amongst office holders see Hindle, *The State and Social Change*, 21–23.

THE VIEW FROM THE OUTSIDE: RELATIONS BETWEEN CROWN AND TOWN

CROWN AND TOWN IN
LATER MEDIEVAL ENGLAND:
BRISTOL AND NATIONAL POLITICS, 1399–1486

PETER FLEMING

With some notable exceptions, the historiography of political relations between Crown and subject in later medieval England has been dominated by the shires and the rural elites, rather than by towns and cities. This is entirely understandable, given that, compared to Flanders or northern Italy, England in this period was a predominantly rural society with an economy based largely on agriculture and its products. On the other hand, market production and trade, both internal and external, were a fundamental part of its economy, and the urban foci of that trade provided resources of money, men, ships, and services whose control was crucial to the effective governance of the realm. English towns, in short, were of immense political importance. Studies of political relations between English towns and the Crown and magnates have tended to focus on the symbiotic relationship between Crown and capital, for obvious reasons, but there has been some discussion of provincial towns in this context.[1]

---

[1] These exceptions include A. Green, *Town Life in the Fifteenth Century*, 2 vols. (London: Macmillan, 1894); A. P. M. Wright, "The Relations between the King's Government and the English Cities and Boroughs in the Fifteenth Century" (D.Phil. diss., University of Oxford, 1965); Susan Reynolds, *An Introduction to the History of English Medieval Towns* (Oxford: Oxford University Press, 1977), 179; Lorraine Attreed, "The English Royal Government and its Relations with the Boroughs of Norwich, York, Exeter and Nottingham" (Ph.D. diss., Harvard University, 1984); eadem, *The King's Towns: Identity and Survival in Late Medieval English Boroughs* (Frankfurt a.M.: Lang, 2001). In addition, Christian D. Liddy has produced important work on relations between towns and the Crown in later medieval England, particularly, in this context, *War, Politics and Finance in Late Medieval English Towns: Bristol, York and the Crown, 1350–1400* (Woodbridge: Boydell Press, 2005). For London, see Jim L. Bolton, "The City and the Crown,

Negotiating the Political in Northern European Urban Society, c.1400–c.1600, ed. Sheila Sweetinburgh, MRTS 434 (Tempe: ACMRS, 2013).   [ISBN 978-0-86698-482-9]

This essay takes Bristol as a case study, with particular emphasis on the fifteenth century. There are good reasons for choosing this particular town for special attention. Bristol ranked as the third wealthiest and most populous urban
community in later medieval England. After London it was England's most significant port. In 1373 it was elevated to the status of a county, the first provincial town or city in England to be given this honour. As a regional capital, its
hinterland included south Wales as well as the English South-west and West
Midlands. During the Hundred Years War, Bristol made major contributions to
the war effort, in the form of money and shipping supplied to the Crown, and
through its situation commanding the south-western approaches.[2] The town's
wealth, strategic position, and relative proximity to London made it a potentially important feature in England's political geography in the central and later
Middle Ages.[3]

This essay focuses on Bristol's relations with the Crown and those magnates
with local interests in the period that begins in 1399 with the deposition of Richard II and the struggle by his usurper, Henry IV, to establish his authority; en-
compasses the dynastic conflict known as the Wars of the Roses; and ends soon
after the accession of Henry Tudor in 1485. For England as a whole, this was a
period of repeated political crises. Bristol's political history in this period mirrors
the national picture.

Political actors, situations, and crises came and went, but in Bristol, as elsewhere, politics was played out within a more stable framework. Bristol's geographical situation and commercial significance, coupled with its position within
the feudal network of magnate landholding and jurisdiction, meant that certain
leitmotifs run through the history of its relations with the English Crown between Conquest and Reformation. There are three main forces at play in this history: the ambitions and demands, respectively, of the urban elite, of the Crown,
and of locally important magnate dynasties. In attempting to understand how
these interacted in a period towards the end of this *longue durée* it is useful to

---

1456–61," *London Journal* 12 (1986): 11–12; R. R. Sharp, *London and the Kingdom*, 3 vols.
(London: Longmans, Green & co., 1894–1995); and the following works by Caroline
M. Barron: "The Government of London and its Relations with the Crown, 1400–1450"
(Ph.D. diss., University of London, 1970); eadem, "London and the Crown, 1451–61," in
The Crown and Local Communities in England and France in the Fifteenth Century, ed. J. R.
L. Highfield and R. Jeffs (Gloucester: Sutton, 1981), 88–109; *London in the Later Middle
Ages: Government and People 1200–1500* (Oxford: Oxford University Press, 2004).

[2] Liddy, *War*, 19–57.

[3] For Bristol's ranking among later medieval English towns, see Alan Dyer, "Ranking Lists of English Medieval Towns," in *The Cambridge Urban History of Britain*, 1: 600–
1540, ed. David Palliser (Cambridge: Cambridge University Press, 2000), 747–70, at
768. For fourteenth-century Bristol, see Liddy, *War*, esp. chapters 2–5, and James Sherborne, *The Port of Bristol in the Middle Ages* (Bristol: Bristol Branch of the Historical Association [hereafter BHA], 1965).

separate the localised from the long term, and to understand how and why these relationships had developed up to the end of the fourteenth century.

From the Conquest to the Black Death

Bristol appears to have originated as a late-Saxon burgh. From the eleventh century onwards, Bristol's geographical situation, looking towards the southern end of the Anglo-Welsh border, meant that it commanded an important strategic position in the Anglo-Norman expansion into South Wales and, then and later, was close to the reserves of men, money, and lordship offered by the Welsh March. By the 1080s the Normans had demonstrated their awareness of Bristol's strategic significance by constructing a castle. The port of Bristol played a prominent role as a base for expansion into Ireland from the 1160s onwards. Bristol's wealth and strategic importance meant that its control was often a major objective in the internecine struggles of medieval England.[4]

Throughout much of the post-Conquest Middle Ages Bristol's history is inseparable from that of two magnate estates. The first is the earldom of Gloucester; the second is the lordship of Berkeley. Their relationship with Bristol before 1399 will now be considered, followed by some discussion of points of crisis in relations between the town and the Crown over the same period.

The manor of Bristol was granted to Robert Fitz Hamon in the 1090s by William II, but it was the former's son-in-law, an illegitimate son of Henry I, Robert earl of Gloucester, who developed the town into a baronial *caput* and major provincial capital. Between 1122 and 1147 he rebuilt the castle as an imposing stone edifice, and founded the priory of St James close by, as a daughter house of the Benedictine abbey of Tewkesbury. During the conflict between King Stephen and forces loyal to the Empress Matilda the support of the marcher lords was crucial to the continued survival of her cause, and her half-brother Robert earl of Gloucester was foremost among them. From 1138 until his death in 1147 Bristol was the centre of Earl Robert's resistance to King Stephen, and the latter was briefly imprisoned in its castle. The future Henry II lived in Bristol under his uncle Robert's guardianship in 1142–1143, and conceived personal ties with both town and earl. As king, Henry's appreciation of the strategic importance of

---

[4] For Bristol in this period, see David Walker, *Bristol in the Early Middle Ages* (Bristol: BHA, 1971). For the castle, Michael Ponsford, "Bristol Castle: Archaeology and the History of a Royal Fortress" (M.A. thesis, University of Bristol, 1979), 27–28; H. M. Colvin et al., *The History of the King's Works*, 6 vols. (London: HMSO, 1963–1982), 2: 578; Peter Fleming, *Bristol Castle: A Political History* (Bristol: BHA, 2004).

Bristol, and suspicion of Robert's son and heir Earl William, led to an increasingly proprietorial attitude to what was still part of the honour of Gloucester.[5]

At some point (perhaps in the mid-1160s) Henry II took Bristol Castle into his own hands and garrisoned it with royal troops as a preventative measure against its further use as a centre of resistance to the Crown. William earl of Gloucester, rankling at this move, joined the rebellion against Henry II in 1174 and expelled the royal garrison, only to be forced to surrender the castle the following year. In 1176 William's daughter and co-heiress Isabel was contracted to marry Henry's son John, the future king, who was at that point named as heir to the earldom. Earl William's loyalties were once again in doubt in 1182 and he was arrested, dying in prison the following year. The honour of Gloucester was confiscated by the king, and Isabel and John's marriage gave Prince John control of the earldom, but with Henry still holding the castle. In 1199 King John refused to relinquish the honour after his first marriage was annulled. Bristol therefore continued as a royal borough, with the castle, the honour court, known as the Earl's Court, held at St James's Priory, and the Barton, the lands attached to the castle that extended over two hundred acres to the north and east of Bristol, also remaining in royal hands. Thereafter, the town, castle, court, and barton usually formed part of the queen's dower. The earls of Gloucester's resentment at their loss would continue to influence their political stance for much of the thirteenth century.[6]

---

[5] *Earldom of Gloucester Charters: The Charters and Scribes of the Earls and Countesses of Gloucester to AD 1217*, ed. Robert B. Patterson (Oxford: Clarendon Press, 1973), 3–9; *Gesta Stephani*, ed. and trans. K. R. Potter (Oxford: Clarendon Press, 1976), 56–57, 88–89, 114–15; *Chronica Magistri Rogeri de Hovedene*, ed. William Stubbs, Rolls Series, 4 vols. (London: Longman, 1868–1871), 1: 193, 197; Matthew Paris, *Chronica majora*, ed. Henry R. Luard, Rolls Series, 7 vols. (London: Longman, 1872–1883), 2: 167, 173; *The Historical Works of Gervase of Canterbury*, ed. William Stubbs, Rolls Series, 2 vols. (London: Longman, 1879–1880), 1: 105, 110; *Annales monastici*, ed. Henry R. Luard, Rolls Series, 5 vols. (London: Longman, 1864–1869), 4: 22 (Thomas Wykes' Chronicle); William of Malmesbury, *Gesta Regum Anglorum*, ed. William Stubbs, Rolls Series, 2 vols. (London: Longman, 1887–1889), 2: 556–57, 572; *The Historia novella of William of Malmesbury*, ed. and trans. K. R. Potter (London: Nelson and Sons, 1955), 50, 61; Robert B. Patterson, "Bristol: An Angevin Baronial Capital under Royal Siege," *Haskins Society Journal* 3 (1991): 171–81. For Geoffrey of Coutances, see John H. Le Patourel, "Geoffrey of Montbray, Bishop of Coutances, 1049–1093," *English Historical Review* 59 (1944): 129–61.

[6] *Chronicle of the Reigns of Henry II and Richard I: Benedict of Peterborough*, ed. William Stubbs, Rolls Series, 2 vols. (London: Longman, 1867), 1: 92; *Rogeri de Hovedene*, 1: 78; *Pipe Roll, 21 Henry II, 1174–75*, Pipe Roll Society 22 (London: Love & Wyman, 1897), 159; *Accounts of the Constables of Bristol Castle in the Thirteenth and Early Fourteenth Centuries*, ed. Margaret Sharp, Bristol Record Society [hereafter BRS] 34 (Bristol, 1982),

The later medieval lordship of Berkeley originated with Robert Fitz Harding, a prominent twelfth-century Bristol burgess. Unusually for a member of the Anglo-Norman elite, he was of English descent. Robert held numerous Bristol properties as a mesne tenant of Robert, earl of Gloucester, but he also purchased from the earl the manors of Bilswick in Gloucestershire, adjoining Bristol to the north, and Bedminster in Somerset, on the south bank of the Avon, encompassing the area of Redcliffe, as well as the nearby Somerset hundreds of Portbury, Bedminster, and Hartcliff. From other lords he acquired, among other properties, the manors of Portbury and of Leigh, a member of Bedminster. Robert Fitz Harding gave sterling support to Earl Robert during his struggles with Stephen. Meanwhile, Roger of Berkeley, royal tenant-in-chief and Gloucester honorial tenant, had supported Stephen, and was consequently dispossessed of his lordship. This Henry had granted to Robert Fitz Harding by 1166. Robert's Berkeley interest was cemented by a double marriage, between his eldest son Maurice and his daughter Helen and Roger's daughter Alice and eldest son Roger. With this transfer of lordship originated the Fitzharding lords of Berkeley, whose descendants still hold Berkeley Castle.[7]

Relations between the Berkeleys and Bristol were sometimes fraught. Redcliffe was a particular bone of contention.[8] By the mid-thirteenth century this part of the Berkeley manor of Bedminster, fronting the south bank of the Avon, had developed into a major commercial centre. In the 1240s Henry III ordered the men of Redcliffe to co-operate with those of Bristol in the construction of a deep-water harbour within the River Frome, running to the north of Bristol; this may well have been perceived by the men of Redcliffe as against their immediate interests, since it gave Bristol a considerable commercial advantage. In 1305 there was a serious outbreak of violence between the two communities. The point at issue was the Berkeleys' claim to separate jurisdiction, including assize of bread and ale and a pillory, in Redcliffe Street, the main thoroughfare

---

73, n. 9; Sherborne, *Port of Bristol*, 3. For Bristol as part of the queen's dower, see Liddy, *War*, 60–80.

[7] Robert B. Patterson, "Robert Fitz Harding of Bristol: Profile of an Early Angevin Burgess-Baron Patrician and his Family's Urban Involvement," *Haskins Society Journal* 1 (1989): 109–22; *A Catalogue of the Medieval Muniments at Berkeley Castle* [hereafter CMMBC] ed. Bridget Wells-Furby, Gloucestershire Record Series 17–18 (Gloucester: Bristol and Gloucestershire Archaeological Society, 2004), 1: xxi–xxiv; Nigel Saul, *Knights and Esquires: The Gloucestershire Gentry in the Fourteenth Century* (Oxford: Clarendon Press, 1981), 62–63.

[8] This paragraph is based on *Bristol Charters, 1155–1373*, ed. N. Dermott Harding, BRS 1 (1930), 18–29, 78–82; *Bristol Charters, 1378–1499*, ed. H. A. Cronne, BRS 11 (1946), 32–41; John Smyth, *The Berkeley Manuscripts: The Lives of the Berkeleys*, ed. John Maclean, Bristol and Gloucestershire Archaeological Society 1 (Gloucester: J. Bellows, 1883), 196–201; *Calendar Patent Rolls, 1301–07*, 347–48, 352, 356; *Calendar Patent Rolls, 1340–43*, 558.

running through the Redcliffe part of the manor of Bedminster. The mayor of
Bristol claimed, on the basis of a royal charter of 1247, that Redcliffe fell within
his jurisdiction. According to allegations made by both sides, the hapless Redcliffe tenants were menaced by the Berkeleys if they refused suit of court at Redcliffe, while the Berkeleys' men were intimidated by those of the mayor. The
violence allegedly spread to nearby market towns. A commission to try the case
found for Bristol, and the liberties of the manor and hundred of Bedminster were
taken into the king's hands. In 1327 Isabella and Mortimer deposed and murdered Edward II. The deed was done at Berkeley Castle, and Lord Berkeley was
a supporter of their short-lived regime. Consequently, his liberties in Bedminster
were returned to him, only to be lost again after the regime's collapse in 1330,
and in 1331 Bristol received a charter confirming its jurisdiction over Redcliffe.
The matter was still not settled, however, and contention flared up again in 1342;
the problem of transpontine jurisdiction would not be definitively solved until
the charter of 1373.

The Crown's acquisition of the Bristol appurtenances of the earldom of
Gloucester, and particularly the castle, brought it into a special relationship with
the town. That this was not always cordial is demonstrated by Bristol's involvement in the Barons' Wars between Henry III and Simon de Montfort. In June
1263 Henry III's son, the future Edward I, established himself at Bristol Castle,
intending to use it as a base from which to attack the rebel marcher lords. However, his men so antagonised the townspeople that they rose up, besieging Edward in the castle. Humiliatingly, Edward was rescued only when Walter, bishop
of Worcester, who had been sent by Simon de Montfort to negotiate with him,
persuaded the Bristolians to allow their lord to leave with the bishop as escort.
Edward left the castle garrisoned with his own men, who held out until April
1265, despite the townspeople's hostility. In June, after the fall of the town of
Gloucester, Simon de Montfort tried to cross the Severn to reach Bristol. Opinion within the town was still largely in his favour, and the Bristolians provided
a small fleet for his passage, but this was destroyed by Edward and the earl of
Gloucester. After de Montfort's defeat and death at Evesham in August, Bristol
had to pay a heavy fine for having supported him.[9]

---

[9] *Gervase of Canterbury*, 2: 221; *Chronica monasterii S. Albani Willelmi Rishanger*, ed.
Henry T. Riley, Rolls Series (London: Longman, 1865), 19, 29; *Flores historiarum*, ed.
Henry R. Luard, Rolls Series, 3 vols. (London: HMSO, 1890), 2: 482–83, 3: 3; *Royal
and Other Historical Letters Illustrative of the Reign of Henry III*, ed. Walter W. Shirley,
Rolls Series, 2 vols. (London: Longman, 1862–1868), 1: 90–91; Sharp, *Accounts*, 71, 75,
82, 89; R. F. Treharne, *The Baronial Plan of Reform, 1258–1263* (Manchester: Manchester University Press, 1971), 164, 193–94, 233, 310; Maurice Powicke, *King Henry III and
the Lord Edward: The Community of the Realm in the Thirteenth Century* (Oxford: Oxford
University Press, 1947), 2: 450, 476, 486–89, 497–500, 787; Margaret Howell, *Eleanor
of Provence: Queenship in Thirteenth-Century England* (Oxford: Blackwell, 1998), 170–71,

The great Bristol insurrection of 1312 to 1316 must be seen in the immediate context of the baronial opposition to Edward II and his favourites, but its roots lay in long-running grievances between the townspeople and the castle constable over the levying of Bristol's annual farm.[10] Before the mid-thirteenth century, the collection of Bristol's farm had periodically been let to the mayor and burgesses, a situation that gave them considerable independence from the castle constable. After 1265, however, the collection of the farm usually rested with the constable, perhaps reflecting the Crown's continuing mistrust of the town following its opposition during the Barons' Wars.

Tensions between the castle constable and the Bristol burgesses reached new heights in 1312. The previous year the baronial opposition, lead by Thomas, earl of Lancaster, had forced Edward II to accept the Ordinances to limit his powers and to banish his favourite Piers Gaveston. The timing of the outbreak of violence in 1312 suggests that the Bristol rebels were seizing the opportunity presented by weakness at the centre and confusion in the provinces. Irritation at the constable's grant of the farm may have been compounded by the actions of the present constable, Bartholomew Badelsmere. Badelsmere had interfered in civic appointments and had misappropriated the wool customs. In the latter activity, he seems to have colluded with a group of fourteen plutocrats who dominated town life, and who were bitterly resented by the majority of lesser burgesses. It was from within this larger burgess group that the rebel leadership emerged. Open warfare broke out between the rebels and the castle garrison, alongside brazen resistance to royal commissioners, among whom was Lord Berkeley. At one point the castle was besieged by the townspeople. The rebellion came to an end in 1316 following the threat of a siege by the earl of Pembroke. The rebels were punished with fines and outlawries, but there were no executions. The rebellion was over, but this was not the end of Bristol's opposition to Edward II and his regime.

Gilbert, the last of the de Clare earls of Gloucester, died at the battle of Bannockburn in 1314. His vast estate was inherited by his daughters.[11] The eldest,

---

224, 228; David A. Carpenter, *The Reign of Henry III* (London: Hambledon, 1996), 249; J. R. Maddicott, *Simon de Montfort* (Cambridge: Cambridge University Press, 1994), 227, 282, 306, 319, 327–28, 332, 334–35, 338–39.

[10] This account of the revolt is based on *Vita Edwardi Secundi*, ed. N. Denholm-Young (London: Thomas Nelson and Sons, 1957), 70–74; *Annales monastici*, 3: 316 (Dunstable), 4: 300 (Wykes); *Flores Historiarum*, 3: 341; Sharp, *Accounts*, 82; *Bristol Charters, 1378–1499*, 47–50; E. A. Fuller, "The Tallage of 6 Edward II (Dec. 16, 1312) and the Bristol Rebellion," *Transactions of the Bristol and Gloucestershire Archaeological Society* [hereafter *TBGAS*] 19 (1894–1895): 171–278; Ponsford, "Bristol Castle," 206–14; Margaret Sharp, "Some Glimpses of Gloucestershire in the Early Fourteenth Century," *TBGAS* 93 (1974): 5–14; Colvin et al., *History of the King's Works*, 2: 580. For Bristol's fee farm, see Liddy, *War*, 60–63, 73.

[11] Michael Altschul, *A Baronial Family in Medieval England: The Clares, 1217–1314* (Baltimore: Johns Hopkins University Press, 1965), 168–69.

Eleanor, brought one-third of Gilbert's earldom to Hugh Despenser the younger. Hugh was granted the constableship of Bristol Castle in 1320 and 1322. His
father, Hugh the elder, earl of Winchester, was given custody of Bristol Castle
and town in 1325. Both were highly unpopular favourites of Edward II. The
castle played a vital role in securing the Despenser lands either side of the Bristol
Channel. In 1326, following Mortimer and Isabella's invasion, the earl of Winchester took refuge in the castle: he may have been there with Edward II, before
the latter's flight to Wales. This was not a good place for a Despenser to seek
refuge, since the enmities of the great insurrection had not been assuaged. Three
years earlier a royal enquiry had found many townspeople to be supporters of the
opposition to Edward II, with a local cult emerging around the gibbeted body of
Henry de Montfort, one of the victims of the purges that followed the defeat of
Thomas of Lancaster at Boroughbridge in 1322. Isabella and her army reached
Bristol prepared for a siege, but the castle garrison deserted Winchester, who was
forced to surrender on 26 October. He was given a peremptory trial, followed by
the full rigours of a traitor's death on the common gallows, to the great delight of
the mob. At the same time a baronial council was held at Bristol, where the king's
young son, the future Edward III, was proclaimed keeper of the realm.[12]

Reviewing the period from the eleventh to the mid-fourteenth centuries, we are
presented with a picture of an urban community whose elite was becoming increasingly ambitious, self-confident, and vociferous. As Bristol grew as a commercial centre, so it found the territorial and jurisdictional limitations imposed
upon it by the feudal landscape of which it was part increasingly irksome; at the
same time, it was developing the resources with which to challenge, in some
cases successfully, those constraints. Or at least this is how it appears from the
extant evidence, and we must allow for the possibility that what seems to be a real
long-term trend is in fact an illusion created by the greater volume and changing
character of evidence as we progress into the later Middle Ages.

Nonetheless, it may still be instructive to review this apparent trend in a
little more detail before addressing the fifteenth century. Until the thirteenth
century, Bristol appears as a pawn in games played by magnates and kings. It
may not be entirely coincidental that Bristol burgesses seem to have found their
voice during the Barons' Wars, when there may have been an attempt to win

---

[12] *Chronica Monasterii S. Albani Thomae Walsingham*, ed. Henry T. Riley, Rolls Series, 2 vols. (London: Longman, 1863–1864), 1: 181, 183; *Chronica Monasterii de Melsa*,
ed. E. A. Bond, Rolls Series, 3 vols. (London: Longman, 1866–1868), 2: 352; *Annales
Monastici*, 4: 347(Oseney); *Flores Historiarum*, 3: 234; J. C. Davies, *The Baronial Opposition to Edward II: Its Character and Policy* (Cambridge: Cambridge University Press,
1918), 94–95, 103; Natalie Fryde, *The Tyranny and Fall of Edward II, 1321–1326* (Cambridge: Cambridge University Press, 1979), 152–53, 189–90.

the allegiance of those beyond the landed aristocracy.[13] Bristolians' hostility to Prince Edward in the 1260s may have been occasioned by nothing more than irritation at the behaviour of his followers, but we cannot rule out the possibility of more profound motivations. In the case of the great insurrection of 1312–1316 there do appear to have been issues of principle as well as purely pragmatic concerns: Bristol's status as a legally constituted commune seems to have been contested.[14] The extent and nature of Bristol's liberties was certainly an issue in its tussles with the Berkeleys over Redcliffe, and efforts to enhance the town's constitutional position and extend the reach of its jurisdiction over the transpontine territories both north of the Frome and south of the Avon lay behind a number of charters. These culminated in the charters of 1373, which constituted Bristol as England's first provincial urban county, with its own county court, sheriffs, and MPs who were knights of the shire rather than mere parliamentary burgesses, and borders that encompassed both Redcliffe and Bilswick.[15]

The insurrection of 1312–1316 also sees the appearance of factionalism as an unmistakable aspect of urban politics, with internecine struggles within the civic elite reflecting the broader conflicts of Edward II's reign. In all probability, leading Bristolians chose, or were forced into, broader political affiliations on the basis of their local interests, and this pattern seems to have been repeated in the fifteenth century. After the work of Caroline Barron and others it goes without saying that internal factionalism, often along the boundary between greater and lesser trades, was also seen in other towns, not least in London.[16]

The Later Middle Ages

In 1399, Bristol's strategic importance once more put it in the foreground of national politics. In July, following Henry Bolingbroke's landing during Richard II's absence in Ireland, both Henry and the king's party in England expected Richard to return through Wales.[17] Bristol Castle was occupied by a

---

[13] Thorlac Turville-Petre, *England the Nation: Language, Literature, and National Identity, 1290–1340* (Oxford: Clarendon Press, 1996), but see Tim William Machan, *English in the Middle Ages* (Oxford: Oxford University Press, 2003), esp. Chap. 2, for a different view.

[14] *Bristol Charters, 1155–1373*, 48–49, 50–51.

[15] Liddy, *War*, 72–80, which makes a compelling case for the 1373 charters as being partly motivated by fears of Crown incursions into Bristol's fiscal autonomy. While these new privileges gave Bristol greater independence, they also, argues Liddy, encouraged its civic elite to see themselves as the Crown's partners in governance (211).

[16] See references in n. 1 above.

[17] For the following paragraph see *Chronicles of the Revolution, 1397–1400: The Reign of Richard II*, ed. Chris Given-Wilson (Manchester: Manchester University Press, 1993),

force of Richard's diminishing band of supporters, led by the treasurer, William Lescrope, earl of Wiltshire, and three king's knights and royal councillors, John Bussy, Henry Green, and John Russell. These Ricardians hoped to establish a bridgehead at Bristol for the king's return to England. Henry moved to block any such attempt. At Berkeley, where he was warmly received by Thomas, Lord Berkeley, Henry was joined by the king's uncle, the duke of York, who had been appointed regent while Richard was in Ireland, and from there they marched to Bristol, reaching it on 28 July. Here they found the castle fortified against them. The defenders were probably several hundred strong. Henry's force may have numbered in the thousands, but a concerted defence of this mighty stronghold could have delayed him long enough for Richard's men to rally and, perhaps, even secure victory. This was not to be. What followed is uncannily reminiscent of the events of 1326. Once Bolingbroke's army had deployed before the castle, the garrison dispersed leaving Wiltshire, Bussy, Green, and Russell with no option but to surrender. All were tried for treason and beheaded apart from Russell who, judged insane, was allowed to live. The pro-Lancastrian chronicler Thomas Walsingham excused Henry's actions by asserting that had he not ordered these three executed the Bristol mob would have torn them apart anyway, so deep was their hatred of Richard's courtiers.

Walsingham's picture of a town committed to Bolingbroke, or at least bitterly opposed to his enemies, is borne out by events in January 1400. A group of Ricardian loyalists—the so-called Epiphany plotters—made an unsuccessful attempt to capture the new king, Henry IV, at Windsor on Twelfth Night and free Richard from captivity. In the immediate aftermath one of the conspirators, Thomas Despenser, earl of Gloucester, great-grandson of Hugh Despenser the younger, tried to flee to Cardiff, but was waylaid crossing the Bristol Channel and delivered up to the mayor of Bristol, Thomas Knappe. Knappe was apparently unable to protect him from the hatred of the Bristol mob and he was lynched. Henry IV is unlikely to have ordered this unlawful act directly, since there was probably not time for news and orders to have been exchanged between mayor and king, but it certainly won his approval and gratitude.

However, within three months of Gloucester's killing, the mood of Bristolians had swung wildly against the representatives of King Henry. According to testimony given three weeks after the event, on 24 April a gang attacked John Stodeley, the Bristol aulnager, responsible for collecting the custom payable on cloth. Stodeley narrowly escaped death. The ringleaders were imprisoned and ejected from the freedom of Bristol.[18] How can we explain, first, Bristol's

34–37, 120, 128, 133–34; and Michael Bennett, *Richard II and the Revolution of 1399* (Stroud: Sutton, 1999), 159–61. For the wider context of Richard II's reign, see N. Saul, *Richard II* (New Haven and London: Yale University Press, 1997).

   [18] London, The National Archives, KB 9/191, fols. 17–19; KB 27/562, rex, mm. 1, 3d, 22; KB 29/45, mm. 11–12; JUST 1/1549; *Calendar Patent Rolls, 1399–1401*, 272, 313,

hostility to Richard and support for Henry, and then this remarkably swift and extreme reversal of public opinion?

While Bristol's hostility to Richard's courtiers may have been part of a general disenchantment with the royal regime, there were also local factors that probably played their part. Bristol had given major financial support to Richard. The town lent over £3,000 to the king in corporate or individual loans, representing about one-quarter of all urban loans to Richard, and making it second only to London as the Crown's biggest urban creditor. Such a record may be seen as evidence of loyalty, and lending could have its rewards in terms of royal patronage and favours, but in the 1390s there is evidence of resistance to royal requests for loans: in 1393 a royal official seems to have returned empty-handed from a visit to find lenders in the town.[19] In addition to loans and taxation, itself a particularly contentious issue under Richard, Bristol also contributed to the royal finances through the supply of shipping and the payment of customs.[20] There is evidence of resistance to the latter, in the form of a spate of investigations into customs evasion in Bristol in the 1390s. Among those Bristol merchants who had goods forfeited for non-payment of customs was John Barnstaple, mayor in 1395–1396, 1401–1402, and 1405–1406.[21] The customs collectors were among the few officials within Bristol who were directly appointed by the king, and as such they would have been very noticeable as Crown representatives. The customs house was not free of controversy: in 1398 two Bristol merchants complained of serious malpractice among the customers.[22]

Richard II's campaigns to pacify Ireland from 1397 to 1399 placed additional burdens on the port of Bristol. The ban on the export of victuals from Ireland caused disruption to what was an important element in Bristol's trade, as did the requisitioning of ships to transport armies across the Irish Sea.[23] Another point of contention related to what were perceived to be attacks on Bristol's jurisdictional

---

315, 521; *Calendar Close Rolls, 1399–1402*, 143, 195; *The Little Red Book of Bristol* [hereafter *LRBB*], ed. F. B. Bickley, 2 vols. (Bristol: Arrowsmith, 1900), 2: 74–75; *Parliament Rolls of Medieval England, 1275–1504*, ed. Chris Given-Wilson (Woodbridge: Boydell Press, 2005), 3: 457, m. 14; J. H. Wylie, *The Reign of Henry the Fourth* (London: 1884), 1: 120; *The Chronicle of Adam Usk, 1377–1421*, ed. Chris Given-Wilson (Oxford: Clarendon Press, 1997), 130–31.

[19] Liddy, *War*, 24, 29, 41–43. For the benefits to be derived from being a royal creditor, see Attreed, *King's Towns*, 157–58.

[20] Liddy, *War*, passim.

[21] *Calendar Close Rolls, 1396–99*, 52, 504, *Calendar Close Rolls, 1399–1402*, 114; *Calendar Close Rolls, 1396–99*, 271, 325.

[22] *Calendar Patent Rolls, 1396–99*, 590; London, The National Archives, SC 8/213/10625.

[23] *Calendar Patent Rolls, 1396–99*, 119, 438, 511; *Calendar Close Rolls, 1396–99*, 327, 331.

independence. In the 1390s Bristol petitioned Parliament about infringements perpetrated by both the Admiralty Court and the court of Marshalsea.[24]

These issues may have been serious irritants, but on their own are unlikely to have driven Bristolians to bay for the blood of Richard's supporters. The missing motivation probably lay not with the townspeople themselves but with their local magnate, Lord Thomas Berkeley. By the 1390s Berkeley held not only the extensive Berkeley inheritance but also the lands of his wife, Margaret, daughter and sole heiress of Warin, Lord Lisle, an estate worth around £600 per annum. Under Lord Thomas the Berkeley fortunes would reach their greatest extent. At his death in 1417 the value of his estates amounted to over £1,600 per annum.[25] In the 1390s he could reasonably expect to have been recognised as the natural leader of Gloucestershire political society, but Richard II's personal intervention upset the local balance of power. In 1397 he created Thomas Despenser as earl of Gloucester. Richard's promotion of the new earl within Gloucestershire undermined Berkeley's position and set him at loggerheads with the king. This was undoubtedly a major factor in Berkeley's declaration for Bolingbroke in 1399, and for his continuing support for Henry IV until at least 1406.[26] Bolingbroke had his own reasons for executing Wiltshire, Bussy, and Green, but Berkeley is unlikely to have pleaded on their behalf. When it comes to the lynching of Thomas Despenser in January 1400, we can surely suspect his agents of orchestrating the mob.

Bristol was not alone in its swift *volte-face* in the first year of Henry IV's reign.[27] Once again, however, there were particular local points of contention. Relations began to sour almost immediately after Henry's coup. On 16 September—a fortnight before Henry's accession—a commission was appointed to enquire as to the whereabouts of the jewels, goods, and chattels of the king and his retinue, which had been left at Bristol. The fall of the castle had been followed by its sacking and the theft of its valuable contents. Similar enquiries were made early in 1400 concerning the goods of the conspirators that may have found their way to Bristol with the earl of Gloucester. Investigations continued until 1402. Accusations made before the Exchequer implicated a number of Bristolians, including Mayor Thomas Knappe, in alleged attempts to conceal the Ricardians' treasure. The Crown's assumption that there was a conspiracy of silence within

---

[24] London, The National Archives, SC 8/225/11246; *Calendar of Charter Rolls*, vol. 5, nos. 353, 1341–1417; *LRBB*, 1: 173.

[25] *CMMBC*, 1: xl–xliii; Bridget Harvey, "The Berkeleys of Berkeley, 1281–1417: A Study in the Lesser Peerage of Late Medieval England" (Ph.D. diss., University of St Andrew's, 1990), passim.

[26] Saul, *Richard II*, 384; *CMMBC*, 1: xl–xliii

[27] Michael Bennett, "Henry of Bolingbrooke and the Revolution of 1399," in *Henry IV: The Establishment of the Regime, 1399–1406*, ed. Gwilym Dodd and Douglas Biggs (York and Woodbridge: Boydell Press, 2003), 9–33, at 25–30.

Bristol may have been correct, but its badgering of the townspeople is likely to have weakened support for the new regime.[28]

Another cause of resentment probably related to the Crown's position as creditor. There may have been creditors still waiting for reimbursement for their loans to the previous regime, and for these, Henry's refusal to honour the debts of his predecessor would have been deeply frustrating.[29] However, these were not the direct causes of the major outbreak of violence against the Bristol aulnager. For these, we need to look elsewhere.

On 15 September 1399 Bolingbroke granted the merchants of Bristol remission of the tunnage and poundage customs dues from that date on, in recognition of the great charges of the merchants for the defence of the realm. Three months later King Henry had to issue a proclamation that these customs that had been levied before 15 September had to be paid; his action was in response to the news that many merchants had refused to pay sums due from before that date.[30] The merchants' more generous interpretation of this grant probably rested on promises Bolingbroke had made in July 1399, when, in an effort to win support, he had announced the abolition of all peacetime taxation.[31] On 1 April 1400 commissioners were appointed to investigate Bristol merchants' evasion of the duty on cloth.[32] The appointment of this commission seems to have been the immediate cause of the 24 April uprising.

Between July 1399 and January 1400 events in Bristol played an important part in the success of Henry IV, both in terms of ensuring his successful usurpation and in foiling Ricardian attempts to unseat him. As far as we can tell, Henry was swept to power on a wave of popular support; and yet, that enthusiasm was fast dissipating within a year of his usurpation. While the support of some Bristolians for Bolingbroke in July 1399, including their participation in the murder of the Despenser earl of Gloucester six months later, may have been prompted by Lord

---

[28] *Calendar Patent Rolls, 1396–99*, 596; *Calendar Patent Rolls, 1399–1401*, 312; *Calendar Patent Rolls, 1401–05*, 199; *Calendar of Inquisitions Miscellaneous, 1399–1422*, nos. 130, 139–41, 152–53; London, The National Archives, E 101/513/5; E 401/619, 13 July; E 159/177 recorda, Easter Term, r. 17d, 19v; E 159/182 recorda, Easter Term, r. 5; E 159/185 recorda, Trinity Term, r. 4–4v.

[29] Liddy, *War*, 24–57; Anthony Steel, *The Receipt of the Exchequer, 1377–1485* (Cambridge: Cambridge University Press, 1954), 144–45. London, The National Archives, E 401/619–57 passim; *Calendar of Fine Rolls, 1399–1405*, 319.

[30] *Calendar Close Rolls, 1399–1402*, 25. A fragmentary petition to Henry IV from the merchants of Bristol and London concerning remission of poundage may relate to this matter: London, The National Archives, SC 8/122/6076.

[31] Douglas Biggs, *Three Armies in Britain: The Irish Campaign of Richard II and the Usurpation of Henry IV, 1397–99* (Leiden and Boston: Brill, 2006), 179; Wylie, *Henry the Fourth*, 1: 193–94, 198; *Usk*, 130–31.

[32] *Calendar Patent Rolls, 1399–1402*, 398–99; London, The National Archives, E 122/17/3; E 401/621, 21 January; *Calendar Fine Rolls, 1399–1405*, 95–96.

Berkeley, the uprising of April 1400 shows that there was at least a faction within the town that could act independently of Berkeley influence, and in violent opposition to royal policy, when they felt their financial interests were under threat.

Bristol's position within the seigniorial geography of mid-fifteenth-century England made political involvement inescapable as the nation slid into civil war in the 1450s. The Berkeleys were no longer the force they had been in the lifetime of Lord Thomas, and after his death in 1417 the family, and their estates, were torn asunder by an inheritance dispute. The protagonists were, on one side, Lord Thomas's daughter Elizabeth (d. 1422), and her husband Richard Beauchamp, earl of Warwick (d. 1439), and on the other James, Lord Thomas's nephew. By the terms of an entail of 1349 James was the rightful heir, but the earl of Warwick was not prepared to let legal niceties get in the way of a rich inheritance, and among much else the manor and hundred of Bedminster and the hundreds of Hartcliff and Portbury passed to the earl and countess.[33] Elizabeth died in 1422 and Richard Beauchamp married Isabel, the daughter of that Thomas Despenser, earl of Gloucester, who was murdered in Bristol in 1400. Their daughter Anne married Richard Neville, son of the earl of Salisbury, and known to historians as 'the Kingmaker'; through this marriage he succeeded to the Warwick earldom and, by 1450, he had been able to overcome other claimants and acquire Bedminster, Hartcliff, and Portbury together with the rest of the Beauchamp inheritance.[34] In addition, he acquired the Bristol appurtenances of the honour of Gloucester, namely the Earl's Court, and the manor and hundred of the Barton.[35]

Richard, Duke Edward's son and heir to the duchy of York, had estates in Wiltshire and Somerset, including Easton-in-Gordano, just outside Bristol, which he held of the former Berkeley manor of Portbury, and thus of the

---

[33] *CMMBC*, 1: xliii–xlvi, 516, 520–21; Peter Fleming and Michael Wood, *Gloucestershire's Forgotten Battle: Nibley Green, 1470* (Stroud: Tempus, 2003), chap. 1.

[34] Michael Hicks, *Warwick the Kingmaker* (Oxford: Blackwell, 1998), 48–49.

[35] Richard II had granted these properties to Thomas Despenser, and in 1402 they were granted for life to Edward, duke of York. On York's death in 1415 they passed to Humphrey, duke of Gloucester. After Humphrey's death in 1447 they reverted to Anne, daughter of Henry Beauchamp, duke of Warwick, granddaughter of Isabel Despenser, and on her death in 1449 they passed to the Kingmaker: Hicks, *Warwick the Kingmaker*, 46–47, 49, 123; Ponsford, "Bristol Castle," 180–92; Sharp, *Accounts*, xxiv, xxxvi–lxiii. A 1424 receipt from the feodary of Earl's Court for aid for the marriage of Elizabeth, daughter of Lady Isabella, countess of Warwick, daughter and heir of Thomas Despenser, is Taunton, Somerset Archive and Record Service, T\PH\pls/1/16. See *Calendar Patent Rolls, 1399–1401*, 134, for Edmund duke of York's acquisition of the Barton in 1381. For Humphrey duke of Gloucester's acquisition of the Barton, see *Calendar Patent Rolls, 1429–36*, 504. For Anne Beauchamp as the duke of Warwick's heiress to the Barton after the death of Gloucester, see *Calendar Patent Rolls, 1441–46*, 391.

earl of Warwick.[36] Between them, York and Warwick could have exercised a stranglehold on Bristol's political life had they so wished, but only occasionally could Bristol have occupied anything like their full attention. When it did, their involvement plunged Bristol into the heart of national politics.

In the early 1450s it seems to have been the duke of York who had the greater influence in Bristol.[37] In 1451 Thomas Yonge, one of the town's MPs and the duke of York's steward of Easton-in-Gordano, sponsored a petition in parliament that the duke be recognised as heir presumptive to the childless king.[38] He was almost certainly doing so with at least the acquiescence of some of the town's leaders. His actions would not have pleased Warwick, who at this time joined with Henry VI's government in resisting York.[39] Bristol may have been implicated in York's disastrous march on Dartford in March the following year. A general pardon was promulgated on 7 April 1452. The mayor and common council of Bristol bought a pardon in May, as did thirteen other Bristolians, including Thomas Yonge; this strongly suggests that they had something in their very recent past about which they felt uneasy.[40] In 1453 an approver accused a group of prominent Bristolians of casting spells to bring about Henry VI's descent into madness; this accusation was not taken seriously, but that it was made suggests

---

[36] P. A. Johnson, *Duke Richard of York, 1411–1460* (Oxford: Clarendon Press, 1988), 14–15; Michael A. Hicks, "The Career of George Plantagenet, Duke of Clarence, 1449–1478" (D.Phil. diss., University of Oxford, 1975), 308, tables XVI and n. The duke of York held Bridgwater: *Bridgwater Borough Archives, V: 1468–1485*, ed. Robert W. Dunning, T. D. Tremlett, and T. B. Dilks, Somerset Record Society 70 (Frome: Butler & Tanner, 1971), xii–xiii. For Easton-in-Gordano as a manor held of Portbury, see *Calendar of Inquisitions Post Mortem, 1422–27*, no. 487.

[37] The events of c. 1450–1471 in Bristol are treated in greater detail in Peter Fleming, "Politics and the Provincial Town: Bristol, 1451–1471," in *People, Places and Perspectives: Essays on Later Medieval and Early Tudor England*, ed. Keith Dockray and idem (Stroud: Nonsuch, 2005), 79–114.

[38] Johnson, *Richard of York*, 63, 73, 98–100, 241; Ralph A. Griffiths, *The Reign of King Henry VI: The Exercise of Royal Authority, 1422–1461* (London: Benn, 1981), 671, 674, 692, 704 n. 61, 748; *Letters and Papers Illustrative of the Wars of the English in France during the Reign of Henry VI*, ed. Joseph Stevenson, Rolls Series, 2 vols. (London: Longman, 1861–1864), 2: 770; Eric W. Ives, *The Common Lawyers of Pre-Reformation England* (Cambridge: Cambridge University Press, 1983), 480; Josiah C. Wedgwood and A. D. Holt, *History of Parliament: Biographies of the Members of the Commons House, 1439–1509* (London: HMSO, 1936), 981–82; J. T. Driver, "Parliamentary Burgesses for Bristol and Gloucestershire, 1422–1437," *TBGAS* 74 (1955): 113–21; A. F. Pollard, "Yonge, Sir Thomas (c. 1405–77)," rev. N. Ramsay, *Oxford Dictionary of National Biography* 60: 817–18.

[39] Anthony J. Pollard, *Warwick the Kingmaker: Politics, Power and Fame* (London: Hambledon Continuum, 2007), 22–23.

[40] *Bristol Charters, 1378–1499*, 127–32; London, The National Archives, C 67/40 passim; Robin L. Storey, *The End of the House of Lancaster*, 2nd ed. (Gloucester: Sutton, 1986), 101–2.

that by then Bristol was considered a likely home for anti-Lancastrian subversion.[41] In the same year, York and Warwick became allies in opposition to the Lancastrian court faction. Further pardons purchased by Bristolians in January 1458, possibly following a visit from the Lancastrian Queen Margaret, may also indicate suspect loyalties.[42]

Given Bristol's strategic position, at the nexus of routes from Ireland, Wales, the South-west, and the West Midlands, it would have made good sense for the Yorkists to cultivate support in the town in the period leading up to their seizure of the throne in 1461. This was particularly the case after the rout of the Yorkists at Ludford in October 1459. With the Lancastrian court based in Coventry, York now in exile in Ireland, and Warwick ensconced at Calais, Bristol controlled two possible approaches to London: York's from a landing in south Wales (and Bristol itself might have given York a suitable bridgehead), and the route from a landing in the South-west, which could conceivably have been made by either duke or earl. In addition, if Bristol was held by the Yorkists, it might provide a base from which communications between Coventry and London could be threatened.

In all probability, Bristol was under Yorkist control soon after the Yorkist earls of Warwick and Salisbury entered London in early July 1460, if not earlier. Later that month Bristol supplied ships to bring the duke of York back from his Irish exile.[43] In September 1460, the same month that York finally crossed the sea from Ireland, the Lancastrian duke of Somerset landed in the South-west and joined with the earl of Devon to raise troops. They were to rendezvous with a large Lancastrian army mustering at Kingston-upon-Hull. They started north in December, passing through Bath, Cirencester, Evesham, and thence to Coventry, but avoiding Bristol, the obvious gateway to the Severn Valley route to Evesham and the West Midlands. They were probably deterred by a show of strength and a discharge of cannon from Bristol Castle, apparently wrested from Lancastrian control by the mayor, William Canynges (Thomas Yonge's half-brother), on the orders of York. Canynges also seems to have seized a consignment of two thousand pounds of gunpowder, saltpetre, and sulphur from Henry May, a Bristol burgess of Irish origin, who was intending to supply it, along with quantities of wheat, to James Butler, or Ormond, earl of Wiltshire. The earl of Wiltshire held manors in Wiltshire and Somerset but came of a major Anglo-Irish family.[44] He evidently accompanied Somerset and Devon on their march

---

[41] London, The National Archives, KB 9/273 m 2; KB 27/776 rex m 4ᵈ; Anthony Gross, *The Dissolution of the Lancastrian Kingship* (Stamford: Paul Watkins, 1996), 21–22.

[42] A. E. Hudd, "Two Bristol Calendars," *TBGAS* 19 (1894–1895): 124; London, The National Archives, C 67/42 passim.

[43] *Calendar of Inquisitions Miscellaneous,* 8: 162–63.

[44] John Watts, "Butler, James, First Earl of Wiltshire and Fifth Earl of Ormond (1420–1461)," *Oxford Dictionary of National Biography* 9: 149–51; London, The National

north.[45] That the Yorkists recognised Bristol's strategic importance is demonstrated by the appointment of Edward earl of March, the son of York, as its castle constable on 14 November 1460, less than a month after his father's public declaration of his claim to the throne.[46] Somerset was once more a threatening presence in the Bristol region soon after Edward's accession in March 1461, when the king repeated his father's command to the mayor and common council to hold the castle against the duke.[47]

While Bristol's governing elite was predominantly Yorkist in sympathy in 1460–1461, Henry May's actions show that its burgess class was not of one opinion. His is not the only instance of Lancastrian support within the town in this period. John Borough, or Burgh, yeoman of the Crown, gauger and water bailiff in the port of Bristol in 1456–1457, was rewarded in January 1460 for his good service against the Yorkists.[48] After the Yorkist seizure of London there was a purge of Bristol's customs officials: of the sixteen individuals who held office during the period between the end of York's second protectorate in February 1456 and July 1460, only one, the Neville retainer Robert Strangeways, was reappointed.[49] In August 1460 the Yorkists commissioned the mayor to suppress riots and disturbances, and these may well have been motivated by political factionalism.[50] In September 1461, six months after Edward's seizure of the throne, the Lancastrian rebels Sir Baldwin Fulford, former sheriff of Devon, and John Heysaunt, a former Bristol customs collector, both executed in Bristol, were alleged to have been recruiting Bristolians to their cause.[51]

However strong Bristol's Lancastrian faction may have been, it was clearly not in the ascendancy in 1460–1461. In 1461 Bristol supplied ships, men (including a detachment that fought at Towton), and money for the Yorkist war effort.[52] Such overt partisanship had its risks. After the second battle of St Albans in February 1461, we are told, "the quene with her counsell had graunted and yeve leve

Archives, C 140/3/29, mm 6, 18; Hicks, "Career of George Plantagenet, Duke of Clarence," 258–62.

[45] *The Great Red Book of Bristol*, ed. E. W. W. Veale, BRS, Pt. 4, 136–38; Cora L. Scofield, *The Life and Reign of Edward IV* (London: Longmans, Green, 1923), 1: 117; Stevenson, *Letters and Papers*, 2: 774–75; Michael K. Jones, "Beaufort, Henry, second Duke of Somerset (1436–64)," *Oxford Dictionary of National Biography* 4: 632–33.

[46] *Calendar Patent Rolls, 1452–61*, 632–33; *Calendar Close Rolls, 1454–61*, 467.

[47] Veale, *Great Red Book of Bristol*, Pt. 1, 137.

[48] *Calendar Patent Rolls, 1452–61*, 275, 329, 350, 354, 579.

[49] *Calendar Fine Rolls, 1461–71*, 4–5, 7, 70–22, 146, 148, 198, 200.

[50] *Calendar Patent Rolls, 1452–61*, 275, 329, 350, 354, 517, 579, 608; *Calendar Fine Rolls, 1461–71*, 4–5, 7, 70–72, 146, 148, 198, 200.

[51] London, The National Archives, KB 9/297, mm. 123–35.

[52] Veale, *Great Red Book of Bristol*, Pt. 1, 137, Pt. 3, 77–78; Griffiths, *Henry VI*, 882 n. 96; *Calendar Patent Rolls, 1461–67*, 100. Loans: London, The National Archives, E 401/877, E 404/72/1 no. 83.

to the northurmen forto spoyle and robbe [. . .] the townes of Couentre, Brystow, and Salesbury wyth the shyrys withynne rehersed, as for payment and recompense of theyre sowde and wages, as the comon noyse was among the peple at that tyme [. . .]."[53] Bristol's commitment to the Yorkists in 1460–1461 may usefully be compared to the political stance of Coventry, about two days' ride to the north. Prominent as Margaret's headquarters in the later 1450s, Coventry saw sufficient hostility to the Lancastrian cause in the immediate aftermath of the second battle of St Albans to cause Lancastrian emissaries to run for their lives after the mayor declared himself unable to protect them from the angry mob.[54] With Bristol, Coventry, and probably Gloucester declaring for Edward of York, there was no refuge in the South-west Midlands for the Lancastrian army following its rebuff by London. Had these three towns held for Lancaster, the political history of later fifteenth-century England might have been very different.

The success of either side in the febrile winter of 1460–1461 depended on the commitments and calculations made by a small number of individuals in key positions. Most were not acting out of long-held convictions, and it is probably wrong to imagine that the duke of York or his son had a deep-rooted and numerous faction in Bristol; in fact, it probably extended little further than the immediate circle of Thomas Yonge and his half-brother William Canynges. But this was enough.

Most Bristolians, along with most Londoners, probably remained uncommitted until it seemed safe to make a public show of support for the Yorkists, and dangerous not to.[55] As in 1399, there were pragmatic reasons for the switch of loyalties. The loss of Gascony in 1453 triggered a temporary collapse of Bristol's wine and cloth trade. At the same time, attacks on Channel shipping increased, as did the Crown's demands for money to shore up both a doomed war effort and a regime that looked to be on the point of collapse.[56] By contrast the earl of Warwick, as captain of Calais, was sponsoring naval exploits in the Channel which, however questionable their morality and strategic efficacy, were earning him plaudits among English merchants.[57] At a more prosaic level, another

---

[53] *An English Chronicle, 1377–1461: A New Edition*, ed. William Marx (Woodbridge: Boydell Press, 2003), 98; *An English Chronicle of the Reigns of Richard II, Henry IV, Henry V, and Henry VI*, ed. J. S. Davies, Camden Society 64 (London: Camden Society, 1856), 109.

[54] Peter Fleming, "Coventry and the Wars of the Roses," Dugdale Society Occasional Paper, 50 (Dugdale Society/Shakespeare Birthplace Trust, 2011), 12–17.

[55] Bolton, "City and the Crown, 1456–61"; Barron, "London and the Crown, 1451–61."

[56] *The Overseas Trade of Bristol in the Later Middle Ages*, ed. Eleanora M. Carus Wilson, BRS 7 (1937), 210–12, 218–19, 222–24.

[57] Colin Richmond, "The Earl of Warwick's Domination of the Channel and the Naval Dimension to the Wars of the Roses, 1456–1460," *Southern History* 20–21 (1998–99): 1–19, at 2; Hicks, *Warwick*, 138–48.

possible cause of disaffection lay with a dispute between Bristol and Queen Margaret over the payment of her annuity of £102 15*s* 6*d* from the fee farm, which had been granted as part of her dower. This dispute began in 1451 and rumbled on for another eight years.[58]

In very broad terms, the picture in the 1450s and early 1460s is similar to that found in the late 1390s and early 1400s: a combination of Bristol's share of general dissatisfaction with a regime deemed to be ineffectual and corrupt and local antagonism over financial exactions. In both cases there was magnate involvement, but whereas in 1399–1400 the Berkeleys had long-standing seigniorial links and physical proximity to the town, as well as a particular personal motive for involvement, in the second case personal loyalties to York and Warwick were less deeply rooted and probably more limited in extent. There are other differences. The Berkeleys, of course, were not claimants to the throne; York eventually, and briefly, was. If we are correct in imagining, in 1400, the Berkeleys' agents egging on the mob to lynch Despenser against the mayor's best efforts, then it suggests that they had cultivated the support of the masses rather than the civic elite. In the 1450s York had on his side, in the Yonge-Canynges family, the wealthiest of the town's plutocrats, while his enemies were to be found beyond this inner circle.

Bristol's involvement in the Readeption of 1470–1471 raises further parallels. Warwick's growing dissatisfaction with Edward IV burst forth in July 1469, when he defeated Edward's favourite, the earl of Pembroke, at Edgecote and then had him executed. By now the earl had consolidated his influence in Bristol and its region, having held the former Berkeley and Despenser/Gloucester properties there for twenty years. Until Warwick's rift with Edward in 1469 there was no need for Bristolians to choose between them. When the choice had to be made, the most powerful faction opted for Warwick. Soon after Edgecote a fugitive brother of the earl of Pembroke was killed in the town.[59] Together with the execution of the earl of Devon in Bridgwater, the killing of the Herberts effectively removed the uppermost layer of royal authority in the West Country. The executions at Bristol and Bridgwater were almost certainly carried out by order of Warwick.

A Bristol detachment fought for William, Lord Berkeley, at the battle of Nibley Green in March 1470, where his adversary, Viscount Lisle, Pembroke's son-in-law, was killed. Their feud was the latest manifestation of the struggle for the Berkeley inheritance that had been under way since Lord Thomas's death

---

[58] London, The National Archives, E 368/225 recorda, Michaelmas, mm. 20–21; E 401/863; *RP*, 5: 223b, 518a; *Calendar Close Rolls, 1447–54*, 222, 225.

[59] Peter Fleming, *Bristol and the Wars of the Roses*, Bristol Branch of the Historical Association pamphlet (Bristol: BHA, 2005), 18–21.

in 1417.[60] Bristol's involvement was probably encouraged by the mayor, John Shipward, together with his son and namesake, and another prominent Bristol merchant, Philip Mede, father-in-law of Lord Berkeley's brother Maurice. Those Bristolians who fought for Berkeley probably did so out of personal, rather than wider political, loyalties, even though the Berkeleys had not been an influential seigniorial force within Bristol since before Warwick's entry into the Beauchamp and Despenser/Gloucester inheritance. The present lord, William, was the claimant by tail male, which put him on the side that had been disinherited by Elizabeth and Richard Beauchamp, through whom the present Earl Warwick enjoyed his share of the Berkeley lands, but Berkeley's opponent at Nibley Green was closely associated with Edward IV and his Woodville supporters. Supporting Berkeley before Nibley Green was not the same as supporting Warwick, but with the killing of Lord Lisle, Berkeley could not have hoped for anything but hostility from Edward IV. By the autumn, the Lancastrian King Henry VI was briefly restored to the throne with the assistance of Warwick and the duke of Clarence, Edward IV's own brother, in association with Margaret of Anjou, Henry's queen. This gave Berkeley a brief refuge from Edward's anger, and he was an active supporter of this new regime of the 'Readeption'.

In this, Berkeley was joined by an influential group of Bristolians. Warwick and Clarence had passed through Bristol in late March or early April 1470, with perhaps as many as five thousand men, and left their artillery there before embarking at Exeter for exile in France. After Warwick's return in September he revisited Bristol, which gave him a warm welcome. He recovered his artillery and was joined by large numbers of men, among whom may have been a group of Bristolians.[61] On 1 May 1471 Margaret's army entered Bristol where, according to the pro-Yorkist *Arrival of Edward IV,*

> they were greatly refreshed and relevyd, by such as were the Kyngs rebells in that towne, of money, men, and artilarye; wherethrwghe they toke new corage, the Thursday aftar to take the filde, and gyve the Kynge battayll [. . .][62]

---

[60] This paragraph is based on Fleming and Wood, *Gloucestershire's Forgotten Battle,* 62–63, 77, 90 and passim.

[61] Fleming, "Politics and the Provincial Town," 98.

[62] *Historie of the Arrival of Edward IV in England and the Final Recouerye of his Kingdomes from Henry VI,* ed. J. Bruce, Camden Society 1 (London: Camden Society, 1838), 25.

The Bristol contingent that marched with Margaret to defeat at Tewkesbury two days later was probably led by the recorder, Nicholas Hervey, who did not survive the battle.[63]

Support for the Readeption was far from total within Bristol's burgess elite, who were once again divided along factional lines. This split seems to have been more serious than that seen after the Yorkist seizure of power in 1461, when Lancastrian support seems largely to have been confined to those outside the governing elite. Edward IV's limited and discriminating punishment meted out to Bristol after his recovery of power in 1471 suggests that a significant number of his supporters among Bristol's elite clung on during his absence. At Coventry on 12 May, just eight days after Tewkesbury, he sent a letter under the privy seal to Bristol announcing that, "albeit that thinhabitauntz . . . haue not be of soche demeanynges in to late in thaire duetie and ligeaunce as thei aught to haue been of towardes vs," since he had been satisfied that "the offenses haue not be committed by the generalte of the Town, but onely by certain persones of the same," he was inclined "to entrete suche persones as humbly wol sue vn to vs, not by waie of rigoure but with resonable moderacion, punyshing the principall sturrers of rebellion ayenst vs and not a generalte." Such leniency had been urged on Edward by his brother, the erstwhile rebel duke of Clarence, who through his marriage to Warwick's daughter Isabel had now taken the earl's place as Bristol's patron and protector.[64] The order was given for the arrest of a small group of Bristolians, including the recorder, who was of course already dead, and four prominent common councillors, and the mayor was ordered to pass on the names of any other suspects. The mayor himself does not appear to have been under suspicion. The suspected councillors eventually secured pardons.[65]

Once again, local factors may have combined with more general anxieties to turn Bristol from initial support of a usurping king to opposition. While Edward's improved relations with France and more effective keeping of the seas during his first reign had positive effects on Bristol's trade, financial disputes persisted between town and Crown. High taxation, and wrangles over the payment of the fee farm and of Queen Elizabeth Woodville's annuity, had a wearisome familiarity. While trade had improved, in the late 1460s Edward's new Burgundian alliance is unlikely to have been welcomed by Bristol merchants, who feared that it would rekindle Anglo-French antagonism and thereby harm what was still their most lucrative area of operations. Warwick, on the other hand, was known to be working for a French alliance. In such circumstances, he might well

---

[63] *Three Fifteenth-Century Chronicles*, ed. James Gairdner, Camden Society 28 (London: Camden Society, 1880), 184; *English Historical Literature in the Fifteenth Century*, ed. C. L. Kingsford (Oxford: Oxford University Press, 1913), 378.

[64] *LRBB*, 2: 130–32.

[65] *Calendar Patent Rolls, 1467–77*, 274; *Calendar Close Rolls, 1468–76*, n. 843; London, The National Archives, C 67/48, mm 18, 20, 34; C 67/49, m 3.

have seemed the natural champion of Bristol's mercantile interests. Whatever powers of coercion or calls on loyalty his Bristol holdings afforded him, Warwick's political position would have been in alignment with the commercial interests of the town's burgesses.[66]

Edward IV died in his bed and was succeeded by his brother Richard III, who was defeated and killed by Henry Tudor in 1485. Support for the Warwick line died hard in Bristol. As late as May 1486 Nicholas Covell, a Bristol craftsman, allegedly took part in armed demonstrations at Westminster and Highbury. He and his accomplices supposedly plotted the destruction of the king. They carried a standard bearing the device of the ragged staff, a sure sign that they supported the claim of young Edward, earl of Warwick, son of Clarence, incarcerated in the Tower for the crime of being a Yorkist heir to the throne.[67]

Bristol was not an island in a feudal sea, impervious to the currents of seigniorial and royal politics, its inhabitants unconcerned by anything other than the business of making money. To understand its medieval political history fully, one has to understand its relationships not only with the Crown, but also with the Berkeleys and the heirs to the original earldom of Gloucester, be they Despensers, Beauchamps, or Nevilles. Theirs is a constant presence. That said, Bristol's governing elite never reacted to the demands of lordship like Pavlov's dogs.[68] Lordship, and its ability to secure compliance through loyalty, patronage, bribes, threats, and physical coercion, played its part in influencing Bristolians' political stance at any given time, but alongside the more basic imperative of survival so did calculations of commercial advantage and the desire to protect civic liberties. In this, the Bristol burgesses were probably not that different from other contemporary elites, urban or otherwise.

---

[66] Fleming, "Politics and the Provincial Town," 101–3.

[67] London, The National Archives, KB 27/900, rex, m. 10; KB 29/116, m. 15[r]. Bristol had some involvement in Buckingham's rebellion of October 1483, in the persons of two of its customers, John Kymer and Thomas Croft, who had links respectively with Humphrey Stafford, duke of Buckingham, and Anthony Woodville, Earl Rivers, but there may also have been Berkeley encouragement: Louise Gill, *Richard III and Buckingham's Rebellion* (Stroud: Sutton, 1999), 85.

[68] This paragraph owes a debt to Colin Richmond, "After McFarlane," *History* 68 (1983): 46–60.

Brokers in the Cities:
The Connections between Princely Officers and Town Officials in Holland at the End of the Middle Ages (1480–1558)

Serge ter Braake

Introduction

On January the second, 1524, master Reinier Brunt showed us a letter from the Council of Holland, telling him to ensure our consent for a contribution of 6000 guilders, which had been spoken of in our last meeting, [. . .]; to which a majority of the city council (*vroedschap*) voted that this time we shall consent on the condition that master Reinier would swear and give his word that this city [. . .] shall not be asked for any further consents.[1]

Master Reinier Brunt was sent to Gouda in 1524 with a delicate task. He was to ensure that the city council would consent in the levy of an extra subsidy to the prince, Charles V, emperor of the German Empire and king of Spain, but also

---

[1] Free translation from L. M. Rollin-Couquerque and A. Meerkamp van Embden, "Goudse Vroedschapsresoluties betreffende Dagvaarten der Staten van Holland en der Staten-Generaal," *Bijdragen en Mededelingen van het Historisch Genootschap te Utrecht* 37 (1916): 61–181, at 146 (2 January 1524): "Upten IIen Januarij anno XVcXXIIII is verthoent geweest by meester Reynier Brundt zekere lettere van credencie van den raidt van Hollant, achtervolgende diewelcke hy verthoent heeft sijn last van den raidt om die brieven, bedraegende VIm Rijnsgulden, dair in de voirgaende vroescap off gesproken was, te besegelen [. . .]; wairup is gestemmet by de meeste stemmen van de vroescap, dat men voir dese reyse besegelen sal die voirsz. brieven, behoudelick dat meester Reynier voirsz. beloeven sal ende zijn handt dairoff gheven, [. . .] dat men ons weder niet vergen en sal tot meerder besegelinge."

Negotiating the Political in Northern European Urban Society, c.1400–c.1600, ed. Sheila Sweetinburgh, MRTS 434 (Tempe: ACMRS, 2013).   [ISBN 978-0-86698-482-9]

count of Holland and Zeeland. Brunt was one of the officers of the prince attached to the highest princely institution in Holland, the Council of Holland in The Hague. He had been the prince's attorney-general since 1523, responsible for the prince's lawsuits in the Council of Holland, and for the prosecution of criminals. His appearance in the city of Gouda, therefore, as recorded by the city council, might be slightly surprising. It was, after all, not his primary task to persuade the subjects of Holland to pay the prince's subsidies. Normally the governor or influential councillors in the Council of Holland would occupy themselves with this. Not long before Reinier was employed by the prince, however, he had been in the service of Gouda as their 'pensionary' ('pensionaris'), the spokesman of the city during meetings of the States of Holland. Furthermore, he had a brother-in-law living in the city.[2] The personal ties of Reinier with the city made him the most suitable man, a perfect broker or mediator, to convince the citizens of Gouda to agree to this last subsidy of the prince.[3]

At the time more than 50 percent of the population of Holland lived in the cities, which had the most important voice in the States of Holland. The officers of the prince held most negotiations and deliberations with the city elites. Nevertheless, it is clear that the division between the two groups—the representatives of the count and those of the cities—cannot be clearly made. The prince was 'obliged' to appoint (mainly) people from Holland and Zeeland to the regional institutions, and thus it was common for the men in his service to have previously held high offices in a city and/or still to have many family members and other connections there.[4] It could be profitable for both the prince and his subjects for an officer to possess good connections within a city. The prince could rely on a servant who was able to get a lot done on the local level, while the citizens had a 'friend' who could work for their interests on the central level.

This paper focuses on the connections of the highest representatives of the count of Holland, the officers in the Council of Holland and Chamber of Accounts in The Hague, with the elites of the six major cities of Holland.[5] The

---

[2] Algemeen Rijksarchief Brussels, Papiers d'Etat et de l'Audience (= Aud.), inv. no. 1526, fol. 37 (Gerrit van Assendelft to Anton van Lalaing, 9 September 1536).

[3] See, for brokerage in late medieval and early modern societies, W. Blockmans, "Patronage, Brokerage and Corruption as Symptoms of Incipient State Formation in the Burgundian-Habsburg Netherlands," in *Klientelsysteme im Europa der Frühen Neuzeit*, ed. A. Mączak and E. Müller-Luckner, Schriften des historischen Kollegs, Kolloquien 9 (Munich: Oldenbourg, 1988), 117–26.

[4] See also S. ter Braake, "In the Service of Sovereign and Subjects: Conflicting Loyalties of Holland Officials at the End of the Middle Ages (1480–1550)," in *Medieval and Early Modern Culture* 10, ed. R. Suntrup and J. Veenstra (Frankfurt am Main: Peter Lang, 2008), 209–20.

[5] This article is primarily based on different sections of chapters 4 and 5 of my doctoral thesis, written at the University of Leiden and now published: S. ter Braake, *Met recht en rekenschap: De ambtenaren bij het Hof van Holland en de Haagse Rekenkamer in de*

count of Holland often had to rely heavily on his officers to make sure that his commands were implemented and that the negotiations for the levy of new subsidies ('beden') would be concluded successfully. In particular, when the county of Holland and Zeeland became a part of the larger Habsburg personal union at the end of the fifteenth century, the count had to leave the negotiations in the hands of his (capable and loyal, he hoped) regional officers. They played the role of brokers by smoothing the relations between on the one hand the 'state', represented by the prince and his officers, and on the other the subjects, who could not yet be ruled in a strictly or primarily formal and impersonal way.

I will demonstrate how important the personal ties with the cities were for the officers to fulfil their tasks successfully at a time when there was considerable resistance to central policy. The Habsburg princes taxed their subjects for wars which did not directly concern the people of Holland. They imposed trade impediments as a consequence of the same wars and the scarcity of grain. They prosecuted 'heretics' who followed the teachings of Luther and other reformers. The prince, whose interests often differed from those of Holland and who in the course of the sixteenth century rarely set foot in the Low Countries (almost never in Holland), had a less personal connection with the people than had his predecessors, and for these reasons the personal ties of the princely officers to the local people were crucial to furthering his wishes. However, we shall see that these connections were not always beneficial to the prince, but could serve the cities just as well. Finally, I will demonstrate how and why these ties weakened in the course of the sixteenth century and what this meant for the relation between the prince and his subjects shortly before the start of the Dutch revolt in 1568 in which Holland played a leading role.

Political Landscape in the Burgundian-Habsburg Netherlands

The Burgundian dynasty acquired the county of Holland and Zeeland during the second quarter of the fifteenth century. The new count left the government and justice in the hands of a governor ('stadtholder') and a council in The Hague. During the course of the fifteenth century the council became a better-defined institution with specialised officials. The auditing of the accounts of local officers was left in the hands of the masters of the Chamber of Accounts since 1446. In 1477 Mary of Burgundy, sole heir of the Burgundian Netherlands, married Maximilian of Habsburg, only to die five years later; consequently, Holland and Zeeland were absorbed into a larger empire. Their ruler was no longer concerned only with the Burgundian Netherlands but was also German emperor and king

Habsburgse Tijd (Hilversum: Verloren, 2007). A summary in English: https://openaccess. leidenuniv.nl/dspace/handle/1887/12449?mode=more

of Spain. Even though Charles V, Maximilian's grandson, was considered a 'natural ruler' by his subjects in Holland and Zeeland, his priorities clearly lay elsewhere.

The centre of government for the Low Countries, with Flanders, Brabant, and Holland/Zeeland as core regions, was in Brussels and Malines. The central institutions there, presided over by the prince or his regent, made the policy which was to be implemented by the several regional institutions. Flanders, Brabant, and Holland/Zeeland, and later also Utrecht, Ghuelders, and Friesland, had their own institutions for administering justice and implementing the policy from the centre. They were not just instruments of the prince, however: they could to a certain extent also make policy themselves and they gave their advice on many occasions. The Council of Holland seems to have had more latitude in operating independently than did the councils in Brabant and Flanders, probably because it was located farther away from the centre. The three 'core regions' also had their own Chamber of Accounts that were responsible for auditing the accounts of the local officers and maximising the profits from the prince's domains. In Holland the Chamber of Accounts was, just like the Council, located in The Hague.[6]

The subjects, or at least some of them, were represented in the States of Holland. From the fifteenth century onwards the States of Holland convened on 'dagvaarten' (diets), whenever they were summoned by the prince or his representatives. In the course of the fifteenth and sixteenth centuries these diets were held mostly in The Hague. Usually the negotiations were led by the most important officers, the stadtholder, president, and councillors of the Council of Holland and the masters in the Chamber of Accounts.

The voting members of the States of Holland were the nobles and the six major cities of Holland: Dordrecht, Haarlem, Delft, Leiden, Amsterdam, and Gouda. These cities had a population of approximately 10,000 to 14,000 inhabitants at the start of the sixteenth century.[7] Dordrecht was the oldest city

---

[6] For the regional institutions in Holland see M. J. M. Damen, *De staat van dienst: De gewestelijke ambtenaren van Holland en Zeeland in de Bourgondische periode (1425–1482)* (Hilversum: Verloren, 2000); Ter Braake, *Met recht en rekenschap*. For the institutions in Flanders see J. Dumolyn, *Staatsvorming en vorstelijke ambtenaren in het graafschap Vlaanderen (1419–1477)* (Antwerp: Garant, 2003); P. P. J. L. van Peteghem, *De Raad van Vlaanderen en staatsvorming onder Karel V (1515–1555)* (Nijmegen: Gerard Noodt Instituut, 1990); M. Jean, *La Chambre des comptes de Lille: L'institution et les hommes* (Paris: École des chartes, 1992). For Brabant see H. de Ridder-Symoens, "Milieu social, études universitaires et carrière des conseillers au Conseil de Brabant, 1430–1600," in *Recht en instellingen in de oude Nederlanden tijdens de middeleeuwen en de nieuwe tijd: Liber amicorum Jan Buntinx* (Leuven: Universitaire Pers, 1981), 257–301.

[7] J. D. Tracy, *Holland under Habsburg Rule, 1506–1566: The Formation of a Body-Politic* (Berkeley: University of California Press, 1990), 48.

and therefore had the first vote in the States after the nobles, enjoying several privileges which were a thorn in the side of the other cities. Dordrecht, Delft, Leiden, and Gouda were located in the south of Holland and relatively close to The Hague. Haarlem and Amsterdam were located farther away in the north. Since the nobles were exempt from contributing to the subsidies to the prince, and therefore rarely objected to them, the consent of the six major cities was imperative for the ruler.

The representatives of the cities in the States of Holland went to the diets with a certain number of mandates ('last'). When they had to decide something which went beyond their mandates they travelled back to their home cities to consult the city council again (a phenomenon called 'ruggespraak'). The representatives of the prince also had certain mandates, and at times they also had to consult the prince or, more frequently in the sixteenth century, the regent in Brussels. As a result, negotiations could take a long time with representatives travelling back and forth.[8] The portion every city had to contribute to the subsidy to the prince was the root of particularly long-drawn-out negotiations.[9] The princely officers could influence how much 'discount' ('gracie') a city would get on the share they had to contribute. In 1523, for example, Councillor Gerrit van Assendelft told the city council of Haarlem that he would help them to get their discount if they would consent in the subsidy.[10]

The growing physical distance between the prince and his subjects, however, resulted in a less personal kind of rule and also a more visible discrepancy between the interests of the prince and those of the people of Holland. The Habsburg wars damaged the Hollanders' trade; as a result they were less willing to pay the prince's subsidies ('beden' or 'aides'). The persecution of heretics, a consequence of the Reformation, caused dispute because some of the privileges of the major cities of Holland were ignored.[11] While the cities of Holland often agreed

---

[8] For the States of Holland in the fifteenth and sixteenth centuries see H. Kokken, *Steden en Staten: Dagvaarten van steden en Staten van Holland onder Maria van Bourgondië en het eerste regentschap van Maximiliaan van Oostenrijk (1477–1494)*, Hollands Historische Reeks 16 (The Hague: Stichting Hollands Historische Reeks, 1991); J. P. Ward, "The Cities and States of Holland (1506–1515): A Participative System of Government under Strain" (Ph.D. diss., Leiden University, 2001); J. W. Koopmans, *De Staten van Holland en de Opstand: de ontwikkeling van hun functies en organisatie in de periode 1544–1588*, Hollands Historische Reeks 13 (The Hague: Stichting Hollands Historische Reeks, 1990). For the mentioning of mandates for the princely officers: Gemeentearchief Amsterdam, stadsarchief (=GAA), inv. no. 5029/29, 329, 382; inv. no. 5029/32, 359.

[9] J. D. Tracy, *A Financial Revolution in the Habsburg Netherlands: Renten and Renteniers in the County of Holland 1515–1565* (Berkeley: University of California Press, 1985), 36, 53 (table 2), 55–56.

[10] Archiefdienst Kennemerland, Stadsarchief Haarlem (=SAH), inv. no. 3, fol. 132r.

[11] See for further details on the dispute over the privileges Ter Braake, *Met recht en rekenschap*, chap. 5 and the further references there.

over trade and heresy and could form a front against the prince and his representatives, they frequently were in dispute over one another's privileges. This is
exactly why they needed to have 'friends' to help them to defend their interests,
not only against the prince but also against the other cities.

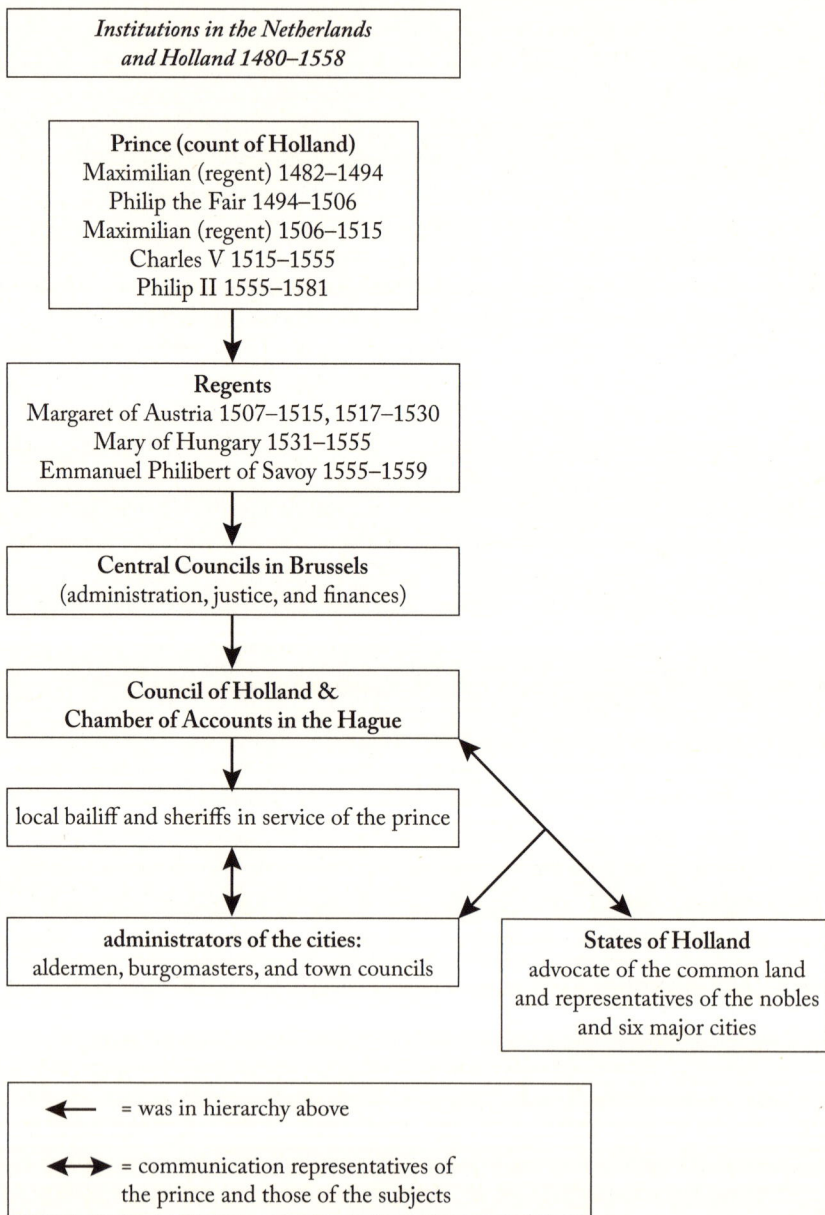

**Institutions in the Netherlands
and Holland 1480–1558**

Prince (count of Holland)
Maximilian (regent) 1482–1494
Philip the Fair 1494–1506
Maximilian (regent) 1506–1515
Charles V 1515–1555
Philip II 1555–1581

↓

Regents
Margaret of Austria 1507–1515, 1517–1530
Mary of Hungary 1531–1555
Emmanuel Philibert of Savoy 1555–1559

↓

Central Councils in Brussels
(administration, justice, and finances)

↓

**Council of Holland &
Chamber of Accounts in the Hague**

↓

local bailiff and sheriffs in service of the prince

↕

administrators of the cities:
aldermen, burgomasters, and town councils

States of Holland
advocate of the common land
and representatives of the nobles
and six major cities

← = was in hierarchy above

↔ = communication representatives of
the prince and those of the subjects

Gift Strategies of the Cities:
"And all services require payment"[12]

The city council of Leiden gave this statement to clarify why they allowed the burgomasters of the city to show 'gratitude' ('dancberheyt') to the men who would help them get a reduction on their contribution to the prince's subsidy. The statement shows just how vague the difference was between the payment of a 'salary' and the distribution of (in our eyes) questionable or even corrupt gifts.[13] It was imperative for the cities to maintain a good relationship with the officers of the prince. They were the ones who could put in a good word for them and make sure they were taxed as little as possible.

These signs of gratitude, the 'gratuiteyten', usually took the shape of money, but sometimes also of other 'valuables', such as timber or a stained-glass window. Depending on the occasion, and especially on the service which was rendered in return for the gift, some of these signs of gratitude could be considered corrupt in the sixteenth century. In the Low Countries, the commonly accepted gifts were wine, beer, fish, or other 'refreshments'. As the Spaniard Bartolomé de las Casas noted at the beginning of the sixteenth century, the 'Dutch' negotiated by dining together.[14] Moreover, the gift of wine to high-ranking visitors, such as princely officers, was a common occurrence in Western Europe. Of course, some welcomes were 'warmer' than others and more than just a welcome based on tradition. At times the accounts show exactly what the motives of the citizens were: "to gain his favour, affection and good recommendation," or "because we trust these officials in this and other matters which this city has to bring up with the prince."[15]

Tradition, however, seems to have played a more prominent role in the pouring of wine than clear attempts to 'influence' high-ranking officials. Wine and meals were served because the officials thought they had the right to such gifts and could be offended if they did not receive it. The amount of wine every officer received was

---

[12] Gemeentearchief Leiden, Secretarie-archief I (=SAL), inv. no. 384, fol. 83v: "Ende dat alle diensten loon vereyschen."

[13] M. Damen, "Corrupt of hoofs gedrag? Geschenken en het politieke netwerk van een laatmiddeleeuwse stad," *Tijdschrift voor sociale en economische geschiedenis* 2, no. 4 (2005): 68–94, at 68–70.

[14] In 1536, for example, two central officers refused a sum of money for their services, but did not protest when they received wine instead: GAA, inv. no. 5029/29, 294. About de las Casas see L. Sicking and R. Fagel, "In the Wake of Columbus: The First Expedition Attempted from the Netherlands to the New World (1517–1527)," *Terrae Incognitae* 34 (2002): 34–45, at 40.

[15] Ter Braake, *Met recht en rekenschap*, 213; Damen, "Corrupt of hoofs gedrag?" 83; V. Groebner, *Liquid Assets, Dangerous Gifts: Presents and Politics at the End of the Middle Ages* (Philadelphia: University of Pennsylvania Press, 2002), 24–25, 31, 65.

practically 'fixed'. The stadtholder received eight jugs of wine, the president four, and the councillors and masters in the Chamber of Accounts two. On the other hand, the representatives of the cities were also guests of high-ranking officers during negotiations. Master of the Chamber of Accounts Vincent Cornelisz,[16] for example, received the representatives of Amsterdam at his home in 1535, a time which was extremely delicate because of problems with heretics in that city. He said that if he were stadtholder he would not be so tolerant, but that he would like to "make peace and friendship" between the stadtholder and the representatives nonetheless. A good reception, especially with plenty of alcohol available, ensured the best available circumstances for tense negotiations.[17]

The officers did not receive gifts only when visiting a city. Most cities sent annual gifts to The Hague, Brussels, and Malines, to maintain good relations with the officers there in general. These annual gifts usually were edible or drinkable and the specialty of the city in question. The officers, and especially the most prominent among them, could count on a yearly supply of wine, beer, butter, cheese, and fish provided by the various cities of Holland.[18]

All these gifts were given primarily out of courtesy or to maintain a good relationship with the princely officers in general. The beneficiaries had no reason to refuse such gifts. But the officers who could render 'special services' to the cities, because of their influence, their office, or a particular assignment, also received gifts of a more questionable nature—especially when the cities hoped to obtain a reduction on the payment of a subsidy, faced a lawsuit, or needed privileges to be defended. It is hard to determine which gifts were 'corrupt'. What we might see as an attempt at bribery, people in the fifteenth and sixteenth centuries might consider an expression of gratitude for exercising an office fairly;[19] an expression not dissimilar to those of the main characters in Shakespeare's *The Merchant of*

---

[16] Cornelisz is an abbreviation for Corneliszoon, son of Cornelis. The use of the patronymic was still rather common in the sixteenth-century Low Countries. Successful men usually adopted a 'real' surname at a later stage in their career. The powerful Vincent Cornelisz, however, appears only as Vincent Cornelisz or simply as 'master Vincent' in the documents.

[17] See in general Ter Braake, *Met recht en rekenschap*, 212–14. For some examples see A. van der Goes, *Holland onder de regeering van keizer Karel den Vijfden, bij den overdragt der Nederlanden aan, en gedurende het bestier van, zijnen zoon koning Philips den Tweeden of verzameling van alle de notulen, propositien, resolutien en andere besognes, in de dagvaarden bij de vergadering van de Staaten dier provincie gehouden, genomen en gedaan door A. van der Goes. . .*, 6 vols. (Amsterdam, 1791), 11 June 1550, 23 August 1553; GAA, inv. no. 5029/29, pp. 148, 260, 266.

[18] Ter Braake, *Met recht en rekenschap*, 215.

[19] See for example the opinion of the city council of Leiden in 1513: SAL, inv. no. 383, fol. 207r: "Ende hoewel die voirs. stede der voirs. zaicken onsculdich was, en zoude nochtans niet behoirlick wesen dat men den ghenen die de stede tot heurder onschult behol pen hebben gheen danckbairheyt bewijsen en zoude." ("And even though the city was

Venice, who offer gifts to the 'young doctor' for giving sound legal advice. One of them even felt so obliged to the 'doctor' that he could not refuse 'him' the very personal ring he received from his wife.[20]

This last category of gifts shows, among other sources, which men were able to put their influence to good use for the cities. The general pattern is that the central officers in Brussels and Malines and a handful of regional officers received gifts from practically all of the cities. We therefore must interpret these gifts as signs of the general influence of these officers and not so much as a 'special bond' with each city. We see for example that the influential councillor Frederik van Renesse, and the master of the Chamber of Accounts Vincent Cornelisz, each received 250 Dutch pounds from the city of Gouda in 1518 for services rendered, an ox and half a barrel of butter in the same year from Haarlem for getting them a reduction in the subsidy to the prince, and stained-glass windows from Leiden in 1521.[21] President Gerrit van Assendelft, the highest officer in Holland next to the stadtholder, also benefited from such gifts, though surprisingly to a lesser extent to the aforementioned men.[22]

What is possibly even more surprising is that the stadtholders received fewer gifts from the individual cities than these men. Probably they were unable to maintain as many local connections as the above-mentioned officers, or were less willing to put their influence to good use for any particular city. It is in any case not the result of their being less influential, since they received major gifts from the States of Holland as a collective for their services to Holland in general.[23]

I will now focus on the more personal ties between the officers and the cities, which were based on more than just their general influence. We shall see that it was imperative for every city to maintain good connections not only with the most influential officers, but also with slightly less prominent and more closely connected men, who could use their influence to the city's benefit.

---

innocent, it would not be decent not to thank the people who helped the city to get them proclaimed innocent.")

[20] Shakespeare's *The Merchant of Venice* (Act 4 Scene i to Act 4 Scene ii; Act 5 Scene i). The role of personal gift-giving concerning legal matters in the sixteenth century has been explored by Natalie Z. Davis, *The Gift in Sixteenth-Century France* (Oxford: Oxford University Press, 2000).

[21] Ter Braake, *Met recht*, 218.

[22] For money, oxen, and timber from Amsterdam, for example: GAA, inv. no. 5014/1, fol. 26^v (money); inv. no. 5014/6, fol. 36 (timber); inv. no. 5014/10, fol. 49^v (oxen).

[23] Ter Braake, *Met recht*, 199.

Case Studies of the Cities

I shall now give some examples of the special connections between the cities and the princely officers. These connections were maintained by both sides. The councillors often were sent to deliberate with the city elites with whom they already had connections.[24] I shall focus on the connections of Dordrecht, the oldest city of Holland, Amsterdam, the up-and-coming city, and three of the other major cities.

Dordrecht

Most princely officers in The Hague either were born in The Hague itself in 'officer families' or had their origins in Dordrecht.[25] Often the prince could benefit from these connections of his officers. Yet sometimes the same connections backfired on him when the officer showed more loyalty to the city than to him.

Floris Oom van Wijngaarden Florisz. and his cousin Floris Oom van Wijngaarden Jansz.,[26] for example, maintained good relations with Dordrecht, although their grandfather had settled in The Hague when he entered the prince's service.[27] Floris Oom van Wijngaarden Jansz. started his career in The Hague in 1496 as a councillor in the Council of Holland. He was removed from his office in 1510, however, because some cities had complained about his conduct. Three years later he was in the service of Dordrecht as their 'pensionary', the city's representative on the diets of the States of Holland, and primarily responsible for protecting the city's privileges.

Floris certainly took his work seriously and eventually was accused of being some kind of demagogue. The Dordrecht privilege to pay only a relatively small part of the subsidies to the prince had already been a point of dispute for decades when Floris became the city's 'pensionary'. Because things looked grim for the citizens, he decided to tell them the story of Esther from the Old Testament, according to him to "comfort them." The Jewish Esther was married to the Persian King Ahasuerus. Haman, the first councillor of Ahasuerus and unaware of Esther's heritage, gave the order that all Jews were to be exterminated. The hero of the story was Mordechai, who had raised Esther, and who told Esther to stand up for her people. Eventually Haman was killed and Mordechai became the king's new first councillor. It is hardly surprising that the central officers in

---

[24] Ter Braake, *Met recht*, 207.

[25] Ter Braake, *Met recht*, chap. 3.1.2. See for the existence of officer families W. Prevenier, "Officials in Town and Countryside in the Low Countries: Social and Professional Developments from the Fourteenth to the Sixteenth Century," *Acta Historiae Neerlandicae* 8 (1974): 1–17.

[26] Florisz. and Jansz. meaning son of Floris and Jan respectively. See above, n. 16.

[27] See for the early Oom van Wijngaardens Damen, *De staat van dienst*, 479–80.

Brussels and Malines accused Floris of inciting hatred toward them. In Floris' analogy we see the citizens of Dordrecht as the oppressed people, the central councillors as Haman (who would meet with disaster), and Floris himself as Mordechai. Other accusations were that Floris had been disrespectful towards the governor and the Council of Holland, and therefore towards his former colleagues, and that he had written a threatening letter to the city of Delft. Eventually Floris was banished from Dordrecht on the order of the prince and had to resign his office.

Nonetheless, Floris was a powerful man; among others he was a friend of the future Pope Adrian VI. Some years later he was reinstated as 'pensionary' and even became active in the imperial inquisition.[28] Floris therefore serves as a perfect example of how important it was for not only the cities, but also for the prince, to keep the influential men in Holland on their side.

Floris' cousin and namesake, Floris Oom van Wijngaarden Florisz., caused less trouble. He was registrar in the Council of Holland for twenty years until he became councillor in 1503. Unlike his cousin he remained a councillor until his death in 1532. He was in the service of the prince for more than fifty years; nonetheless he still kept in touch with the city elites of Dordrecht, as witnessed by two letters from 1521.[29] In the first letter he invites the magistrate to come to his castle of IJsselmonde where a relative would sing his first Mass. Afterwards, writes Floris, they might throw a party. In the second letter Floris mentions that he had received the city's letter, which had been carried to him by his 'relative' Floris van Coulster, who was a magistrate in Dordrecht and the brother of Councillor Abel van Coulster. The Dordrecht magistrate had requested Floris' presence, to which he agrees. Unfortunately we do not know what they talked about. Late in 1527 and again at the beginning of 1528 Floris wrote to the city to have pity on the inhabitants of IJsselmonde, to some extent his personal subjects, who also were citizens of Dordrecht, and not to tax them too highly.[30]

Registrar in the Council of Holland, Arend Sandelijn was born in Dordrecht and did not forget his roots either. Before he became a registrar, and later councillor, he served the city as solicitor before the Council of Holland.[31] In 1528, when he had been the registrar for over a decade, he bought the office of the person responsible for bringing barrels of wine and beer to the city of Dordrecht,

---

[28] S. ter Braake, "Korte biografie van meester Floris Oem van Wijngaarden (c. 1467–1527)," *Holland* 37 (2005): 63–77, at 70–73.

[29] Stadsarchief Dordrecht, stadsarchief, de grafelijke tijd (=GAD), inv. nr. 2.192–193, Floris Oom van Wijngaarden Florisz. to the city magistrate of Dordrecht (8 and 13 August 1521).

[30] GAD, inv. no. 2.199/200 (Floris Oom van Wijngaarden Florisz. to Dordrecht, 30 December 1527 and 21 January 1528).

[31] GAD, inv. no. 2.132, Hendrik de Beauvoir to Floris Oom van Wijngaarden Jansz. (8 September 1514).

with the purpose of aiding his "poor friends" ("arme scamele vrinden") there "as he should" ("als hij schuldich is").[32] Another example is provided by the mediating role of Councillor Cornelis de Jonge and master in the Chamber of Accounts Tielman Oom van Wijngaarden (uncle of the two Florises) during a conflict between the cities of Dordrecht and Schoonhoven. Both of them had roots in Dordrecht.[33]

The connections of Dordrecht with princely officers possibly ensured the city's relatively ready consent to the prince's subsidies. These connections were kept alive during the period under research here. Councillor Cornelis Suys, for example, was the brother-in-law of Boudewijn Drenkwaerd, who in the second half of the sixteenth century represented the city at diets.[34] The citizens on the other hand also benefited from their 'friends' in power. Arend Sandelijn even felt 'obliged' to do something for his poorer friends in the city.

Amsterdam

Jan Benninck was appointed councillor in The Hague in 1510, after he had been sheriff of Amsterdam for fourteen years. His appointment as sheriff ended when the magistrate of Amsterdam leased the office from the prince, which indicates that they were not too happy with his performance at that time and wanted to appoint their own candidate.[35] This might be related to Benninck's trying to interfere too much in local affairs—customarily this fell to the city council ('vroedschap'). When Benninck became a councillor, however, he still often travelled to Amsterdam and its surroundings to represent the prince and deliberate with the subjects.[36] No problems are reported during his time as a councillor, from 1510 until 1535, but after his death he was accused of several abuses.

In 1536 the people of Amsterdam had to exonerate themselves from the problems caused by heretics, followers of Luther and Anabaptists, in the city.

---

[32] Nationaal Archief, Archief Grafelijkheidsrekenkamer, Registers (=RekReg), inv. no. 8, fols. 47–47ᵛ.

[33] GAD, inv. no. 318, fols. 9–10; P.H. van de Wall, *Handvesten, privilegien, vrijheden, voorregten, octrooijen en costumen; midsgaders sententien, verbonden, overéénkomsten, en andere voornaame handelingen der stad Dordrecht: opgezogt, overgezien, met de oorsprongkelijke stukken vergeleeken, en met geschied- en oudheidkundige aanmerkingen opgehelderd*, Tweede deel (vols. IV–VI) (Dordrecht: Van Braam, 1790), 721–23.

[34] Koopmans, *De Staten van Holland*, 247–48.

[35] J. ter Gouw, *Geschiedenis van Amsterdam*, 8 vols. (Amsterdam: Scheltema en Holkema, 1879–1893), 3: 367–68.

[36] For Benninck's journeys as a councillor to Amsterdam see for example GAA, inv. no. 5029/28, p. 189; Nationaal Archief, Archief Grafelijkheidsrekenkamer, Rekeningen (=RekRek), inv. no. 345, fols. 167, 168; inv. no. 347, fols. 104, 105ᵛ–106; inv. no. 355, fols. 101ᵛ–102; inv. no. 356, fols. 94ᵛ, 95ᵛ; inv. no. 357, fols. 95–96; inv. no. 4439, fol. 36; inv. no. 4444, fol. 32ᵛ.

The deceased Jan Benninck was blamed for all of the problems. As a councillor he would have made sure that the city was entirely in the hands of his friends and relatives. He was present during the yearly elections of the burgomasters and aldermen by the city council, notwithstanding that he was a councillor living in The Hague. He claimed that since he had once been an alderman ('schepen') in the city he had the right to be in the city council. According to the accusations he brought "an old and demented man who could barely stand on his feet" ("oudt versuft man die gaen noch staen en mochte") to the city hall (probably a man who was entitled to vote because of an office he had once held), so that he could win the most votes. Rigging the voting in this way would have resulted in a lot of 'incompetent' aldermen keeping Jan Benninck and his fellowship in charge "eternally" ("ten eeuwigen dagen").[37] So we see here a princely officer who used his influence to keep his own local faction in power in Amsterdam. This of course could also be beneficial to the prince, but when one faction is in power for too long there tend to be abuses which in the end are only in the interest of the faction itself.

Jan Benninck's supposed role as a benefactor of heretics was even more striking than his meddling in the city elections, because this went completely against the interests of the prince. Charles V saw the prosecution of heretics as one of his most sacred duties, and Benninck, as his representative as a councillor, should therefore have been active in this field as well, rather than obstructing it. Heresy was a contentious issue in the second quarter of the sixteenth century, and every officer was urged to do his duty well. In 1528 the governor, Anton van Lalaing, threatened the representatives of Amsterdam saying that he knew very well how much heresy there was in the city. Their sheriff, who was appointed by the city's magistrate since they had leased the office themselves, was too weak. Van Lalaing threatened to "better" ("beteren") the sheriff or otherwise lend money himself to pay off the lease of the office.[38] After his death it was claimed that Benninck had received suspect clergymen in his house and had refused to vote in heresy cases before the Council of Holland, saying that the prince had revoked his placards against heresy. When he still was alive, however, his position as a councillor never seems to have been jeopardized.[39] He is an example of a man who had good contacts with both the prince and with a local 'faction' in Amsterdam and in fact was too powerful for either side. The citizens of Amsterdam complained about his trying to monopolize power in the city, and if half of the

---

[37] A. F. Mellink, *Documenta Anabaptistica Neerlandica* (Leiden: Brill, 1975–1988), 5: no. 303; Nationaal Archief, Ambtenaren Centraal Bestuur (=ACB), inv. no. 94.

[38] GAA, inv. no. 5029/28, pp. 299–300, 303–4; inv. no. 5029/29, pp. 19–20, 23; Ter Gouw, *Geschiedenis van Amsterdam*, 4: 157, 161.

[39] J. G. De Hoop Scheffer, *Geschiedenis der kerkhervorming in Nederland van haar ontstaan tot 1531* (Amsterdam: Funke, 1873), 598, 606–7; Mellink, *Documenta*, 5: doc. 303.

rumours about his affinity with heretics were true, he was not a very loyal servant to the prince either.

Reinier Brunt, whom we already met in the introduction to this paper, also had lasting ties with Amsterdam. Two of his daughters were married to the sons of a prominent Amsterdam family.[40] Such marriage alliances were quite common. Most officers originated from the city elites themselves. In 1537 and 1538, when Brunt recently had become a councillor, he deliberated with the Amsterdam representatives about the subsidy to the prince.[41] As attorney-general (1523–1536) he, more than anyone else, had been tasked with the prosecution of heretics. Therefore, and because of his general connections in Amsterdam, it was he who made sure there were loyal and Catholic aldermen and burgomasters in Amsterdam after the outbreak of an Anabaptist revolt there in 1535.[42] In this case it was clearly the prince who was the principal beneficiary of Brunt's connections.

Three of the Other Cities: Gouda, Delft, and Leiden

In the introduction we already mentioned Master Reinier Brunt's close ties with Gouda. His appearance there in 1524 was certainly not the only time he paid the city a visit during his terms as attorney-general and later councillor in the Council of Holland. It was he, for example, who went to Gouda in 1536 to persuade the city to pay for the preparation of some ships. In 1527 he presented the city with the regent's proposal to defend the country against the king of France.[43]

Like Brunt, Jacob Mouwerysz., a native of Gouda, was a former pensionary of the city when he entered the prince's service as a councillor in the Council of Holland. In this capacity he was sent to Gouda often, for a variety of tasks. In 1516, for example, he had to recruit soldiers from the city.[44] Even though he now was in service to the prince, he still occupied himself with the city's assignments,[45] and in recognition of this in 1517 he received a gift of beer which

---

[40] Tracy, *Holland under Habsburg Rule*, 134.

[41] GAA, inv. no. 5029/29, pp. 415, 424.

[42] ACB, inv. no. 94, Reinier Brunt to Anton van Lalaing (10 and 18 January 1536); inv. no. 72, Reinier Brunt to Anton van Lalaing (30 January 1537); Mellink, *Documenta*, 5: nos. 75, 82, 299–300.

[43] Aud., inv. no. 1530, fol. 214 (Gerrit van Assendelft to Anton van Lalaing, 22 August 1536); Rollin-Couquerque and Meerkamp van Embden, "Goudse Vroedschaps-resoluties," 27 April 1537.

[44] Streekarchief Midden-Holland, Oud archief Gouda (=OAG), inv. nr. 1175, fol. 21. For more missions in general: OAG, inv. no. 1175, fols. 19ᵛ–21; inv. no. 1176, fols. 20ᵛ, 24–24ᵛ.

[45] In 1516: OAG, inv. no. 1175, fols 51, 52, 55ᵛ. In 1521: OAG, inv. no. 1179, fol. 57ᵛ.

was double that given to more experienced councillors. In 1518 he received a gift from the city on the occasion of his wedding.[46]

The lack of surviving sources means that the ties of the princely officers with the city of Delft are harder to determine. This is a pity since Delft was, after The Hague and Dordrecht, the most prominent supplier of princely officers. Nonetheless the prince's accounts show that councillors with origins in Delft were often sent there, especially to deal with heresy. Councillor Joost Sasbout was the brother and brother-in-law of two representatives of the city.[47] When there were rumours about an Anabaptist revolt in Delft, it therefore was logical to send Joost to the city to deal with the situation.[48] Councillor Willem Pijnsen, whose parents came from Delft, was sent on missions to deal with heretics relatively frequently. He probably was selected for this not because he was an expert in the field of heresy prosecution, but because, through his parents, he still had connections in Delft. We see that in ten out of these eighteen heresy missions he was sent to that city.[49]

The final 'special' bond I shall examine is that of the city of Leiden with councillor (1515–1528) and later president of the Council of Holland (1528–1558) Gerrit van Assendelft. Van Assendelft was sheriff of the city between 1527 and 1533, and maintained good relations with the Leiden elites after that time.[50] In 1537 he recommended Adriaan Aertsz., a citizen of Leiden, to stadtholder Anton van Lalaing, for the office of usher ('deurwaarder') in the Council of Holland. Gerrit told the governor that the friends of Adriaan Aertsz., who were "among the most notable in the magistrate of Leiden" ("van de principaelsten in de wet van Leyden zijn"), would be very grateful for this.[51]

Seven years later there was a conflict between the city of Leiden and attorney-general Hippolitus van Persijn. The attorney-general had arrested a man from Leiden because, according to him, the city itself was too lenient in cases of heresy. Gerrit van Assendelft was willing to listen to the complaints of the citizens of Leiden, who claimed that according to the *privilegium de non evocando*, they were allowed to deal with the matter themselves. However, the attorney-general refused to give up his prisoner, receiving support from the regent, Mary

---

[46] OAG, inv. no. 1176, fol. 23; inv. no. 1177, fol. 24.

[47] Koopmans, *De Staten van Holland*, 253.

[48] Aud., inv. no. 1529, fol. 172 (Gerrit van Assendelft to Anton van Lalaing, 26 March 1536).

[49] Based on RekRek, inv. no. 4448/4468. "Ander ontfanck extraordinarys geemployeert tot betalinge van de oncosten in 't stuck van de informatien ende executien van de luteryanen."

[50] RekRek, inv. no. 362, fol. 89; inv. no. 368, fol. 124ᵛ.

[51] Aud., inv. no. 1531, fols. 101–101ᵛ (Gerrit van Assendelft to Anton van Lalaing, 16 December 1537).

of Hungary, who said that cases of heresy solely belonged to the prince or his attorney-general.[52]

Conclusions and Cutting the Ties

There were a limited number of central and regional officers with whom *every* city wanted to have a good relationship. These officers were 'showered' with gifts from all sides. What we have seen as well is that there were (less) prominent officers who maintained good relations with one or two particular cities and were willing to advance their particular interests, or were most capable of persuading them to agree to the demands of the prince. Sometimes generations after one of their ancestors had settled in The Hague, these officers still maintained good relations with the cities where they had their roots. Often the officers also had good connections in cities where they had been on the payroll in the past. The men who grew up in a city, worked there, or had ancestors and relatives there enjoyed a level of trust which made them particularly suitable to play the role of brokers, mediating between the interests of the prince and those of the city.

We have seen that the personal ties of the princely officers with the cities could be of great use to the prince when it came to implementing his wishes. When heresy, taxes, or war raised their ugly heads, officers with good relations with the 'locals' were sent to the cities and managed to smooth the relationship between the prince and his subjects. We have also seen, however, that the same contacts could be damaging to the prince's interests. For the citizens the contacts usually were beneficial, but they did not always all feel the benefit of this. The accusations that Jan Benninck and his faction held Amsterdam in their power for decades show that some prominent citizens were not happy with his continuous meddling in the city's affairs. According to the same accusers, it was Benninck who had caused the rise of heresy in Amsterdam, which was to the great sorrow of some of the citizens as well as the prince.

Despite these continuous connections between princely officers and city elites, we see that the bonds slowly diminished in the course of the sixteenth century. In the last quarter of the fifteenth century and first quarter of the sixteenth century it was still common for a man to be first in the service of a city and later in service of the prince, or the other way around, whereas in the second quarter of the sixteenth century most men remained in service of either the prince or the subjects.[53] This slowly created more distance between the princely officers and the cities. Simultaneously, officer dynasties became so integrated into The Hague that the connections with their ancestral city grew thinner every generation, even if this was a very slow process.

---

[52] Van der Goes, *Holland*, 13 October 1544, 7 and 24 February 1545.
[53] Ter Braake, "In the Service."

When these officers gradually resolved themselves into two opposing sides—those representing the prince and those representing the cities—it became harder to smooth relations and implement difficult decisions from the centre without causing serious protest. This made the relationship between the prince and his subjects more tense, especially when Philip II succeeded his father in 1555. The diminishing number of men able to play the role of a successful broker was one of the reasons why the citizens of Holland started to operate more independently from the prince and his officers and eventually were able to revolt successfully against Habsburg rule.

Town, Faith, and Power in Unquiet Times: Prague between the Hussite Pre-Reformation and the Habsburgs' Rule (1436–1526)

Christian-Frederik Felskau

Introduction

Reflections about power are probably as old as mankind's inclination to ponder the shape and meaning of his social life. Not surprisingly, such reflections have an important place within medieval studies.[1] In this field, possibly the greatest impact has been made by Max Weber and Pierre Bourdieu.[2] Weber's theory, according to which power is measured by the possibility of forcing one's own will on others, was complemented by the French sociologist and his studies on symbolic and ritual

---

[1] Recent contributions include *Aspects of Power and Authority in the Middle Ages*, ed. Brenda Bolton and Christine Meek, International Medieval Research 14 (Turnhout: Brepols, 2007); *La pouvoir au Moyen Âge: Idéologies, pratiques, représentations,* ed. Claude Carozzi and Huguette Taviani-Carozzi, Collection le Temps de l'Histoire (Arles: Publications de l'Université de Provence, 2005); *Institutionelle Macht: Genese — Verstetigung — Verlust. Im Auftrag des Sonderforschungsbereichs 537,* ed. André Brodocz et al. (Cologne: Böhlau, 2005). This article uses the following abbreviations for frequently cited periodicals: *DP=Documenta Pragensia; PSH=Pražský sborník historický.*

[2] Compare Christian Hochmuth and Susanne Rau, "Stadt — Macht — Räume: Eine Einführung," in *Machträume der frühneuzeitlichen Stadt,* ed. eidem, Konflikt und Kultur — Historische Perspektiven 13 (Konstanz: UVK, 2006), 13–40, at 24; see also Susan Reynolds, "Secular Power and Authority in the Middle Ages," in *Power and Identity in the Middle Ages: Essays in Memory of Rees Davies,* ed. Huw Pryce and John Watts (Oxford: Oxford University Press, 2007), 11–22, at 12, with short reflections upon Gierke's and Ullmann's ascending or descending theory of power.

Negotiating the Political in Northern European Urban Society, c.1400–c.1600, ed. Sheila Sweetinburgh, MRTS 434 (Tempe: ACMRS, 2013). [ISBN 978-0-86698-482-9]

aspects of power.[3] Recent debates have focused on the question of what power is based upon and the level of its visibility, and the ideas generated from these debates underpin this article: namely, that the relationship between power's appearance and justification is so strong that the two spheres can hardly be separated.[4]

Owing to the attractive nature of power, historiography gives much more attention to the so-called flourishing epochs than to those labelled as stagnant or even decadent.[5] This general observation is confirmed by the turbulent period of Prague's history discussed here, which has received little attention compared to the 'Golden Prague' of Charles IV (1346/47–1378)[6] or the glamorous era of Rudolph II (1576–1611/12).[7] To date relatively little has been written on the time between the acceptance of the Basle *Compactata* by the Diet in Iglau/Jihlava in 1436 and the integration of Bohemia into the Habsburg Empire through the election of Ferdinand I (1526–1564) as king by the assembly of the three estates in Prague in 1526.[8] Undoubtedly, the Hussite Pre-Reformation and its

---

[3] Pierre Bourdieu, *Sozialer Raum und "Klassen": Leçon sur la leçon* (Frankfurt am Main: Suhrkamp, 1995); compare Gerhard Göhler and Rudolph Speth, "Symbolische Macht: Zur institutionentheoretischen Bedeutung von Pierre Bourdieu," in *Institutionen und Ereignis: Über historische Praktiken und Vorstellungen gesellschaftlichen Ordnens*, ed. Reinhard Blänkner and Bernhard Jussen (Göttingen: Vandenhoeck & Ruprecht, 1998), 17–48. For the refusal of power as a structuring principle see Michel Foucault, *Das Subjekt und die Macht*, in *Michel Foucault: Jenseits von Strukturalismus und Hermeneutik*, ed. Hubert Dreyfus and Paul Rabinow (Frankfurt am Main: Athenäum, 1994), 243–61, at 254.

[4] On this topic see *Das Sichtbare und das Unsichtbare der Macht: Institutionelle Prozesse in Antike, Mittelalter und Neuzeit. Im Auftrag des Sonderforschungsbereichs 537*, ed. Gert Melville (Cologne: Böhlau, 2005).

[5] Peter Moraw, "Die Länder der Krone Böhmen, König Johann (1310–1346) und Kaiser Karl (1346/57–1378)," in *Die Blüte der Staaten des östlichen Europa im 14. Jahrhundert*, ed. Marc Löwener, Quellen und Studien des Deutschen Historischen Instituts Warschau 14 (Wiesbaden: Harrassowitz, 2005), 143–68.

[6] For recent studies see *Prague: The Crown of Bohemia 1347–1437*, ed. Barbara Drake Boehm and Jiří Fajt (New York and London: The Metropolitan Museum of Art, Yale University Press, 2005); Ralf Lützelschwab, "Prag, das neue Paris?: Der französische Einfluß auf die Reliquienpolitik Karls IV.," in *Wallfahrten in der europäischen Kultur—Pilgrimage in European Culture*, Tagungsband Přibram, 26–29 Mai 2004, ed. Daniel Doležal and Hartmut Kühne, Europäische Wallfahrtsstudien 1 (Frankfurt am Main: Peter Lang, 2006), 201–19.

[7] For example *Rudolph II and Prague: The Court and the City*, ed. Eliška Fučíková et al., exhibition catalogue (London: Thames & Hudson, 1997).

[8] Summary: Jiří Pesek, "Macht in der Stadtgeschichte Prags–Von der Gründung der Prager Karls-Universität bis zur Gegenwart," in *Die Macht der Städte. Von der Antike bis zur Gegenwart*, ed. Michael Gehler, Historische Europa-Studien 4 (Hildensheim/Zurich/New York: Olms, 2011), 477–90, at 481; fundamental: Václav V. Tomek, *Dějepis mesta Prahy*, 9 vols., Novočeská Biblioteka (Prague: Fr. Řivnáč, 1892–1906), dedicating

consequences caused a serious break for the Bohemian capital, reducing its European ties,[9] its splendour, and not least its demographic size.[10] Though Prague suffered a time of chronic instability, the religious plurality, local government, and wider Bohemian politics coalesced in the town and became entangled in European politics. This makes the epoch preceding the Habsburgs' rule in Prague so interesting for questions of power with a local, urban focus.[11]

The Town and the Re-establishment of Imperial Power: Sigismund and Utraquist Prague

Sigismund of Luxembourg, the eldest son of Charles IV, reigned in Bohemia from 1419 to 1437. The hope expressed at the council of Basle that with Sigismund's return to the Bohemian capital the former ordered status of Central Europe would be re-established, however, remained unfulfilled, if one considers the subsequent

---

vols. 5 to 9 to that era; recently *Dějiny Prahy I: Od nejstarších dob do sloučení pražských měst (1784)*, ed. Pavla Státníková et al. (Prague and Litomyšl: Paseka, 1997), 243–72, 344–47. Ivan Borkovsk and Josef Janáček, *Dějiny Prahy* (Prague: Nakl. polit. lit., 1964); Franz Machilek, "*Praga caput regni*: Zur Entwicklung und Bedeutung Prags im Mittelalter," in *Stadt und Landschaft im deutschen Osten und in Mitteleuropa*, ed. Friedhelm B. Kaiser and Bernhard Stasiewski, Studien zum Deutschtum 17 (Cologne: Böhlau, 1982), 67–126, esp. 98–103.

[9] In particular see František Šmahel, *Die Hussitische Revolution*, 3 vols., MGH Schriften 43–45 (Hannover: Hahn, 2002); Thomas A. Fudge, *The Crusades Against Heretics in Bohemia, 1418–1437: Sources and Documents for the Hussite Crusades*, Crusade Texts in Translation 9 (Aldershot: Ashgate, 2002); see also the chronicle of a contemporary witness, *Die Hussiten: Die Chronik des Laurentius von Březová 1414–1421*, trans., intro., and annot. Josef Burjoch, Slawische Geschichtsschreiber 11 (Graz: Böhlau, 1988).

[10] After the reign of Charles IV in which nearly 60,000 inhabitants were registered as living in Prague, pre-Reformation events resulted in a heavy loss of citizens: see Eduard Maur, "Urbanizace před urbanizací," in *Zrod velkoměsta: Urbanizace českých zemí a Evropa*, ed. Pavel Horská et al. (Prague and Litomyšl: Paseka, 2002), 54–120, at 61, 83. In 1524, only an estimated 25,000 inhabitants lived in the Prague towns: Josef Janáček, *Das alte Prag* (Leipzig: Koehler & Amelang, 1980), 125. According to Hochmuth and Rau, "Stadt—Macht—Räume," 18, at the end of the sixteenth century Prague's population had increased to 70,000 inhabitants.

[11] With references to the capital see Petr Čornej, *Velké dějiny zemí koruny české, Svazek V: 1412–1437* and idem and Milena Bartlová, *Velké dějiny zemí koruny české, Svazek VI: 1437–1526* (Prague and Litomyšl: Paseka, 2004, 2007, respectively); Petr Klučina, *České země za Jiřího z Poděbrad a Jagellovců* (Prague: Albatros, 1994); Jörg Hoensch, *Geschichte Böhmens: von der slawischen Landnahme bis ins 20. Jahrhundert* (Munich: Beck, 1997), 154–84. Unfortunately, I was unable to gain access to the study of Jeanne Ellen Grant, "The Political Side of Hussitism: Late Medieval Law in Bohemia and the Holy Roman Empire" (Ph.D. diss., University of California at Berkeley, 2005).

history of Bohemia and that of the royal town of Prague.[12] Principally, there were two reasons for this failure: on the one hand, the king had to deal with the Bohemian nobility, the majority of whom were critical of him and noticeably few of whom were present at his coronation in St Vitus' Cathedral in 1420.[13] On the other hand, the elderly ruler was not prepared to break up the politically dominant position of the city of Prague in Utraquist Bohemia, which it had gained after the outbreak of the Hussite revolt.[14] The Utraquists were a body of Hussites who fought for the right to receive the Eucharist in both kinds (*utraque specie*); sometimes they are called also 'Calixtines' or 'Adherents of the Chalice'.

In 1435, Sigismund ordered that Vyšehrad and the castle district of Hradčany must seek reconciliation with the prevailingly Hussite citizens of Prague.[15] He also stated that they would not have to pay extraordinary taxes and that the important office of vice chamberlain (*Unterkämmerer, podkomořík*) would always be held by a local person. Consequently, when the king entered the Bohemian capital in August 1436 he took up residence not in the damaged castle, the traditional royal seat, but in the palace built by King Wenceslas IV (d. 1419) in the Old Town near the church of St Benedict, the former settlement of the Teutonic Knights.[16] This was one of two royal residences constructed by Wenceslas; the

---

[12] This hope was expressed by Johannes Schele (d. 1439), bishop of Lübeck and participant in the council of Basle: Günther Hödl, "Zur Reichspolitik des Basler Konzils: Bischof Johannes Schele von Lübeck (1420 bis 1439)," *Mitteilungen des Instituts für Österreichische Geschichte* 75 (1967): 46–65. For general remarks on the type of royal towns see Felicitas Schmieder, *Die mittelalterliche Stadt,* Wissen kompakt (Darmstadt: Wissenschaftliche Buchgesellschaft, 2005), 86; H. Samsonowicz, "Free Royal Cities," in *Oxford Dictionary of the Middle Ages* (hereafter *ODMA*), ed. R. Bjork, 4 vols. (Oxford: Oxford University Press, 2010), 2: 669. The contributions in *DP* 21 (2002) under the title "Osm set let pražské samosprávy" shed light on various aspects of Prague's self-government over time.

[13] For statistical remarks on the nobility after the Hussite revolt see Jiří Jurok, *Česká šlechta a feudalita ve středověku a raném novověku* (Nový Jičín: Dílna, 2000), 94–102. See the 1458 chronicle of Aenea Silvio Piccolomini, *Historia Bohemica. Historie česká,* trans. and ed. Dana Matrínková et al., Clavis monumentorum litterarum regnum Bohemiae 4, Fontes rerum Regni Bohemiae 1 (Prague: KLP, 1998), 118–20: "pauci nobiles Pragensium [. . .]."

[14] About the fate of the Utraquist party see Zdeněk V. David, *Finding the Middle Way: The Utraquists' Liberal Challenge to Rome and Luther* (Washington, DC: Woodrow Wilson Center Press, 2003); Wilhelm Baum, *Kaiser Sigismund: Hus, Konstanz und Türkenkriege* (Graz: Styria, 1993), 272–76.

[15] According to Jaroslav Kadlec, *Přehled českých církevních dějin,* 2 vols. (Řím: Zvon, 1987), 1: 289, only the parish church of St Benedict in the Old Town remained in the hands of the Roman Catholics.

[16] This residence, completed in 1385, consisted of two courtyards and a palace with an adjacent tower, connecting the existing tower of the Old Town with what is today known as Celetná Street: Barbara Drake Boehm and Jiří Fajt, "Wenceslas IV," in *Prague:*

other was close to the brothers of the Holy Sepulchre in the New Town, and the two were intended to demonstrate his balanced relationship to the two most important city communities.[17]

On 26 August 1436 King Sigismund conducted a solemn ceremony at which considerable numbers of the leading nobility were present,[18] where he received the oath of loyalty from the councillors of all Prague's towns: that is, the Old Town, the New Town on the right of the Moldau, and the heavily damaged Lesser Town, the *civitas minor* (also called *Kleinseite, Malá strana*) on the other side of the Moldau. At the same time, he restored the former independent position of the New Town, which it had lost temporarily when the councillors of the Old Town—at that time prevailingly adherents of the Catholic faith—took over control in 1434.[19] To counter this apparent loss of royal power, he tightened his control on the civic authorities by again taking the right to appoint new councillors. At the time, the council of the Old Town became dominated by the moderate Hussites, some of whom had even participated in the revolution and who now started to distance themselves from their former leader Jan Velvar. The leader of

---

The Crown of Bohemia, 91–103, at 96, no. 39; for the king's motives see Ivan Hlaváček, "Hof und Hofführung König Wenzels IV.," in *Deutscher Königshof, Hoftag und Reichstag im späteren Mittelalter*, ed. Peter Moraw, Vorträge und Forschungen 48 (Stuttgart: Thorbecke, 2002), 105–36, at 113.

[17] Architecture as a manifestion of power is described by Werner Paravicini, "Das Gehäuse der Macht: Einleitung und Zusammenfassung," in *Das Gehäuse der Macht: Der Raum der Herrschaft im interkulturellen Vergleich*, ed. idem, Mitteilungen der Residenzen-Kommission der Akademie der Wissenschaften zu Göttingen, Sonderheft 7 (Kiel: Selbstverlag, 2005), 7–14. For the topic of urban residences in general see Jens Friedhoff, "Administration: Architektonische Verzahnung von Stadt und Residenz," in *Höfe und Residenzen im spätmittelalterlichen Reich: Bilder und Begriffe*, ed. W. Paravicini, 2 vols., Residenzenforschung 15.1 (Ostfildern: Thorbecke, 2005), 1: 244–47. For a description of the building, erected in the late 1390s, see Pavel Kalina and Jiří Koťátko, *Praha 1310–1419: Kapitoly o vrcholné gotice* (Prague: Libri, 2004), 139.

[18] For the presence of the higher noble families in the city: *Cronica Bartossi de Drahonicz*, ed. Jaroslav Goll, Fontes Rerum Bohemicarum 5 (Prague: Nákl. nadání Františka Palackého, 1893), 591–628, at 619, with the mention of Meinhard of Neuhaus, Alessone of Sternberg, and Hinko of Pirnstein in the first line. On interreligious marriages see the remarks of Petr Maťa, "Vorkonfessionelles, überkonfessionelles, transkonfessionelles Christentum: Prolegomena zu einer Untersuchung der Konfessionalität des böhmischen und mährischen Hochadels zwischen Hussitismus und Zwangskatholisierung," in *Konfessionelle Pluralität als Herausforderung: Koexistenz und Konflikt in Spätmittelalter und Früher Neuzeit. Winfried Eberhard zum 65. Geburtstag*, ed. Joachim Bahlcke et al. (Leipzig: Leipziger Universitätsverlag, 2006), 307–32, at 309, 325.

[19] The following remarks are mainly based on *Dějiny Prahy*, 1: 243–47. On the development of the council system in the Prague towns see Jaromír Čelakovský, "O vývoj středověkého zřízení radního v městech Pražských," *Sborník příspěvků k dějinám hlavního města Prahy* 1. 2 (1920): 257–302.

those opposed to Velvar was Pešík of Kunvald, and this faction was reinforced by the appointment of Pešík's brother, Jan of Kunvald (d. 1440), to the office of royal lower chamberlain, Jan residing "At the silver star" between present-day Dlouha Street and Týnská Street.[20]

The adherents of Velvar and the non-consecrated Archbishop John Rokycana (1431–1471), who was not approved of by the Apostolic See and against whom the king took increasingly resolute action, noticed with disfavour their declining importance, especially when, at the instigation of Sigismund, the elderly Christian of Prachatiz/Křišťan z Prachatic (before 1370 to 1439) was elected to the office of archepiscopal ecclesiastical administrator in 1437.[21] After the death of his predecessor Konrad of Vechta in 1431, Rokycana had become the leader of the Utraquist Church and was supported by the so-called Lower Consistory of this confession.[22] Within the Consistory, located close to the Tein church, the country estates and the towns possessed voting rights.[23] Although it was seen as acceptable on a personal level by the king and his successors, Rokycana's position came under attack from certain sectors of the metropolitan chapter, especially the chapter of Vyšehrad and the houses of several religious orders that had returned to the town during the years 1436–1437.[24] Moreover, of the forty-

---

[20] Description; Ružena Baťková, s.v. "čp. 612," in *Umělecké památky Prahy: Staré město, Josefov*, ed. Pavel Vlček et al. (Prague: Academia, 1996), 414; depiction: *Dějiny Prahy*, 1: 244.

[21] On the early career of Rokycana see T.A. Fudge, "Reform and the Lower Consistory in Prague," in *The Bohemian Reformation and Religious Practice*, ed. Zdeněk V. David and David R. Holeton (Prague: Main Library, Academy of Sciences of the Czech Republic, 1996–), 2: 67–96, esp. 69; idem, "John of Rokycan," *ODMA* 4: 1419.

[22] Fudge, "Reform and the Lower Consistory," esp. 70. In the times of the administrator Wenceslas/Václav the Younger (b. 1417, d. 1497), promoted by Bishop Rokycana, the proceedings took place in the chapel of Bethlehem: Šmahel, *Die Hussitische Revolution*, 3: 1875–78. For a concise biography of Rokycana see Jaroslav Boubín, "Rokycana, Jan (c. 1390–1471)," in *Encyclopedia of the Middle Ages*, 2 vols. (Cambridge: James Clark, 2001), 2: 1250; Milan Šimek, *Role Jana Rokycany při jednávání kompaktát*, on http://www.filosof.cz/prace/rokycana.pdf. On the early synods see *Staré letopisy české*, ed. Alena M. Černá et al., Fontes rerum Bohemicarum, series nova, 2 (Prague: Centrum medievistických studií, 2003), 48.

[23] For further details see Jiří Kejř, "Zur Entstehung des städtischen Standes im hussitischen Böhmen," in *Städte und Ständestaat*, ed. Bernhard Töpfer, Forschungen zur mittelalterlichen Geschichte 26 (Berlin: Akademie-Verlag, 1980), 195–213.

[24] Shortly after his return to Prague, Sigismund, accompanied by Bishop Filibert of Coutances, who later on preached at the Tein church, and several legates, appointed nineteen new clergymen; see James P. Palmitessa, "Wer besaß die Kirchen und Klöster in Prag vor dem Dreißigjährigen Krieg?," in *Konfessionelle Pluralität*, 431–58, at 443. For the reorganisation of religious life and administration see Šmahel, *Die Hussitische Revolution*, 3: 1866–77.

four pre-Hussite parishes only twenty-three remained. Most were headed by Utraquist clergy, but the parishioners had gained considerable autonomy thanks to the ending of patronage rights, allowing them far greater influence on the public life of the city.[25] Yet those few surviving Catholic religious houses whose members did not flee all suffered extensive difficulties: some were subject to internal schism, while others were deprived of their autonomy through the installation of urban office bearers, as in the case of the unique order of Bohemian origin, the Knights with the Red Star.[26]

However, pressure from the royalists and the Catholic nobility grew to such an extent that Rokycana had to leave Prague in the summer of 1437, going into exile in eastern Bohemia where he stayed until 1448 when he returned to the Tein church (St Mary's), the designated metropolitan church of the Utraquists.[27] Nearly two months after Rokycana's departure, King Sigismund's unconcealed animosity towards the more radical branch of the Hussites became manifest in the hanging of more than sixty former adherents of the radical leader Jan Žižka (1360–1424). Among these was the seditious and powerful nobleman Jan Roháč of Dubá, who was executed in front of the city hall on the Old Town's central marketplace.[28] The king's stance was backed by local, wealthy aristocratic families such as the Rosenbergs, the Sternbergs, the Hasenburgs, and the Wartenbergs who expected to benefit from it.[29]

---

[25] F. Šmahel, "Prag in der zweiten Hälfte des 15. Jahrhunderts," in *Zentralität in Ostmitteleuropa an der Wende vom Mittelalter zur Neuzeit*, ed. Evamaria Engel (Berlin: Akademie-Verlag, 1995), 185–12, at 196; Palmitessa, "Wer besaß die Kirchen und Klöster," 439. A listing of all clerics is entailed in Tomek, *Dějepis*, 9: 339–47.

[26] J.B. Palmitessa, "The Knights with the Red Star and the Renewal of Ecclesiastical Property," in *The Bohemian Reformation and Religious Practice*, 5: 359–70, at 363.

[27] For the inauguration festivities of the new church bells in 1436 see Petr Čornej, "Slavnosti husitské Prahy," *DP* 12 (1995): 75–103, at 100. Studies on the episcopal see in Prague include Anna Petitova, "La résidence de l'évêque comme centre du pouvoir ecclésiastique à travers l'exemple de Prague: réflexion sur la destinée d'un lieu de pouvoir," in *Lieux du pouvoir au Moyen Age et à l'epoque moderne: Textes réunis et présentés par Michał Tymowski* (Warsaw: Wyd. Uniwersytetu Warszawskiego, 1995), 173–84; Zdeňka Hledíková, "Biskupské a arcibiskupské centrum ve středověké Praze," *PSH* 27 (1994): 5–25.

[28] Petr Čornej and Bohdan Zilynski, "Jan Roháč z Dubá a Praha: Konec Jana Roháče — pověst a skutečnost," *PSH*, 20 (1987): 35–60; For a short treatment see Jiří Otter, *Fünf Rundgänge durch Prag auf den Spuren der böhmischen Reformation* (Prague: Artep, 2000), 29. In 1433 Jan Roháč of Dubá owned a house, registered under čp. 837a, situated closely to the horse market in the Old Town: *Dějiny Prahy*, 1: 258.

[29] For the distribution of the country's high offices among the noble lineages see Jurok, *Česká šlechta*, 69, table 69; 71, table 1. A major contribution to this topic was made recently by Petr Mat'a, *Svět české aristokracie (1500–1700)* (Prague: Nakl. Lidové noviny, 2004).

The death of Sigismund in early December 1437 did not ease the situation, and the decision of the Diet (*Landtag, zemský sněm*), agreed in Prague later that month, to appoint six noblemen as speakers of the Bohemian kingdom could not balance the loss of royal power.[30] At a meeting in the Charles College of Prague's university the moderate Hussites and many of the most influential Roman Catholic noblemen (who had urban residences, often in the more prestigious Old Town)[31] decided to accept Albrecht of Habsburg, Sigismund's son-in-law, as the future king. They were opposed by the more radical Utraquists around Velvar who supported the candidacy of the Polish prince Kasimir/Kazimierz from the Jagiello dynasty.[32] The council of the Old Town, however, was able to thwart the anticipated resistance of this group by arresting and incarcerating Velvar and several of his supporters as well as banishing other citizens from the city. Consequently, Albrecht was solemnly crowned in St Vitus' Cathedral in June 1438 and was able to reward this allegiance to his house by confirming Pešík of Kunvald and his friends, amongst them Pavel of Dětřichovic, in their official positions. The moderate Hussites were able to strengthen their position still further when a failed attempt by the supporters of the Polish candidate to occupy Prague that summer offered them an opportunity to persecute their opponents. Furthermore, their political ascendancy was not checked by the unexpected death of Albrecht in 1439, nor by the refusal of Albrecht III of Bavaria (1401–1460) to take the crown. In that situation, the governance of Prague controlled by Pešík of Kunvald and the castle governor (*Burgmeister, purkmistr*) of the New Town, Pavel of

---

[30] The acts of this institution, mostly gathered at Prague, were published in *Archiv český čili Staré písemné památky české i morawské z archivůw domácích i cizích*, ed. František Palacky et al., 37 vols. (Prague: Kronberger i Řiwnáč, 1840–1944), 6: 395–450, no. 47. This source is also easily accessible through the internet: http://www.psp.cz/eknih/snemy/. The men appointed were Ulrich of Rosenberg, Meinhard of Hradec, Aleš Holický of Šternberk, Hanuš of Kolovrat, Nikolaus Zajíc of Hasenburg, and Sigmund of Wartenberg. An interesting epistolary collection is in *Království dvojího lidu: České dějiny let v soudobé korespondenci*, ed. Petr Čornej (Prague: Odeon, 1989), 41–62, nos. 1–10.

[31] Within the Old Town, the residences of the higher noble families were traditionally concentrated in two areas, one close to the House of the Landtafeln/dům Zemských desek (*tabulae terrae*, here with the pre-1419 owners of Kunstádt z Waldeck, Hradec, Landštein, Rosenberg), the other between the royal court and the house of the estates, named U černého orla (čp. 493), here with the pre-1419 owners as the mint master Peter Zmrzlík of Schweißing/Petr Zmrzlik of Svojšína, Jindřich Lefl of Lažan, and Jan of Vlašimí.

[32] According to Hoensch, *Geschichte Böhmens*, 154, Kasimir, who was elected by the Utraquists as king of Bohemia on 27 May 1438, was choosen because the Polish nobles opposed the initial option of Władisław III (1424–1444) as candidate, insisting on his residential duty in Silesia.

Dětřichovic, who served the Rosenberg dynasty, could operate under conditions of high independency.[33]

Urban Government in Times of Absent Royal Power

The inner political stability of the Prague towns between 1438 and 1448, especially in comparison with the preceding revolutionary years, is mirrored by the relatively low fluctuation of the city councillors. Members of these urban governing bodies, which differed in size between that of the Old Town (eighteen members), the New Town (twelve), the Little Side (twelve), and the castle districts (six each), could only be fully entitled burghers, and officially they were elected annually.[34] Exceptions to this precondition, however, were numerous, showing that the election was far from being a democratic or controlled procedure. Among the council of the Old Town, only twenty-nine councillors alternated within these ten years, while in the corresponding body of the New Town no more than fifteen persons can be identified.[35] The leading position of Pešík of Kunvald and Pavel of Dětřichovic was so strong that, what with already having a decisive role in the urban council, they were able to execute the office of the castle's governor from 1440 to 1448.[36] Seeking to revive conservative Hussitism, they adopted a policy of reconciliation by appointing the former Hus-followers Jan Příbram (d. 1448) and then Prokop of Pilsen (d. 1457) to the office of administrator of the Chalice church after the death of Christian of Prachatiz, and in this they benefited from the assistence of the highest burgrave (*höchster Burggraf, nejvyšší purkrabí*) Meinhard von Hradec (d. 1449) and of the Prague captain (*Hauptmann, hejtman*)

---

[33] A list of the higher and lower nobility for the year 1440 can be found in *Velké dějiny zemí koruny české*, 6: 68; Tomek, *Dějepis*, 9: 95; see also Robert Šimůnek, "Rožmberská klientela 15. století, část 1," *Výběr* 37.3 (2000): 186–93. See also Michal Fiala and Jakub Hrdlička, "Řídící vrstva v počatcích českých měst na přikladu pražské aglomerace," *DP* 15 (1997): 13–24.

[34] See the remarks of Hana Páthová in *"Liber Vetustissimus Antiquae Civitatis Prageusis 1310–1518,"* ed. eadem, *Documentia Prageusia Monographia* 25 (Prague: Scriptorium, 2011), 142–45. For a comparison with the neighbouring German towns see Joachim Eibach, "Burghers or Town Council: Who was Responsible for Urban Stability in Early Modern German Towns?" *Urban History* 34 (2007): 14–26.

[35] For a summary of the structure and organisation of the town councils see Šmahel, "Prag in der zweiten Hälfte des 15. Jahrhunderts," 194, here also with a distinction between the 'council of the seniors' and the 'great commune'. For the first see Karel Hrubý, "*Senior communitas*—eine revolutionäre Institution der Prager hussitischen Bürgerschaft," *Bohemia* 13 (1972): 9–43. A list of all councillors and urban magistrates is provided in Tomek, *Dějepis*, 5: 77–111; 9: 265–324. The six councillors of the Hradschin and the Vyšehrad were not part of this statistical survey.

[36] *Dějiny Prahy*, 1: 245.

Hanuš of Kolovrat (1390–1450).[37] This comparatively harmonious cohabitation of Hussites and Catholics was best demonstrated by the existence of two administrators in Prague at the top of the two church organisations. The Catholic administrator was instructed by the metropolitan chapter which had relocated to Zittau/Žitava south of the capital. The chapter was allowed to re-establish its administration with all office holders in Prague—though only temporarily—from 1440 onwards.[38]

This period of stability was owed primarily to the political acumen of Pešík and Pavel who, against a background of differing doctrinal positions within the population, managed to strenghten the position of the moderate Hussite groups. At the same time, the desire of the Prague citizens to live peacefully and their readiness to adapt to the Hussite way of life also contributed to this success.[39] However, the city's financial situation was precarious after the Hussite Pre-Reformation, the only beneficiaries being war-profiteers.[40] Nonetheless, soon after peace was restored attempts were made to repair the damage at least to the castle districts of Hradschin and Vyšehrad, and at a slower rate also to the suburban settlements.[41]

Prague During the Government of Georg of Podiebrad

Those holding extreme Hussite views gained support from those in east Bohemia, and for leadership they looked to the nobleman Georg of Podiebrad and Kunstadt (1420–1471)[42] and to the exiled Bishop Rokycana. Podiebrad's career began as a member of the country's court (*Landgericht, zemský soud*) at the end

---

[37] For older biographies see František M. Bartoš, *Literární činnost M. Jana Rokycany, M. Jana Příbrama, M. Petra Payna* (Prague: ČAVU, 1928); Jaroslav Prokeš, *Mistr Prokop z Plzně*, Husitský archiv 3 (Prague: Společnost Husova musea, 1927).

[38] Zdeňka Hledíková provides a detailed description: "Pražská metropolitní kapitula, její samospráva a postavení doby husitské," *Sborník historický* 19 (1972): 5–48.

[39] Petr Čornej, "Praha husitská," in *Praha—Čechy—Evropa: 1100 let kulturní, hospodářské a politické metropole střední Evropy. Publikace k výstavě Clam-Gallasův palac, 7. dubna—1. června 2003* (Prague: Scriptorium, 2003), 32–38, at 37; K. Hrubý, "Struktury a postoje husitských skupin pražského politického systému," *Acta Universitatis Carolinae—Historia Universitatis Carolinae Pragensis* 9. 1 (1968): 29–78.

[40] Šmahel, *Die Hussitische Revolution*, 3: 1773; at greater length Josef Janáček, "Městské finance a investice: Praha 1420–1547," *Československé časopis historický* 25 (1977): 408–26.

[41] For a summary of these aspects see Machilek, *"Praga caput regni*," 98.

[42] A fundamental resource is Rudolf Urbánek, *Věk poděbradský*, 4 vols., České dějiny 3 (Prague: Laichter, 1915–1962); for a concise biography see Otakar Odložilík, *The Hussite King: Bohemia in European Affairs 1440–1471* (New Brunswick: Rutgers University Press, 1965), and R. Šimůnek, "George of Poděbrady," *ODMA* 2: 699–700.

of the 1430s, when he became active in the politics of the estates and established a vast dominion in the territory of his origin. His career was enhanced by the death of his companion, the moderate adherent of the Chalice Hynek Ptáček z Pirkštejna (d. 1444), who fought vigorously in the battle of Lipan/Lipany (1434) on the side of the Prague Chalice alliance.[43] For Podiebrad, Jan Čabelický (d. 1513), and their followers, the capture of Prague Castle in 1443 strengthened their religious convictions, contributing to an escalation in the level of religious conflict in spring 1448. At the same time, the papal legate Juan Carvayal (1390–1469) entered the town to negotiate in the Vyšehrad Castle on the situation of the clergy, the compliance of the *Compactata*, which were exposed to public view on a panel attached to the chapel of the Holy Spirit at the cattle market, and the episcopal status of Rokycana.[44] Probably as a consequence of Carvayal's actions and the growing pressure of the Catholic nobility, headed by the magnate Ulrich (II) of Rosenberg (1403–1462), the highest burgrave Meinhard of Hradec and several local knights broke away from the Chalice confession.[45] The impending loss of the capital to this increasingly Catholic consortium provoked the intervention of Georg of Podiebrad, who shortly afterwards was appointed to the office of the country's administrator (*Landesverweser, zemský správce, gubernator*).[46] In September 1448 he seized Prague with a troop of 9,000 men, and meeting no serious resistance he arrested Meinhard.[47] He also forced Pešík and Pavel, the leading councillors, to resign from their posts. They fled from Prague, while the metropolitan chapter moved again to the (Catholic) Moravian town of Pilsen, since Rokycana—like John Velvar—was expected to return from exile. Beyond Prague, however, the Catholic movement could, despite the shift of power in the capital, enjoy prosperity. For instance, the Observant Franciscan Giovanni

---

[43] Miroslav Plaček and Peter Futák, *Páni z Kunštátu: Rod erbu vrchních pruhů na cestě k trůnu* (Brno: Lidové Noviny, 2006), 374–80.

[44] For summaries of these events see Kadlec, *Přehled českých církevních dějin*, 1: 293–95; Milena Bartlová, *Eine Neudatierung des sog. Raigener Altars und revidierte Chronologie der böhmischen Tafelmalerei des 15. Jahrhunderts* (Prague: Virtus, 1999), 15. The text of the *compactata* in Czech and Latin is to be found in *Archiv český*, 3: 398–444. For the *compactata* see *Dějiny Prahy*, 1: 242.

[45] On Ulrich II see Anna Kubíková, *Oldřich II. z Rožmberka* (České Budějovice: Veduta, 2004); Thomas Wünsch, "Gemeinwohl dezentral: Zu Begriffsinhalt und -verwendung des *obecné dobré* in der politischen Korrespondenz des Ulrich II. von Rosenberg (1403–1462)," in *Konfessionelle Pluralität*, 167–82, at 178.

[46] Machilek, "*Praga caput regni*," 98.

[47] Šmahel, *Die Hussitische Revolution*, 3: 1841; František Palacký, "Vlastenecké dějiny I: Dobytí Prahy skrze p. Jiřího z Poděbrad léta příčiny jeho," *Časopis Českého musea* 1 (1827): 37–83; for a broader discussion of the estate's resistance see Zdeněk Vibíral, "Religious Identities and Political Discourse in Early Modern Bohemia," in *Mighty Europe 1400–1700: Writing an Early Modern Continent*, ed. Andrew Hiscock, Cultural Identity Studies 3 (Oxford: Lang, 2007), 85–96, at 88.

di Capestrano (d. 1456), who dared not enter Prague, still managed to convince people from other towns and the countryside of the benefits of the reform movement of his order, including noblemen with close links with Prague such as Wenzel/Václav of Wolfstein.[48]

After these favourable changes for the Chalice movement in Prague and other regions of the country, Georg of Podiebrad focused on securing and extending his power. Having convinced not only his own faction but also unexpectedly the more radical Tábor to accept the *Compactata* in 1452,[49] his recognition as the country's administrator was ensured (a year earlier Emperor Friedrich III [1452–1493] had confirmed him in the office of country marshal [*Landesmarschall*]).[50] Even the short reign of Ladislaus V Postumus (Pohrobek)—who was crowned in Prague cathedral in 1453 having been king of Hungary since 1440 and for a long period under the emperor's guardianship—could not weaken Podiebrad's position.[51] Although the Catholic nobility, again under the leadership of Ulrich of Rosenberg, had pressed the emperor to ensure Ladislaus' enthronement, it made little impact on the situation in Prague because the new king needed to devote

---

[48] Petr Hlaváček, "Bohemian Franciscans Between Orthodoxy and Nonconformity at the Turn of the Middle Ages," in *The Bohemian Reformation and Religious Practice*, 5 (Prague: Academy of Sciences of the Czeck Republic, 2004), 167–89, at 171.

[49] For some of the religiously defined differences between the Taborites and the Utraquists see Jiří Kejř, "Teaching on Repentance and Confession in the Bohemian Reformation," in *The Bohemian Reformation and Religious Practice*, 5, 89–116, at 106; also F. Šmahel, "Tabor and Taborites," *ODMA* 4: 1591.

[50] I. Hlaváček, "Beiträge zur Erforschung der Beziehungen Friedrichs III. zu Böhmen bis zum Tode Georgs von Podiebrad (1471)," in *Kaiser Friedrich III. und seine Zeit*: *Studien anläßlich des 500. Todestages am 19. August 1493/1993*, ed. Paul-Joachim Heinig, Forschungen zur Kaiser- und Papstgeschichte des Mittelalters, Beihefte zu J.F. Böhmer, *Regesta Imperii*, 12 (Cologne: Böhlau, 1993), 279–98; see latest contributions in *Eger 1459. Fürstentreffen zwischen Sachsen, Böhmen und ihren Nachbarn: dynastische Politik, fürstliche Repräsentation und kulturelle Verflechtung*, Saxonia 13, ed. André Thieme and Uwe Tresp (Wettin-Löbejün: Stekovics, 2011).

[51] F. Šmahel, "Středověké slavnosti, svátky a radostné chvíle (Uvodní zamyšlení)," *DP* 12 (1995): 33–44, at 38. See moreover the contribution of Petr Čornej on the festivities in Hussite Prague: *DP* 12 (1995): 75–104. In the precincts of this event, several representatives of noble families received the accolade: see Werner Rösner, "Reise- und Länderbeschreibungen in autobiographischen Zeugnissen des Adels im Spätmittelalter," in *Erkundung und Beschreibung der Welt: Zur Poetik der Reise und Länderberichte*, ed. Xenja von Ertzdorff and Gerhard Giesemann (Amsterdam and New York: Rodopi, 2003), 87–108, at 96. About the relation of the Prague citizens to Ladislaus see Aenea Silvio Piccolomini, *Historia Bohemica*, 254: "Pragenses gubernationi suae nihil morati se commisere." See the most recent edition, including the earliest translations (Old Czech and Middle New German): Aenea Silvio Piccolomini, *Historia Bohemica*, ed. Joseph Hejnic et al., 3 vols., Beiträge zur slavischen Philologie und Kulturgeschichte, Reihe B, 20/1–3 (Cologne: Böhlau, 2005).

most of his time to matters in Hungary. On one of his rare visits to Prague, for a joint synod of the Catholic and Utraquist clergy in 1454 (at the castle and in the Carolinum), he accepted Rokycana as bishop.[52] Two years later Ladislaus fled to Prague in a vain attempt to escape the plague, but his presence had no greater effect on the balance of power in the city.

For the university, founded by Charles IV and located in the Old Town between the fruit market and the Old Town's square, the capture of Prague by Podiebrad and his followers was a disaster.[53] Even though Emperor Sigismund, at the request of the Prague towns, had confirmed in a charter ('Majestätsbrief') dated 1435 that the confiscated properties of the colleges had to be returned, Podiebrad's occupation of the town nullified all possible efforts to restore the university's international reputation because the German-speaking (Catholic) scholars had to flee for a second time to escape from the Calixtines.[54] When, in April 1460, Rokycana pushed through the election of his follower Wenceslas the Younger to the office of dean of the Faculty of Arts, the continuing tension between the Utraquist majority and the Catholic minority reached its peak, leading to the expulsion of Master Niklas of Hořepník. In the end, the obligatory implementation from 1462 of the oath on the Chalice by all entering scholars only resulted in the permanent exclusion of those of different faith from the university.[55] Despite this shift towards a more provincial outlook, the university experienced an increasing interest in humanistic views, though the rigid traditionalism of the Utraquist milieu remained the dominant feature.[56]

---

[52] Blanka Zilynská, "Synoden im utraquistischen Böhmen 1418–1531," in *Partikularsynoden im späten Mittelalter*, ed. Nathalie Kruppa and Leszek Zygner, Veröffentlichungen des Max-Planck-Instituts für Geschichte 219, Studien zur Germania Sacra 29 (Göttingen: Vandenhoeck & Ruprecht, 2006), 377–86, at 382.

[53] *A History of Charles University*, ed. František Kavka and Josef Petráň, 2 vols. (Prague: Karolinum, 2001); F. Machilek, "Kirche und Universität im Spätmittelalter: die Gründungen Prag und Erfurt," in *Universitäten im östlichen Mitteleuropa zwischen Kirche, Staat und Nation—Sozialgeschichtliche und politische Entwicklungen*, ed. Peter Wörster, Völker, Staaten und Kulturen in Ostmitteleuropa 3 (Munich: Oldenbourg, 2008), 165–93, at 186.

[54] The text of the royal letter appears in *Privilegia civitatum Pragensium: Privilegia měst Pražských*, ed. Jaromír Čelakovský, Codex Juris Municipalis regni Bohemiae 1 (Prague: Grégor, 1886), 218, nr. 134. For a summary of the most important occurences see Šmahel, *Die Hussitische Revolution*, 3: 1879.

[55] Urbánek, *Věk poděbradský*, 4: 235–49.

[56] Urbánek, *Věk poděbradský*, 4: 235–49; Šmahel, *Die Hussitische Revolution*, 3: 1883, 1885. For more detail see Pavel Spunar, "Literární činnost utrakvistů doby poděbradské a jagellonské," in *Acta reformationem bohemicam illustrantia: Příspěvky k dějinám utrakvismu*, vol. 1 (Prague: Kalich, 1978), 165–269; a brief case study is Ota Halama, "Petrarkův spis *Sine titulo*, utrakvisté a Bratří jagellonské epochy," in *Evropa a Čechy na konci středověku: Sborník příspěvků věnovaných Františku Šmahelovi*, ed. Eva Doležalová et al. (Prague:

In economic and political terms the government of Podiebrad, especially his early years, was undoubtedly successful. The construction industry prospered, even against a background of high emigration, voluntary and forced, of the German-speaking population.[57] The Tein church was extended in order to make it a metropolitan church. Conceptually it had to be seen as equivalent to the cathedral of St Vitus and, for this reason, soon after 1463 a tower was erected on its northern side and the gable of the western facade was ornamented with a golden chalice and the slogan *Veritas Dei vincit* in huge letters.[58] Additionally, the Burgrave Johann Zajímač of Kunstadt (d. 1460), installed by his distant relative Podiebrad, recruited new settlers, mostly from the already existing communities in Prague, to settle under the Vyšehrad Castle on the right of the Moldau, which became an independent small municipality named the Vyšehrad Mountains (*Vyšehrader Berge, Hory Vyšehradu*).[59] At the same time the citizens of the New Town embellished their city hall with a high tower, demonstrating their strength and elevated self-conception (1452–1456).[60] Not surprisingly, the burghers of the Old Town even surpassed such endeavours when they began to extend their city hall, adding an architecturally similar tower to the lower building with its astrological clock and ornamenting its facade.[61] In the Old Town, Georg

---

Centrum medievistických studií, 2004), 433–48. One of the examples is the bachelor and chancellor of the New Town, Prokop of Prague: see Marie Bláhová, "Pražská inteligence v pozdním středověku," *DP* 22 (2004): 51–66, at 64–66.

[57] Jiří Pešek, "Národnostní skupiny, menšiny a cizinci ve městech: Praha středověku i novověku ve středoevropském srovnání," *DP* 19 (2001): 9–16. In the records of 1457–1516 of new inhabitants, of the 1062 new burghers only fifteen had a German name; see Šmahel, "Prag in der zweiten Hälfte des 15. Jahrhunderts," 189. For the proportions in the Pre-Hussite era in comparison see Jaroslav Mezník, "Národností složení předhusitské Prahy," *Sborník historický* 17 (1970): 5–30.

[58] Machilek, "*Praga caput regni*," 98, with further references. For the selection of the cathedral as the remaining favoured burial place see Pavel Král, "Tod, Begräbnisse und Gräber: Funeralrituale des böhmischen Adels als Mittel der Repräsentation und des Andenkens," in *Macht und Memoria: Begräbniskultur europäischer Oberschichten in der Frühen Neuzeit*, ed. Mark Hengerer (Cologne: Böhlau, 2005), 421–48, at 432.

[59] A detailed genealogy of the Kunstadt family is accessible on the internet: http://genealogy.euweb.cz/bohemia/kunstat.html. See Richard G. Plaschka, *Nationalismus, Staatsgewalt, Widerstand: Aspekte nationaler und sozialer Entwicklung in Ostmittel- und Südosteuropa*, Schriftenreihe des Österreichischen Ost- und Südosteuropa-Instituts 11 (Munich: Oldenbourg, 1985), 22.

[60] Karel Kibic, "Novoměstská radnice v Praze a její nejstarší jádro," *Staletá Praha* 9 (1979): 213–30. In 1464 the Little Town began to build a bridge tower.

[61] For the steps in the architectural development of the city hall see Janáček, *Das alte Prag*, 103, table 15. See also Arnold Bartetzky, "Die Beziehungen zwischen Stadt und Krone im Spiegel von Rathausdekorationen des Spätmittelalters und der Frühen Neuzeit," in *Krakau, Prag und Wien: Funktionen von Metropolen im frühmodernen Staat*, ed. Marina Dimitrieva and Karen Lamprecht, Forschungen zur Geschichte und Kultur

of Podiebrad was elected king of Bohemia by a provincial Diet. He even received support from many Catholic nobles, thereby stimulating a courtly culture to develop in the town around the main church of the Chalice movement.[62]

These concrete symbols of the city's development were matched by the stability of its administration, the population of the whole probably totalling 30,000 inhabitants at this time.[63] During the rule of Podiebrad, which lasted nearly twenty-three years, only 102 councillors of the Old Town are known, of whom Jan Trefan (fourteen times), Pavel Cisper (thirteen times), and Samuel Velvar (twelve times) are recorded the most frequently among the members of this governing body. Of their counterparts from the New Town only sixty-seven councillors have been identified.[64] Podiebrad, the 'king of two peoples', gained support because of his concern to combat the rising Unity of Brethren movement (*Brüderunität, Jednota bratská, Unitas Fratrum*) most notably from the New Town council.[65] The Unity was established under the leadership of the lay theologian Peter of Chelčitz/Petr Chelčický (c. 1390–c. 1460), who had preached in the 1420s in the Bethlehem chapel in Prague and who argued for an absolute renunciation of power and possession by the reformed church.[66] While its supporters were concentrated in Chelčický's home area, the region around the

---

des östlichen Mitteleuropa 10 (Stuttgart: Steiner, 2000), 44–58, at 46, illus. 375. In addition to the embellishment, a house donated by Mikeš Kožešník was integrated into the complex after 1458.

[62] A record of his election is inserted into the manuscript Prague, Archiv hl. města Prahy, Sbírka rukopisů, nr. 2085, with reference in *Praha—Čechy—Evropa*, 124, nr. 88; see also Leszek Belzyt, "Sprachlich-kulturelle Pluralität in Prag und Krakau im 15. und 16. Jahrhundert: Topographie und Entwicklungstendenzen im Vergleich," *DP* 19 (2001): 25–36, at 32.

[63] According to the numbers given by L. Belzyt, "Demographische Entwicklung und ethnische Pluralität in den größten Städten Ostmitteleuropas," in *Zentralität in Ostmitteleuropa an der Wende vom Mittelalter zur Neuzeit*, ed. Evamaria Engel, Forschungen zur Geschichte und Kultur des östlichen Mitteleuropa 1 (Berlin: Akademie-Verlag, 1995), 61–70, at 69, Prague experienced a slow increase of inhabitants between 1450 and 1500.

[64] The statistical data are based on *Dějiny Prahy*, 1: 247. For a more detailed insight into the councillors of the New Town see Kateřina Jíšová, "Novoměstské radní elity v 15. Století," *DP* 22 (2004): 81–96, at 82, 84.

[65] Rudolf Říčan, *The History of the Unity of Brethren: A Protestant Hussite Church in Bohemia and Moravia*, trans. Daniel Crews (Bethlehem, PA: The Moravian Church in America, 1992).

[66] See Jaroslav Boubín, "Pojem svobody u Petra Chelčického," in *Od knížat ke králům: Sborník u příležitosti 60. narozenin Josefa Žemličky* (Prague: Nakl. Lidové noviny, 2007), 454–65. From his literary work see *Das Gift der heiligen Kirche: Eine Polemik um die Macht der Kirche in der Zeit der böhmischen Reformation. Die Replik von Chelčický an Bischof Rokycana*, ed. Christian Staffa, Dahlemer Hefte 12 (Berlin: Alektor-Verlag, 1993), 57–70.

'Eagle Mountains' (*Adlergebirge, Orlické hory*), even the Utraquist bishop Rokycana sympathised with the ideas of this congregation; but once the confraternity, officially founded in 1457, decided to meet regularly with its supporters in
Prague, primarily under the protection of Jan Přibram at the Emmaus monastery
(*Na Slovanech*), it was considered as a threat.[67] Thereupon several of its members,
amongst them the leader Gregor named Krajčí (d. 1474), were arrested in March
1461 and incarcerated in the gaol of the New Town (by this time Podiebrad had
restored Charles IV's decree against heretics precisely for that purpose).[68] Under the precondition of a revocation of all clauses counter to the *Compactata* the
detainees were released shortly afterwards. Hence the Unity of Brethren gained
further popularity in Prague as well as in the Bohemian lands in general.

After the death of Pope Calixtus III (1455–1458), who was extremely interested in the possibility of an agreement, Podiebrad's relationship with the Roman Catholic Church deteriorated following the election to the papal throne as
Pius II of the humanist, historian, and uncompromising opponent of the Bohemian Utraquists Enea Silvio Piccolomini (d. 1464). In part this was thanks to
his previous office as an imperial secretary in Austria, where he became quite
familiar with the Bohemian situation, as his *Historia Bohemica* demonstrates.[69]
Initially, a compromise between king and pope seemed feasible: a legation from
Rome sought to mediate regarding Silesia's recognition of Podiebrad, and negotiations began on the topic of restoring ecclesiastical properties.[70] At the peak of
this 'little Counter-Reformation', the bishop of Breslau/Wrocław, Jost of Rosenberg (1456–1467), preached in St Vitus' Cathedral in 1461 against the Chalice
and therefore against the Utraquists.[71] These events, coupled with the king's in-
tention to become a Catholic, sparked an uprising in Prague which was fomented
by Rokycana. As a result Podiebrad took an oath of affiliation to the Utraquist
faith and swore to defend the *Compactata*.

---

[67] For more detailed information see Šmahel, *Die Hussitische Revolution*, 3: 1900–11.

[68] Michael Tönsing, "*Contra hereticam pravitatem*: Zu den Lucceser Ketzererlassen
Karls IV. (1369)," in *Studia Luxemburgensia: Festschrift Heinz Stoob zum 70. Geburtstag*,
ed. F.B. Fahlbusch and Peter Johanek (Warendorf: Fahlbusch, 1989), 285–311.

[69] Josef Hejnic, "Enea Silvio de Piccolomini (Pius II) und das Prager Domkapitel
zu St Veit auf der Prager Burg im 15. Jahrhundert," in *Studien zum Humanismus in den
böhmischen Ländern: Ergänzungsheft*, ed. Hans-Bernd Harder and Hans Rothe, Schriften
des Komitees der Bundesrepublik Deutschland zur Förderung der Slawischen Studien
13 (Cologne: Böhlau, 1991), 19–28; still of value is Hermann Markgraf, "Das Verhältniß
des Königs Georg von Böhmen zu Papst Pius II. 1462–1464," *Forschungen zur deutschen
Geschichte* 9 (1869): 217–58.

[70] These remarks are mainly based on Claus Bernet, s.v. "Georg von Podiebrad,"
in *Biographisch-Bibliographisches Kirchenlexikon*, ed. Friedrich W. Bautz et al., 26 vols.
(Nordhausen: Bautz, 1975–), 21 (2003): cols. 1183–1203.

[71] Václav Filip and Karl Borchardt, *Schlesien, Georg von Podiebrad und die römische
Kurie* (Würzburg: Verein für Schlesische Geschichte, 2005), 109.

The king's growing importance with regard to imperial politics is document-ed amongst others by the so-called 'Prague peace camp' of November 1461, dur-ing which he was able to achieve a general cease-fire between the German dukes and princes, and to instigate the first steps in his famous world peace manifesto.[72] In response to these developments Pius II, in 1462, annulled the Basle *Compactata* and demanded that Podiebrad should align himself to the papacy. The king re-fused. Instead, he called a synod in Prague — of seven hundred clerics, including two hundred Catholics — which strengthened the king's position concerning his defence of the *Compactata*.[73] Yet soon afterwards the text of the secret oath that Podiebrad had taken to return to the Roman Catholic faith was published. This provoked the arrest and torture of the papal nuncio Fantino de Valle, who had argued at the Diet in Prague on St Laurence's day for the papal power to depose the king if he did not accept the withdrawal of the *Compactata*.[74] With Fantino's sudden release on 27 October 1462, Podiebrad tried to remedy the situation, but probably it was the approaching threat of a Turkish attack on the Christian kingdoms, as well as Podiebrad's commitment to establishing a common defence policy, which prevented more resolute sanctions by the Apostolic See against his disobedience.[75] Furthermore, Bohemia's neighbouring Christian rulers saw no reason to isolate Podiebrad; rather they sought to enter into further discussions and even convened a Diet of the Holy Roman Empire (*Reichstag*) in Prague in 1463.[76] The following year Podiebrad ignored another summons to Rome to jus-tify his faith, while Pope Paul II's (1417–1471) absolution of the Bohemians from their oath of loyalty to the king had no greater effect.[77] In contrast, the position

---

[72] Gerhard Messler, Tractatus pacis generalis toti christianitati fiendae: *Das Welt-friedensmanifest König Georg von Podiebrad. Ein Beitrag zur Diplomatie des 15. Jahrhun-derts,* Studien und Dokumente 10/11 (Karlsruhe: Johannes-Mathesius-Verlag, 1973).

[73] Zilynská, "Synoden im utraquistischen Böhmen," 383.

[74] Fudge, "Reform and the Lower Consistory," 85. For the participation of the Prague towns in these councils see I. Hlaváček, "Husitské sněmy," *Sborník historický* 4 (1956): 71–109.

[75] On the cooperation between Podiebrad and the diplomat Antonius Marini in this project see Heiner Timmermann, "Einigungs- und Friedenspläne im Europa der Neu-zeit," in *Gesichter Europas,* ed. Michael Salewski and idem, Dokumente und Schriften der Europäischen Akademie Otzenhausen 105 (Berlin: LIT, 2002), 59–85, at 64.

[76] On 29 June 1463 at the congress in Prague, he reached an agreement with the Hohenzollern Margrave Albrecht of Brandenburg (named Achilles, 1414–1486), in which Podiebrad agreed to several concessions in feudal regulations for a peace treaty. In the Imperial Diet in Prague which lasted 8–24 August 1463, these items were again negotiated: Bernet, "Georg von Podiebrad," col. 1199.

[77] The first document is published in Filip and Borchardt, *Schlesien, Georg von Podie-brad,* 222–31, no. 23; the second one in *Scriptores rerum Silesicarum,* ed. G.A. Stenzel et al., 17 vols. (Breslau: n.p., 1835–1895), 9: 135–49.

of the Utraquist bishop Rokycana was strengthened through a *disputatio* between the Catholic and the Utraquist consistories, convened by Podiebrad in 1465.[78]

Internal opposition to Podiebrad came from the higher aristocracy (*Herrenstand*) when at a meeting in Zittau they elected the highest burgrave and former supporter of Podiebrad, Zdeněk von Sternberg (1410–1476), as their leader. This Catholic league, the so-called *Liga von Grünberg*, comprised Bohemian nobles as well as those of the Moravian estates, the town of Breslau, and a considerable number of prelates.[79] Despite this increasing and soon military resistance to Podiebrad, the proclaimed crusade against the 'heretical king' in 1468 did not receive much support from the German princes to whom it was addressed.[80] Nonetheless, the rival king Matthias Corvinus (d. 1490), who was elevated to this position by the Catholic League in 1469, did pose certain problems for Podiebrad and his successor, the strict Catholic Vladislav/Władysław (II) Jagiełło.[81] Yet Matthias never gained the core lands of Bohemia, controlling instead huge areas of Moravia and parts of Silesia.

During Podiebrad's supremacy, the Prague towns were able to harness their economic potential, allowing them to some extent to recover from their earlier international political isolation. This led to an increase in self-confidence among the capital's leading citizens, and as the councillors and the leading patriciate strove for power they revived older traditions and sought to acquire further legal

---

[78] Fudge, "Reform and the Lower Consistory," 75; Odložilík, *The Hussite King*, 296, no. 315. A list of all administrators and members of this institution in V. Tomek, "O církevní správě strany podobojí v Čechách od r. 1415 až 1622," *Časopis českého muzea* 22 (1848): 365–83, 441–68, at 463–68.

[79] Joachim Bahlcke, *Regionalismus und Staatsintegration im Widerstreit: Die Länder der Böhmischen Krone im ersten Jahrhundert der Habsburgerherrschaft (1526–1619)*, Schriften des Bundesinstituts für ostdeutsche Kultur und Geschichte 3 (Munich: Oldenbourg, 1994), 53; František Palacký and Zdeněk Sternberg, *Dějiny rodu Sternbergů: Geschichte der Familie Sternberg*, Do nitra askiburgionu 14 (Moravský Beroun: Moravská expedice, 2000), esp. 35.

[80] Edition: Filip and Borchardt, *Schlesien, Georg von Podiebrad*, 236–38, no. 26. Compare Peter Hilsch, "Die Kreuzzüge gegen die Hussiten: geistliche und weltliche Macht in Konkurrenz," in *Konfessionelle Pluralität als Herausforderung*, 201–16, at 214.

[81] Josef Macek, *Jagellonsky věk v českých zemích (1471–1526)*, 4 vols. (Prague: Academia, 1991–1999), offers an extensive study on the epoch; short remarks by Urszula Borkowska, "Edukajca i mecenat artystyczny Władysława Jagiellończyka króla Czech i Węgier," in *Polacy w Czechach, czesi w Polsce X–XVIII wiek*, ed. Henryk Gmiterek and Wojciech Iwańczak (Lublin: Wyd. Uniwersytetu Marii Curie-Skłodowskiej, 2004), 193–208. On the occasion of his nomination and coronation as Bohemian king, a huge celebration was organized in the town on 15/16 June; see for instance *Staré letopisy české do r. 1509*, Narodní knihovna v Praze, Sign. XXII A 1, fols. 400–405; description of the source by Jiří Pražák, *Katalog rukopisů křižovnické knihovny nyní deponovaných ve Státní knihovně ČSR* (Prague: SK ČSR, 1980), 98–100.

privileges.[82] With regard to the latter, the Old Town had taken the first initiative when, in the 1440s, the authorities had collected together evidence of its rights, including the alleged ancient privilege of Sobieslaw II (d. 1180) whereby the German settlers had been granted extensive autonomy, allowing them to control the local Jewish community.[83] The New Town followed suit with a treatise on rights, liberties, letters of privilege (*Gnadenbriefe*), and other documents.[84] In terms of the construction of urban identity, the nobility provided another model, namely the establishment of a coat of arms that could be displayed in various ways.[85] Even though such initiatives predate the Hussite government, the final and royally approved form was established under Vladislav's rulership, and once again the Old Town took the lead, decorating its restyled southern facade with its own and a whole series of other emblems.[86] In addition, owing to the growing financial power of the leading citizens and other social groups the local churches received a considerable increase in *pro animae* donations, especially in the Utraquist parishes, and, furthermore, a sizeable investment in buildings more generally can be noticed.[87]

---

[82] An introductory study is Halina Manikowska, "Political Identities of Towns in Central Europe during the Late Middle Ages," in *Political Culture in Central Europe (10th–20th Century), Part I: Middle Ages and Early Modern Times*, ed. eadem and Jaroslav Pánek (Prague: Institute of History, 2005), 135–62.

[83] F. Šmahel, "Die Prager Judengemeinde im hussitischen Zeitalter," in *Jüdische Gemeinden und ihr christlicher Kontext in kulturräumlich-vergleichender Betrachtung von der Spätantike bis zum 18. Jahrhundert*, ed. Christoph Cluse et al., Forschungen zur Geschichte der Juden, Abteilung A, 13 (Hannover: Hahnsche Buchhandlung, 2003), 341–63, at 345.

[84] Šmahel, "Prag in der zweiten Hälfte des 15. Jahrhunderts," 192.

[85] *Böhmische Stadtsiegel aus der Sammlung Erik Turnwald* (catalogue), ed. Aleš Zelenka (Munich: Oldenbourg, 1988), 90.

[86] Šmahel, "Prag in der zweiten Hälfte des 15. Jahrhunderts," 192; Jiří Čarek, *Městské znaky v českých zemích* (Prague: Academia, 1985), 305–14. Research has not yet offered a precise dating of the decoration: see Rostislav Nový, "Nejstarší heraldické památky Staroměstské radnice v Praze," *PSH* 22 (1989): 33–70, at 60; *Praha—Čechy—Evropa*, 124, no. 92 (Emperor Friedrich III meliorates the coat of arms of the Old Town, 1475).

[87] The gifts for the soul of the higher patriciate of the New Town show are discussed by Kateřina Jíšová, "Spása duše a očistec u novoměstských měšťanů: K religiozitě novoměstského měšťanstva v pozdním středověku," in *Evropa a Čechy na konci středověku*, 253–68; see also the classic study by John Klassen, "Gifts for the Soul and Social Charity in Late Medieval Bohemia," in *Materielle Kultur und religiöse Stiftung im Spätmittelalter*, Österreichische Akademie der Wissenschaften, Phil.-hist. Klasse 54, Veröffentlichungen des Instituts für mittelalterliche Realien-forschung Österreichs 12 (Vienna: Verlag des Instituts für Mittelalterliche Realienkunde Österreichs, 1990), 63–82.

Prague under Jagiellonian Rule

Following the succession of Vladislav Jagiello, a great-grandson of Charles IV, the balance of power between the two major religious confessions in Bohemia and Prague shifted noticeably. The most visible sign of these changes was the return of the metropolitan chapter, the arrival of many Catholic burghers, and the reoccupation of several abandoned or dissolved monasteries.[88] At the same time life at the royal court in Prague was more and more dominated by the Catholic nobility.[89] The Utraquists, for their part, put forward plans to reform their ecclesiastical organisation under the elected administrator Koranda (1471–1497), Rokycana's successor. Simultaneously, the provosts and deans of the metropolitan chapter embarked on a strategy of liturgical reform.[90] As part of these endeavours several attempts were made to persuade the adherents of the Unity of Brethren to accept the fundamental Utraquist conventions of faith.[91]

King Vladislav enforced the re-introduction of Catholicism insofar as he replaced the Utraquist governing patricians of the Podiebrad era by obedient councillors, who linked their promotion "in an unscrupulous manner with the most miserable greed for plunder."[92] Thereafter the Utraquists took advantage of the temporary absence of the king, who had fled to Kuttenberg/ Kutná Hora because of the outbreak of pestilence, to instigate a revolt in 1483 with the support of their first foreign consecrated bishop Augustin Luciani.[93] In the course of this uprising, sustained principally by people of lower social status, the Catholic clergy and

---

[88] Hoensch, *Geschichte Böhmens*, 165.

[89] For the court offices from 1480 onwards see Macek, *Jagellonský věk*, 1: 322–29. *Hofkultur der Jagiellonendynastie und verwandter Fürstenhäuser/The Culture of the Jagiellonian and Related Courts*, ed. Urszula Borkowska and Andrea Langer, Studia Jagellonica Lipsiensia 4 (Ostfildern: Thorbecke, 2010); Jaroslav Pešina, "Die Tafelmalerei am Jagellonenhof in Prag 1471–1526," *Acta historiae artium Academiae Scientiarum Hungaricae* 19 (1973): 207–30.

[90] Katherine Walsh, "Liturgische Reformbemühungen der Prager Domherren in nachhussitischer Zeit," in *Kirchliche Reformimpulse des 14./15. Jahrhunderts in Ostmitteleuropa*, ed. Winfried Eberhard and Franz Machilek (Cologne: Böhlau, 2006), 255–76, esp. 266; Barry F. H. Graham, "The Evolution of the Utraquist Mass, 1420–1620," *Catholic Historical Review* 92 (2006): 553–73, states that the Utraquists retained the (Latin) Prague use of the mass of the Roman Catholic Church.

[91] His election was executed on an Utraquist synod: Zilynská, "Synoden im utraquistischen Böhmen," 383.

[92] Šmahel, *Hussitische Revolution*, 3: 1862.

[93] See the biographies of the two foreign Utraquist bishops Augustin of Santorin (1482–1493) and Filipp of Villanova (1504–1597): Winfried Eberhard, "Augustin Lucian de (von Santorin) Bessariis, (d. 1493)," "Filippo von Villanuova (Novavilla), (d. 1507)," in *Die Bischöfe des Heiligen Römischen Reiches: Ein biografisches Lexikon*, ed. Erwin Gatz et al., 4 vols. (Berlin: Duncker & Humblot, 1994–1998), 2: 51, 724 respectively; *Velké dějiny*

councillors, as well as Germans and Jews, were expelled from the town.[94] These attacks did not spare the resident canons and monks, and the Observant Franciscans, who only a year earlier had received permission to settle in the monastery of St Ambrose, and the Austin canons from the prestigious foundation 'Charles' Court' (*Karlshof*), had to leave Prague.[95] The riots had a lasting effect on the local political landscape because the three Prague towns agreed in October 1483 on a pact of mutual support,[96] and in the aftermath King Vladislav moved from the royal residence in the Old Town to the traditional seat in the castle (1485), which was afterwards expanded to a permanent fortress equipped with firearms.[97]

The re-established union of the Utraquist towns compelled the Catholic majority of the Bohemian nobles to revise their religious programme, and in the longer term the alliances among the estates that had previously followed a moderate Utraquist agenda dissolved.[98] The most important consequence of this process was the religious peace, announced in 1485 during a Diet in Kuttenberg, which obliged Catholics and Utraquists to observe mutual tolerance and respect of the other's faith and property.[99] The same was not applied, however, to the adherents of the Unity of Brethren, who had meanwhile gained ground in Prague notwithstanding King Vladislav's severe persecution. For example, leaders of the confraternity, like the Polish scholar Michael Wittman who preached at the church of St Egidius in the Old Town, were arrested and tortured, before disappearing

---

zemí koruny české, 6: 445. According to Macek, *Jagellonsky věk*, 1: 319, annex 1, Prague underwent epidemics again in 1505, 1507, and 1508.

[94] F. Šmahel, "Pražské povstání 1483," *PSH* 19 (1986): 35–102; Kamil Boldan, "Passio Pragensium—tištěná relace o pražskám povstání 1483," *DP* 19 (2001): 173–80. An interesting external source is the still unpublished chronicle of Jakob Twinger von Königshofen (Straßburg, 1495/96), Gießen Universitätsbibliothek, MS 179, fols. 316ᵛ–319ᵛ, with his account of a Hussite revolt in Prague.

[95] F. Machilek, "Einführung: Beweggründe, Inhalte und Probleme kirchlicher Reformen des 14./15. Jahrhunderts (mit besonderer Berücksichtigung der Verhältnisse im östlichen Mitteleuropa)," in *Kirchliche Reformimpulse*, 1–124, at 74; Hlaváček, *Bohemian Franciscans*, 181. In 1496, when several Orders could return to the city, the Franciscan Observants were ignored.

[96] On the defence system in Prague see P. Klučina, "Organizace a dislokace voské husitské Prahy," *Staletá Praha* 14 (1984): 89–94.

[97] Machilek, *"Praga caput regni,"* 100; J. Frolik, "Prague Castle," *ODMA* 3: 1353–54.

[98] W. Eberhard, *Monarchie und Widerstand: Zur ständischen Oppositionsbildung im Herrschaftssystem Ferdinands I. in Böhmen* (Munich: Oldenbourg, 1985), 70.

[99] See W. Eberhard, "Entstehungsbedingungen für öffentliche Toleranz am Beispiel des Kuttenberger Religionsfriedens von 1485," *Communio viatorum* 29 (1986): 129–54; Jaroslav Pánek, "The Question of Tolerance in Bohemia and Moravia in the Age of the Reformation," in *Tolerance and Intolerance in the European Reformation*, ed. Peter Grell and Bob Scribner (Cambridge: Cambridge University Press, 1996), 231–48, at 235.

without leaving any trace (1480).[100] Others were more fortunate and, under the terms of the Kuttenberg peace, they were offered an opportunity to try to prove the validity of their heretical beliefs using the Bible or else leave the country.

The Utraquist cities, headed by Prague, observed with suspicion the increasing predominance of the nobility in national politics—a nobility who managed to enhance its position in the quarrel over the composition of the country's court (*Landrecht*), reconciled in 1487: this supreme court henceforth was composed of the four highest country office holders, twelve *barones*, and eight knights.[101] Ten years later, the predominance of the high nobility once again was strengthened by a treaty administering the allocation of the country's highest offices (1497).[102] These rights were confirmed once more by Vladislav's 'Regulation of the Country' (*Landesordnung, Vladislavské zřízení zemské*) in 1500.[103] The cities tried to expand their options, in particular through a marked growth in external commercial relations as exemplified by the 1481 trade contract of Prague with the town of Nuremberg.[104] The intermediary judgement of the king in the conflict between the towns and the nobility in 1502 momentarily eased the clash,[105] but notwithstanding these struggles their influence lasted until 1517.[106]

---

[100] Říčan, *The History of the Unity of Brethren*, 48; Michael Welte, "Lukas von Prag," in *Biographisch-Bibliographisches Kirchenlexikon*, 5: col. 419s., has a synthesis of Lucas's most important writings.

[101] Robert Novotný, "Dvorská a zemská hierarchie v pozndě středověkých Čechách," in *Dvory a rezidence ve středověku*, Mediaevalia Historica Bohemica, Supplementum 1 (Prague: Historický ústav AV ČR, 2006), 145–61, at 156, with further references to the installation of the Chamber Court (*Kammergericht/ Komorní soud*).

[102] Jaroslav Pánek, "Der böhmische Adel zwischen Jagiellonen und Habsburgern," in *Die Länder der Böhmischen Krone und ihre Nachbarn zur Zeit der Jagiellonenkönige (1471–1526)*, ed. Evelin Wetter, Studia Jagellonica Lipsiensia 2 (Ostfildern: Thorbecke, 2005), 143–50, at 145.

[103] J. Pánek, "Český stát a stavovská společnost na prahu novověku ve světle zemských zřízení," in *Vladislavské zřízení zemské a počátky ústavního zřízení v českých zemích: Sborník příspěvků z mezinárodní konference konané ve dnech 7.–8. prosince 2000 v Praze*, ed. Karel Malý and idem (Prague: Historický ústav Akademie věd České republiky, 2001), 13–16.

[104] In short see Václav Ledvinka, "Prag," in *Böhmen und Mähren: Handbuch der historischen Stätten*, ed. Joachim Bahlcke et al., Kröners Taschenausgabe 329 (Stuttgart: Kröner, 1998), 470–91, at 482; Ferdinand Seibt, "Nürnberg und Böhmen in der vorindustriellen Welt," in *Nürnberg: Eine europäische Stadt in Mittelalter und Neuzeit*, ed. Helmut Neuhaus, Nürnberger Forschungen 29 (Nuremberg: Verein für Geschichte der Stadt Nürnberg, 2000), 235–47. Latest see *DP* 29 (2011), dedicated to the topic "Prague-Nüremberg: a partnership of regional metropolises."

[105] *Staré letopisy české*, fols. 406–423. For a list of the towns joining the city's union see *Velké dějiny zemí koruny české*, 6: 522. The Lesser Town did not participate in it.

[106] Bohdan Zilynskyj, "Městský stav v boji se šlechtou na počátku 16. Století," *Folia Historica Bohemiae* 6 (1984): 137–61.

Yet the depositing of the Bohemian 'country panel' (*Landtafel, Tabula*), the register of the nobility's estate and legal transactions, in Prague Castle in 1512 does indicate an additional factor in the growing importance of the capital.[107] Two years later a delegation of Prague citizens, as representatives of the Old and the New Towns and with the support of Bartholomäus of Münsterberg (a grandson of King Podiebrad), received the municipal law of Nuremberg, which hitherto had applied to the Lesser Town and the *civitas* of Budín only, thus giving them the right to elect their own councillors (1514).[108] Further privileges were acquired in 1518 when the Old Town allied itself with the New Town, under the leadership of the mayor (Primator) Jan Pašek of Vrat/Jan Pašek z Vratu (d. 1533) and with the assistance of the magnate Zdeněk Lev of Rosental (1470–1535), to set up a joint government (*Stadtregiment*) which took its seat in the city hall of the Old Town.[109] Such a policy of mutual assistance was expanded to include other cities as Prague attempted to strengthen its political position.[110] One way of demonstrating the capital's successes was through its cityscape: the community of the Old Town began the construction in 1475 of a tower in the king's honour, the

---

[107] See Hájka z Libočan, *Kronika česká podle originálu z r. 1541*, ed. V. Flajšhans (Prague: České akademie věd a umění, 1929), fol. 465a; H. Goldblatt, "Annals and Chronicles, Central/Eastern Europe: Slavic Chronicles, Chronographs, and Histories," *ODMA* 1: 70–71. On this registration of the nobles' property see Pavla Burdová, *Desky zemské Království českého* (Prague: Státní ústřední archiv v Praze, 1990); Stanisław Grodziski, "Das böhmisch-österreichische Hypothekenrecht und seine Bedeutung für Galizien," in *Ius commune*, Veröffentlichungen des Max-Planck-Instituts für europäische Rechtsgeschichte, Sonderhefte, Texte und Monographie 15 (Frankfurt am Main: Klostermann, 1981), 189–206, at 192.

[108] See Macek, *Jagellonský věk*, 3: 44; edition of the privilege in *Privilegia civitatum Pragensium*, 1: 349–53. Walter Popp, "Marktrecht, Stadtrecht, Stadtrechtsfamilien im Osten, insbesondere die Stadtrechtskreise von Nürnberg, Eger und Prag," *Fürther Heimatblätter* N.F. 28 (1991): 86–94. The Prague citizens already obtained the same commercial liberties as the burghers of Nuremberg, decreed by Charles IV and reconfirmed by Emperor Sigismund in 1436; see Jiří Kejř, "Das böhmische Städtewesen und das 'Nürnberger Recht'," in *Der weite Blick des Historikers: Einsichten in Kultur-, Landes- und Stadtgeschichte. Peter Johanek zum 65. Geburtstag*, ed. Wilfried Ehrbrecht et al. (Cologne: Böhlau, 2002), 113–24, at 121.

[109] Macek, *Jagellonsky věk*, 3: 42–45; Zigmund Winter, *Kulturní obraz českých měst: Život veřejný v XV a XVI věku*, 2 vols. (Prague: Matice česká, 1890–1892), 1: 666.

[110] Jiří Pešek, "Některé problémy bádání o spojené Praze z let 1518–1528," *DP* 4 (1984): 186–97, at 187; Antonín Kostlán, "K hospodářskému zázení spojené Praze 1518–1528," *DP* 4 (1984): 218–20. See for instance the offer of support to the 'castle master' and the council of the town of Kauřim/Kouřim 18 November 1520: *Království dvojího lidu*, 280, no. 148. A biography that is still of value is by V. Tomek, "Žiwot M. Jana Paška z Wratu," *Časopis Českého Musea* 18 (1844): 17–53.

so-called 'powder tower' (*Pulverturm, Prasná brána*)[111] at its north-eastern exit, and around 1520 the renaissance window was installed on the eastern facade of the city hall with the meaningful inscription *Praga caput regni*.[112] Regardless of whether this burgeoning self-confidence of the urban elites of the Prague towns was due to increased trade or social mobility, it added massively to the wealth of the capital.[113] At the same time, the expansion of royal architecture within the cityscape visually demonstrated the king's contribution to this upswing. The most prominent of these royal building projects was the massive Vladislav Hall at Hradschin castle [Fig. 8.1], begun in 1493 under the architect Benedikt Ried (d. 1534).[114] Evidently, this enormous throne and tournament hall was designed to compensate the Bohemian higher nobility for the loss of the court and their

---

[111] Jan Royt, "*Renovatio regni*: Zum Charakter der Kunst in Böhmen unter den Jagiellonen Wladislaw II und Ludwig II," in *Die Jagiellonen: Kunst und Kultur einer europäischen Dynastie an der Wende zur Neuzeit*, ed. Dietmar Popp and Robert Suckale, Wissenschaftliche Beibände zum Anzeiger des Germanischen Nationalmuseums 21 (Nuremberg: Germanisches Nationalmuseum, 2002), 227–32.

[112] Bartetzky, "Die Beziehungen zwischen Stadt und Krone," 48; Jiřina Hořejši and Petr Heřman, "*Praga caput regni*: Glosy ke kulturní historii Staroměstské radnice," *Staletá Praha* 19 (1989): 33–54, at 49. On the various meanings of *caput*, which is not necessarily identical to the modern term 'capital', see Evamaria Engel and Karen Lamprecht, "Hauptstadt—Residenz—Metropole—Zentraler Ort: Probleme ihrer Definition und Charakterisierung," in *Zentralität in Ostmitteleuropa*, 11–32, at 14.

[113] Tomek, *Dějepis*, 8: 414–71, on the changing urban elites in Prague during the first half of the 15th century. On the topic in general see *Poteri economici e poteri politici secc. XIII–XVIII*, ed. Simonetta Cavaciocchi, Atti della settimana di studi, Istituto Internazionale di Storia Economica F. Datini, Prato, 30 (Florence: Le Monnier, 1999); also Janos M. Bak, "Probleme einer vergleichenden Betrachtung mittelalterlicher Eliten in Ostmitteleuropa," in *Das europäische Mittelalter im Spannungsbogen des Vergleichs: Zwanzig internationale Beiträge zu Praxis, Problemen und Perspektiven der historischen Komparatistik*, ed. Michael Borgolte, Europa im Mittelalter 1 (Berlin: Akademie-Verlag, 2001), 49–64. For the debate on the distinction between the urban and noble patriciate see Jaroslav Čechura, "Městská šlechta—součast pražského patriciátu? (K otázce kontinuity pražského patriciátu 14.–16. století)," *DP* 9 (1991): 57–76; Hana Pátková, "Dosavadní ediční zpřístupnění rukopisu 986 Archivu hlavního města Prahy," *DP* 21 (2002): 15–27, with further literature on urban charters.

[114] Thomas DaCosta Kaufmann, *Höfe, Klöster und Städte: Kunst und Kultur in Mitteleuropa, 1450–1800* (Cologne: Böhlau, 1998), 62; *Höfe und Residenzen im spätmittelalterlichen Reich: Bilder und Begriffe*, ed. Paravicini, 2: 5, plate 4; *Europas Fürstenhöfe: Herrscher, Politiker und Mäzene 1400–1800*, ed. Arthur G. Dickens (Graz: Styria, 1978), 134; see also the overview by Viktor Kotrba, "Baukunst und Baumeister der Spätgotik am Prager Hof: Kurt Bauch zum siebzigsten Geburtstag," *Zeitschrift für Kunstgeschichte* 31 (1968): 181–215; and Frolik, "Prague Castle;" also H. Látal, "Benedikt Ried," *ODMA* 1: 247.

Fig. 8.1: Prague, Vladislav Hall at Hradschin castle. *Photo: Petrus Silesius (GNU Free Documentation Licence: available at www.commons.wikimedia.org/wiki/File:Prag_Vladislav-Saal.jpg)*

courtly lifestyle, since after the unexpected death of his rival Matthias Corvinus Vladislav moved his residence to Ofen/Obuda in the Hungarian kingdom. [115]

Prospective Remarks: Prague in the Transition to the Habsburgs' Reign

The career of mayor Jan Pašek—initially dean of the university in 1496; chancellor of the Old Town from 1498 to 1511; [116] ennobled in 1504; juryman (*Schöffe*) from 1515 to 1518 and thereafter mayor—is indicative of both the increasing importance of the urban chancelleries in particular and the possibilities of Prague's policy of in time bridging between the Jagellonian and the Habsburg rule in general. Because Pašek arranged the union of the two most important Prague towns on his own authority, he was dismissed by the last Jagellonian king, Louis II (b. 1506, in Prague 1516–1526), during the king's visit to Prague in 1523. [117] Yet he was in a position to use successfully the local political unrest, caused partly by the growing conflicts between the increasing number of Lutherans, sometimes called new Utraquists, and the old Utraquists. [118] The new Reformation in Germany found an early fertile soil in some circles of the Bohemian nobility, but even more in the Utraquist patriciate and also at the university. In 1521 Thomas Müntzer (d. 1525) described his first concept of a new evangelical church known as the so-called 'Prague manifesto.' [119] Such new ideas were adopted by a prominent local protagonist, the ordained master Gallus Cahera, who preached at the Tein church and was the first of now four administrators of the Utraquist

---

[115] The bearers of the highest country office in the year 1500 are listed in *Velké dějiny zemí koruny české*, 6: 515.

[116] The volume *Stadt, Kanzlei und Kultur im Übergang zur Frühen Neuzeit — City Culture and Urban Chanceries in an Era of Change*, Medieval to Early Modern Culture/ Kultureller Wandel vom Mittelalter zur Frühen Neuzeit 4, ed. Rudolf Suntrup and Jan R. Veenstra (Frankfurt am Main: Peter Lang, 2004) is confined to West European towns. For Prague see the brief discussion by I. Hlaváček, "Pražské městské kanceláře a kancelář dvořská v pozdním středověku," *DP* 21 (2002): 29–38.

[117] Václav Bůžek, "Cizinci ve vlastním království: Pobyt Ludvíka Jagellonského a Marie Habsburské v Čechách na přelomu let 1522–1523," in *V komnatách paláců v ulicích měst: Sborník příspěvků věnovaných Václavu Ledvinkovi k šedesátým narozeninám*, ed. Kateřina Jísová (Prague: Scriptorium, 2007), 233–43, at 241.

[118] Based on the concise discussion by Zdeněk V. David, "The Strange Fate of Czech Utraquism: The Second Century," *Journal of Ecclesiastical History* 46 (1995): 641–68, at 652.

[119] Thomas Müntzer, *Prager Manifest*, intro. Max Steinmetz, trans. Winfried Trillitzsch, comm. Friedrich de Boor and Hans-Joachim Rockar (Leipzig: Zentralantiquariat der Deutschen Demokratischen Republik, 1975).

Church.[120] Nonetheless, it was not only this change in the religious landscape which brought the career of Jan Pašek to an end, but rather the growing re-establishment of imperial power that led to his dismissal for the second time by Ferdinand I in 1528. In a longer perspective it seems that the Prague towns were no more able to widen their framework of action on the political stage, at least within Bohemia, as they had been able to achieve during the Jagiellonian era.[121] However, in the ensuing contest with the newly-established estates and a powerful royal authority, the towns would suffer further setbacks after the failed revolt of 1547. But even if the goal of self-government was not achieved fully by the Prague towns, the Bohemian capital continued to experience rising prosperity as its citizens benefited from the stability and the new splendour brought to it by the Habsburg dynasty.[122] This strengthened royal power was able to alleviate the confessional, religious tensions and challenges without deleting their effects in the long run.[123]

---

[120] The new Utraquist master Wenceslas Roždalovský sent Luther Hus's tractate *De ecclesia* together with an invitation to Prague: see Zdeněk Kučera, "Prag," in *Theologische Realenzyklopädie*, ed. Gerhard Müller (Berlin and New York: de Gruyter, 1977–), 27 (1997): 172–80, at 175; see also Eberhard, *Konfessionsbildung und Stände in Böhmen 1478–1530*, Veröffentlichungen des Collegium Carolinum 38 (Munich: Oldenbourg, 1981), esp. 139, 144–50. On Cahera see Malcom D. Lambert, *Medieval Heresy: Popular Movements from the Gregorian Reform to the Reformation* (Oxford: Blackwell, 2002), 406. B. Zilynská, "Utrakvističtí církevní 'hodnostáři'—součást městské elity?" *DP* 22 (2004): 117–24, discusses the question of the ties between urban and Utraquist elites.

[121] In a wider framework, compare these two syntheses: F. Šmahel, "Das böhmische Ständewesen im hussitischen Zeitalter: Machtfrage, Glaubensspaltung und strukturelle Umwandlungen," in *Die Anfänge der ständischen Vertretungen in Preußen und seinen Nachbarländern*, ed. Hartmut Boockmann (Munich: Oldenbourg, 1992), 219–46; and Kejř, "Zur Entstehung des städtischen Standes im hussitischen Böhmen," passim.

[122] Václav Bůžek, "From Compromise to Rebellion: Religion and Political Power in the First Century of the Habsburgs' Reign in Bohemia and Moravia," *Journal of Early Modern History* 8 (2004): 31–45. For the 'topography of power' as a case study of the Charles bridge see Howard Louthan, "Breaking Images and Building Bridges: The Making of Sacred Space in Early Modern Bohemia," in *Sacred Space in Early Modern Europe*, ed. Will Coster and Andrew Spicer (Cambridge: Cambridge University Press, 2005), 282–301.

[123] See latest: *Confession and Nation in the Era of Reformations: Central Europe in Comparative Perspective*, ed. Eva Doležalova and Jaraslov Pánek (Prague: Institute of History, 2011).

Afterword

Negotiating the political: the view from London

Caroline M. Barron

To one who has studied the history of the city of London in the fifteenth and sixteenth centuries these essays are of considerable interest because they provoke reflection on similarities and differences. For smaller towns, or those operating with powerful external pressures, negotiating the political, or the creation and maintenance of a communal identity, was much harder than it was for the city of London. The study of a single city, and in particular a well-established and comparatively stable city such as London, can induce a form of myopia which assumes that what is true of the city within one's sights is true of all cities everywhere. These essays serve as an important corrective, and provoke a London historian to consider what is distinctive about England's capital city and what was commonplace.

Size, of course, makes a considerable difference. Prague, with some 30,000 inhabitants, was probably the only town discussed here which could rival London where the population having sunk as low, perhaps, as 40,000 in 1400 had reached 200,000 by 1600. Osnabrück, Bristol, and the Dutch towns of Dordrecht, Haarlem, Delft, Leiden, Amsterdam, and Gouda may have had between 10,000 and 14,000 inhabitants, Canterbury about 6,000, and Bury St Edmunds, Dover and Sandwich about 3000 each. And the physical size of the town and the number of people living there obviously made a great difference to the ways in which urban identities, whether individual or communal, were created and maintained. A single sermon criticising a single individual would not have caused the storm in London that it did in Canterbury in 1593. As Paula Simpson points out, in a provincial society "much attention was paid to honour, shame, and reputation;

Negotiating the Political in Northern European Urban Society, c.1400–c.1600, ed. Sheila Sweetinburgh, MRTS 434 (Tempe: ACMRS, 2013). [ISBN 978-0-86698-482-9]

matters which were regularly negotiated in the local community through gossip and hearsay. . ." In London there was plenty of gossip and hearsay but it was fragmented into a hundred different parishes and the political impact was, thereby, reduced. The achievements of John Smyth in Bury, notable as they were, would have been easily outshone by the wealth and benefactions of any number of London merchants in the later fifteenth century.

By comparison with many of the towns discussed here, London in the fifteenth and sixteenth centuries had a relatively stable governing system: the struggles with the Crown which had dominated the city in the thirteenth century had their final sputtering in 1392 but, by the fifteenth century, London and the Crown had settled into a generally symbiotic relationship. By contrast, many of the Continental towns were locked in conflict with their rulers: the autonomy of Osnabrück was contested by the bishop and cathedral chapter; and in England numerous towns had yet to resolve sometimes long-running disputes over lordship: that of Bury St Edmunds involving the abbey which lay at the heart of the town. The separate townships which made up the city of Prague were in almost continuous conflict with each other and with the king of Bohemia. But since the king was often absent in Hungary his influence was diluted by distance. In the same way the Hapsburg prince of Holland, since he was also an emperor, was not often a visible presence in his Dutch principality. By contrast the kings of England—and their governments—were only a mile away from London at Westminster and, apart from Henry V, were rarely out of the country. So the mayor of London could visit the offices of government and royal ministers could, in turn, visit London, and there was no need for the City to employ agents, as the Dutch towns did, to represent their interests at court. Certainly on occasion gifts were passed to royal officers to influence judicial or Council decisions but, for the rulers of the City of London, royal power was immediate and not remote. If they needed to bend a royal ear they could ride to Westminster in a morning and deal with the matter.

Although the rulers of London were frequently subjected to royal influence, particularly in financial matters, they were not exposed to pressure from great magnates living in the surrounding counties. Peter Fleming's essay demonstrates the extent to which the mayor and aldermen of Bristol were influenced by the "seigniorial geography of mid-fifteenth-century England." The rivalry between the lords of Berkeley and the earls of Gloucester and between those who, later in the period, inherited their estates, had a marked impact on the policies that could be pursued by the mayors of Bristol. In the same way the Catholic nobility played a highly significant role in the tortured politics of fifteenth-century Prague and in Dover in the late sixteenth century it was outsiders—the gentry commissioners and Crown appointees—who carried most weight in deciding the form, future, and financing of the redeveloped Dover harbour. London was never, by this period, subjected to this kind of external magnate pressure. In part this may have been because there were no large magnate estates in the vicinity of London, but it was also because the city collectively was wealthier than any individual member of the English aristocracy.

A certain hostility to the Church, or to the clergy, was probably a feature of most medieval towns. But the intensity of that hostility varied greatly. Clearly if the landlord of the town were a bishop or religious house this could intensify the conflicts, as in Bury in the late fourteenth century, although such conflicts were much less sharp later. In Osnabrück there was sufficient tension between the town and the prince bishop and his cathedral clergy for the townsmen to build a new town hall "as a counterweight to the Cathedral and the Cathedral Close," and in the popular rising of 1488 there were demands for the release of common land enclosed by the Church and attacks on the sexual misbehaviour of the clergy. Even before the Reformation, Prague was racked by religious disputes within and without the Roman Catholic Church. Such religious divisions intensified in the second quarter of the sixteenth century as can be seen in the Dutch towns (particularly Amsterdam) and elsewhere in Europe. In the smaller English towns such as Canterbury or Sandwich social and class divisions might split open along sectarian lines. The ability of urban communities, whether Prague or the Dutch cities or small English towns, to negotiate these fierce religious conflicts depended upon the ability of the rulers of the towns to put the security and well-being of the community above religious principles and beliefs. This rarely happened but, strangely enough, in sixteenth-century London, as Ian Archer has demonstrated, the unity of governing purpose among the twenty-six aldermen transcended religious difference and held the city together through the upheavals of the later sixteenth century. Doubtless much of this stability was achieved by using an iron fist rather than a velvet glove, but the turbulence of Prague shows what the rulers of London had to fear.

By contrast with England these continental towns appear to have had quite a ruthless judicial system. Sixty of the followers of Jan Žižka were hanged in Prague, some of them in front of the city hall in the central marketplace. Certainly there were public executions in English towns, but they were the executions not of townsmen but, rather, of rebellious (or unfortunate) aristocrats who were brought to the towns for execution, such as Hugh Despenser, earl of Winchester who was executed in Bristol in 1326/7, or the royal courtiers Sir John Bussy, Sir Henry Green, and the earl of Wiltshire in 1399. After the executions of the victims of the Merciless Parliament in 1388, when the Londoner Nicholas Brembre had been executed for his support for Richard II's absolutist style of government, no Londoner was sufficiently involved in high politics to suffer during the civil wars of the fifteenth century. Executions took place *in* London, but they were not *of* London. Those who were executed in London during the revolt of Jack Cade in 1450 were men from outside the city: they were not Londoners. It seems to have been far more dangerous to rule Paris or Prague or Ghent or Bruges than it was to rule London or Bristol, although the mayor of Canterbury was executed in 1471 following the failure of the rebellion against Edward IV.

In contrast, several men of Bristol who had also supported the same rebellion, including four prominent common councillors, were, in the end, pardoned rather than executed. Would this have been the outcome in towns on the Continent?

The embellishment of the physical environment of the town was common to all these urban communities regardless of size. But their priorities and choice of motifs of course varied. Many towns built, or rebuilt, their town halls in the fifteenth century: whether the small towns of Bury St Edmunds or Sandwich, or the substantial towns of Prague or Osnabrück. The inhabitants of the New Town in Prague added a high tower to their city hall in the 1450s which, in turn, provoked the men of the Old Town to do the same for their town hall but, in their case, they added an astrological clock. Many towns on the Continent built clock towers as symbols of urban independence and, perhaps, to assert merchant time over church time. When the Londoners rebuilt the Guildhall in the fifteenth century they saw no need for a clock tower: perhaps because there were already clocks on the towers of several of the parish churches, and possibly also they felt no compulsion to assert mercantile time in opposition to clerical time. When the rulers of London came to consider the decoration of the façade of their new Guildhall, like the men of Osnabrück, they chose largely secular rather than religious motifs. At Osnabrück there were seventeen niches for statues which included Charlemagne, Ceres and Flora, the Virgin Mary and the Nine Worthies. In London there were seven niches occupied by Christ in Majesty, Moses and Aaron representing Law and Learning, and the four cardinal virtues of Justice, Fortitude, Temperance, and Prudence. Statues of these four cardinal virtues appeared also on the sixteenth-century well in the square in front of the town hall at Osnabrück which was known as the Council Well. This emphasis on the Roman civic virtues, and especially the importance of justice within the urban community, is apparent in many late medieval towns. And it was the failure of the judicial system which provoked the contentious sermon in Canterbury. Unjust or corrupt judges were to be severely punished even if not necessarily flayed—the punishment meted out by Cambyses, king of Persia in the sixth century BC, to the corrupt judge Sisamnes. Representations of justice, or injustice, were themes often chosen by civic rulers when decorating their civic halls. In the fifteenth century, Bruges, Louvain, and Brussels all chose to decorate their town halls with painted scenes of just and unjust judges. The most famous civic representation of just government is that painted in the early fourteenth century by Ambrogio Lorenzetti in the Palazzo Publico in Siena. Although the smaller towns discussed here could not afford expensive sculptural decoration or paintings for their guildhalls, yet the need for impartial justice was as keenly felt within smaller urban communities as in those that were larger and wealthier. As Plato had argued in fourth-century BC Athens, it was justice which lubricated political communities.

Although the spoken word was, clearly, very important in knitting together the inhabitants of these towns, regardless of size, yet all these essays demonstrate the crucial, and increasing, role played by the written word. And it was the use of the written word, rather than simply voices or fists, that would ultimately enable the lesser or poorer members of urban societies to influence policy and to negotiate their way into the political arena within their communities. In London, in the conflicts of the later fourteenth century, the artisan citizens, led by John of Northampton, pushed through reforms in the ways in which the city was governed, and these changes were written down in English in a volume known as the Jubilee Book (because it was compiled in the fiftieth year of the reign of Edward III). It was the written text which was believed to be so contentious, and, to end controversy, the book was publicly burnt in 1387. But the increasing significance of the written record is everywhere apparent. In Osnabrück the city ordinances, recorded in the municipal register, were supposed to be read out every year, and the rebels of 1488 demanded access to this volume. The growing importance of Prague as the capital of the country was marked in 1512 by the deposition in the city's castle of the land register of the estates of the nobility. John Smyth's benefactions to Bury, recorded for posterity in *Jankyn Smyth's Book,* together with his will and charters relating to his endowed lands, were all to be read out every year, and at Sandwich the mayor and jurats had a copy of the chantry foundation charter read out to them before they removed an offending chantry priest.

There is little in these essays about the poorest members of these urban communities, and one might ask how these people negotiated the political, or were able to influence the course of events. It is largely the urban elites in Bury or Osnabrück or Dover who have left a political trail which we can follow in the surviving records. But the urban poor, who probably made up a majority of the population in the towns and cities considered here, were not necessarily excluded from influencing political events because they could not read. Especially in towns, those who could read shared the information to be found in newsletters and posted bills with those who could not. The advent of printing vastly enlarged the reading stock available in towns and fanned the flames of urban discontent. Negotiation was always largely carried on through speech, fierce at times, and sometimes by blows which might be fatal but, increasingly, negotiating the political was dependent upon the written word: the pen was slowly proving to be mightier than the sword.

Index

Note: page references in *italics* refer to illustrations; references to footnotes are denoted by 'n' and the footnote number.